W9-BGH-873

PIETIST AND WESLEYAN STUDIES

Editors: David Bundy and J. Steven O'Malley

This monograph series will publish volumes in two areas of scholarly research: Pietism and Methodism (broadly understood). The focus will be Pietism, its history and development, and the influence of this socioreligious tradition in modern culture, especially within the Wesleyan religious traditions.

Consideration will be given to scholarly works on classical and neo-Pietism, on English and American Methodism, as well as on the social and ecclesiastical institutions shaped by Pietism (e.g., Evangelicals, United Brethren, and the Pietist traditions among the Lutherans, Reformed, and Anabaptists). Works focusing on leaders within the Pietist and Wesleyan traditions will also be included in the series, as well as occasional translations and/or editions of Pietist texts. It is anticipated that the monographs will emphasize theological developments, but with close attention to the interaction of Pietism with other cultural forces and to the sociocultural identity of the Pietist and Wesleyan movements.

1. Gregory S. Clapper, *John Wesley on Religious Affections.* 1989.
2. Peter Erb, *Gottfried Arnold.* 1989.
3. Henry H. Knight III, *The Presence of God in the Christian Life: John Wesley and the Means of Grace.* 1992.
4. Frank D. Macchia, *Spirituality and Social Liberation: The Message of the Blumhardts in the Light of Wuerttemberg Pietism.* 1993.
5. Richard B. Steele, *"Gracious Affection" and "True Virtue" according to Jonathan Edwards and John Wesley.* 1994.
6. Stephen L. Longenecker, *Piety and Tolerance: Pennsylvania German Religion, 1700–1850.* 1994.

Piety and Tolerance
Pennsylvania German Religion, 1700–1850

by
Stephen L. Longenecker

Pietist and Wesleyan Studies, No. 6

The Scarecrow Press, Inc.
Metuchen, N.J., & London
1994

#29597519

British Library Cataloguing-in-Publication data available

Library of Congress Cataloging-in-Publication Data

Longenecker, Stephen L., 1951-
    Piety and Tolerance: Pennsylvania German Religion, 1700-1850
/ by Stephen L. Longenecker.
        p. cm. -- (Pietist and Wesleyan studies ; no. 6)
    Includes bibliographical references (p. xxx-xxx) and index.
    ISBN 0-8108-2771-9 (alk. paper)
    1. Pennsylvania--Church history--18th century. 2. Pennsylvania--
Church history--19th century. 3. German Americans--Religion. 4.
Pietism--Pennsylvania--History. 5. Religious tolerance--
Pennsylvania--History. I. Title. II. Series.
    BR555.P4L66 1994
    277.48--dc20   93-48988

Based on the author's Ph.D. dissertation, "Democracy's Pulpit:
Religion and Egalitarianism among Early Pennsylvania Germans."
Baltimore, MD: The Johns Hopkins University, 1990.

Copyright©1994 by Stephen L. Longenecker
Manufactured in the United States of America
Printed on acid-free paper

To Timothy L. Smith

HOLY SPIRIT LIBRARY
95 0466
CABRINI COLLEGE, RADNOR, PA.

Contents

Editors' Foreword

Stephen Longenecker opens to us a panoramic view of the pluralistic subculture of colonial Pennsylvania German Protestantism, with its roots in German Pietism. His contention is that the roots of American religious toleration have an important source in the array of German-American church folk, sectarians, and indigenous revivalists who manifested in various ways the invigorating ferment of continental Pietism. This work serves to balance the preponderance of studies that have overlooked the Germans of the Middle Colonies in the course of locating the roots of American religious pluralism in the New England Puritans.

A central concern is his demonstration of how Pietism, as a significant movement in European Protestant history, distinctively affected the formation of American religion, particularly with regard to the central issue of religious toleration. Based upon a careful use of primary sources, Longenecker offers a balanced, chronological interpretation of the colonial Pennsylvania German religious scene, including the confessional traditions, Anabaptists, Radical Pietists, and finally the camp meeting revivalists. A distinctive feature of the study is the extensive analysis given to the major representatives of the latter group, through his treatment of the literature of the Evangelical Association and the United Brethren in Christ. Of particular significance is the early contribution made by these groups to the budding antislavery impulse in American history.

With the publication of the work, the Pietist and Wesleyan Studies series has moved beyond a concern for the theological and institutional aspects of Pietism to a consideration of its larger, pervasive contribution to the cultural life of the nation.

David Bundy
Associate Professor of
  Church History
Librarian
Christian Theological
  Seminary
Indianapolis, IN

J. Steven O'Malley
Professor of Church History and
  Historical Theology
Asbury Theological Seminary
Wilmore, KY

Foreword

The significance to the larger religious culture of the collective experience of the diverse sects which settled in colonial early Pennsylvania continues to call for the kind of research, analysis, and explication which Stephen L. Longenecker demonstrates in *Piety and Tolerance*. American religious and intellectual studies have not neglected this subject, but the Pennsylvania context, and particularly the Pennsylvania German, has not provided the setting for most of the inquiries. The struggles for religious tolerance by religious dissenters such as Roger Williams in the face of laws of religious establishment in New England, or the victories won by the surprising political coalition of Baptists and Jeffersonians in Virginia, naturally make for more lively history than an account of the progress of tolerance in Penn's colony where the legal religious establishment was the non-establishment of any sect. There, the struggle was not to create the possibility of pluralism but to demonstrate how to make it work.

In spite of the prior attention of a small group of well-known American church historians, such as F. Ernest Stoeffler, Donald F. Durnbaugh, and Timothy L. Smith, Longenecker's mentor, the story of the Pennsylvania religious experience largely remains untold. The present work marks a significant response to that reality. Its extensive analysis of the contributions of Pennsylvania Germans in the Anabaptist, Pietist, and revivalist traditions to the growth of religious tolerance in American society joins an expanding stream of scholarship that seeks to broaden our understanding of the pluralistic and complex roots of the religious culture of the United States. Longenecker's account demonstrates how Pennsylvania's legal context radically reversed the fortunes of exclusion that German Anabaptists had experienced in Europe and how their response to their legally-established religious rights in Pennsylvania helped to forge the accepted standards for interrelationships between religious sects and the state. But, even more importantly, it reveals how, in a religiously pluralistic society, the relationships among the Pennsylvania German religious sects generated their own impetuses to the growth of religious tolerance as they participated in certain religious and cultural movements that encouraged the egalitarianism inherent in their own history, theology, and experience to come to the fore.

The Dunkers or German Baptists and the Mennonites, whom Longenecker deals with most extensively, generated their first impetus to tolerance by their very presence in the new colony. In their former homelands in Europe they had been the subjects of almost universal religious and social discrimination by Lutheran, Reformed, or Catholic authorities. In their new home the situation was completely reversed. Lutherans and constituents of other dominant religious traditions in Europe suddenly found that they had to live on equal legal status and in competitive reality with proponents of all sorts of Anabaptist "heresy," even the more radical ones.

But more than legal pressure was at work to encourage the development of a religious tolerance that eventually became an important building block of American religious experience. A pervasive and enduring strain of Pietist experiential spirituality inherent in Anabaptism by the time of its establishment in America was also an integral part of the theology of many of the early Lutheran and Reformed clergy and laity who settled there. This common experiential element encouraged an egalitarianism that tended to leap over the cultural chasms traditionally created by variant creeds and rituals. The validation of the authority of personal religious experience encouraged the empowerment of all persons and the weakening of the authority traditionally lent to theology and ideology in religion. In the end, the acknowledgement of their common acceptance by God allowed for a more ready openness between sects and acceptance of "the other."

Longenecker rightfully recognizes that much of the toleration which developed among the many sects in Pennsylvania was a practical response to the necessities of the legal and social restrictions of life in the colony. Nevertheless, he also rightfully realizes that a theological commitment to the universality of the Gospel appeal as proclaimed by Pennsylvania German revivalists of whatever strand was equally significant in its development. This conviction that every person was equal before God in the most important of human concerns--his or her personal salvation--made most Dunkers, Mennonites, Evangelicals, United Brethren, and German Methodists strong opponents of slavery. Their historical experience of appeal to a higher power and passive resistance to governmental and ecclesiastical injustice, when called for, also made them open opponents of laws and causes that sought to support or justify its continuance. *Piety and Tolerance* introduces us to a host of Dunkers and Mennonites, generally quite unknown by most religious historians, who witnessed to their beliefs by living out their convictions on human brotherhood whether they were living in north or south.

Longenecker's extensive research on the Pennsylvania German revival is especially helpful. It significantly enriches our understanding of American revivalism. The strains of Pietism that interlaced Lutheran, Reformed, Moravian, and German Anabaptist communities in early Pennsylvania helped to create a religious milieu that was supportive of innovations such as union churches supported by cooperating Lutheran and Reformed congregations, interdenominational meetings encouraged by even such a staunch Lutheran as Henry Melchior Muhlenberg, interdenominational religious papers such as Christopher Sauer's, and above all the rise of Pennsylvania German revivalism with all the accoutrements of nineteenth-century American revivalism. The awakenings among the Pennsylvania Germans commonly portrayed the interdenominationalism, extempore preaching, pointed and person-oriented praying, the public place of women, and the emphases on freedom of the will and perfectionism reminiscent of the phenomenon. And all of this as early and maybe earlier than the expressions of the first awakening in New England under Edwards or in New Jersey under Frelinghuysen. Even the Pennsylvania Dutch "big meetings" and "bush meetings" forecast the coming of the camp meetings that were to become a standard feature of American revivalism.

From early on the religious situation in Pennsylvania demonstrated the patterns of religious life that would become common to much of America as the last vestiges of religious establishment were shaken off in the first decades of the nineteenth century. This excellent study represents a challenge to other historians to continue to mine the largely untapped potential for enlarging our understanding of American religion represented by the Pennsylvania religious experience.

Melvin E. Dieter
Professor Emeritus of Church
  History and Historical Theology
Asbury Theological Seminary
Lyndhurst, Virginia

Preface

This study explores the roots of tolerance in early America, particularly in Pennsylvania. Traditionally, according to Michael W. Zuckerman, scholars have looked to New England for the "keys to America's past."[1] One popular textbook of American religious history, for example, claims that Protestant revivalism emerged from the descendants of Massachusetts Bay,[2] while another finds no lasting legacy from the middle colonies, only a "chaos of cults" in which religion succeeded merely because it survived.[3]

It is mistaken, however, to probe for America's history solely in New England, a region of little ethnic variety that treasured conformity. If what marks American democracy is respect for the rights of all, then perhaps a more diverse area, such as the middle colonies, prompted the tradition of tolerance. *Piety and Tolerance*, therefore, looks to early Pennsylvania Germans to determine the influence of German Protestantism, particularly Pietism, in promoting understanding and cooperation. German Christians, themselves an early American minority, were a surprisingly pluralistic subculture that included Radical Pietists, Anabaptists, Wesleyans, Lutherans, and Reformed, and yet Pietism became part of each tradition.

Defining Pennsylvania Germans is surprisingly troublesome. For German settlers who followed the Great Valley south and itinerant preachers whose circuits crisscrossed colonies and states, political boundaries meant little, making Germans in western Maryland and Virginia's Valley part of the larger Pennsylvania German population. Occasionally this study taps these sources. The book halts in the mid-

---

[1] Michael W. Zuckerman, "Introduction: Puritans, Cavaliers, and the Motley Middle," *Friends and Neighbors: Group Life in America's First Plural Society*, ed. Zuckerman (Philadelphia: Temple University Press, 1986), 11.

[2] Sydney E. Ahlstrom, *A Religious History of the American People* (New Haven: Yale University Press, 1972), 7.

[3] Edwin Scott Gaustad, *A Religious History of America* (New York: Harper and Row, 1966), 99.

nineteenth century when expansion into the mid-west and Ontario and the arrival of a fresh wave of German immigrants blurred the distinctivenesss of Pennsylvania Germans, causing them to be less identifiable.

Piety and Tolerance begins with an introduction to the theology of Pietism and then discusses the Old World society that emigrating Germans left behind. The low socio-economic status of German nonconformists and the absence of tolerance makes Pennsylvania even more remarkable. Then the book examines in approximate chronological order each of the subgroups within Pennsylvania German Pietism: Radical Pietists, Anabaptists, eighteenth-century church Germans, and the campmeeting revivalists of the next century. The book concludes by investigating the Pietists' application of their faith to slavery, the dominant ethical issue of the first half of the nineteenth century. Portions of this book have appeared elsewhere, including the Johns Hopkins American History Seminar, the Shenandoah Valley Regional Studies Seminar, the Kansas Institute for Nonviolence, and the Johns Hopkins/Bretton Woods Conference on American Religious History.

I am indebted to numerous friends and colleagues for improving my work. The staffs of the following libraries were always helpful: the Johns Hopkins University, Bridgewater College, Lancaster Mennonite Historical Society, Lancaster Theological Seminary, Franklin and Marshall College, Millersville University, Towson State University, the United Methodist Archives at Drew University, Lovely Lane Methodist Historical Society, Moravian College, National Archives, Seminary of Evangelical Theology, Eastern Mennonite College, and Lutheran Theological Seminary. A generous grant from the Glenmeade Foundation funded this project. Bridgewater College's Flory Fund for the Humanities financed a research trip to Pennsylvania, and my fellow members of Bridgewater's Forum for Religious Studies have been stimulating and supportive. David J. Rempel Smucker and Lloyd Zeager at the Lancaster Mennonite Historical Society graciously shared their expertise, and Reginald Washington was my guide through the maze at the National Archives, quickly sending me along the best path. The librarians at Bridgewater College, especially Thelma Hall and Ruth Greenawalt, provided professional and constructive assistance. I am grateful to Donald F. Durnbaugh, Al Keim, John B. Frantz, Richard K. MacMaster, and Mack Walker for comments on individual chapters. Carl Bowman's insights on Church of the Brethren history have been exceptional, and his reading of a late draft noticeably improved the text. The advice of Don Bird and Tom Umbel, my partners on a research project at Johns Hopkins, was valuable, and the Religious History Seminar at Johns Hopkins, including Glenn Spann and Heather Warren, was similarly helpful. Sherri Emmert and Mendy Howard assisted with time-saving clerical skills. Earl Ziegler and Fred Bernhard encouraged me to begin this adventure, and Marie Bucher, Eva O'Diam, Mark and Dawn Ottoni-Wilhelm, Amy Worline Ervin, and the Shull Computing Center at Bridgewater also provided assistance. The advice, encouragement, and wisdom of my advisor, Timothy L. Smith, have been exceptional and invaluable; words cannot express what he has done for me. Special gratitude goes to my family--Ada, Lew, and Carol--for understanding the many hours I spent away from them pursuing this project. To all who helped, thank you. The errors that remain despite their best efforts are mine.

Abbreviations

AHR	*American Historical Review*
ATJ	*Asbury Theological Journal*
BLT	*Brethren Life and Thought*
CH	*Church History*
JSH	*Journal of Social History*
JR	*Journal of Religion*
LCQ	*Lutheran Church Quarterly*
MQR	*Mennonite Quarterly Review*
MH	*Methodist History*
PA	*Pennsylvania Archives*
PMBH	*Pennsylvania Magazine of History and Biography*
PMH	*Pennsylvania Mennonite Heritage*
WMQ	*William and Mary Quarterly*

INTRODUCTION

An Egalitarian Theology

God is pleased, proclaimed a hymn written by the seventeenth-century theologian August Hermann Francke, when believers promise Christ to come to Him "with heart and tongue."[1] Francke's words, drawn from Pietism, expressed theological egalitarianism by extending salvation to anyone, regardless of gender, age, nation, or social rank, willing to accept Christ's lordship. This religious doctrine arrived in Pennsylvania with many of the earliest German colonists.

The cornerstone of Pietism, as constructed by its seventeenth-century Lutheran and Calvinist founders, was an emphasis on inner experience as vital to individual salvation. According to Pietists, the Christian faith had atrophied through the rationalizations of the scholastic theologians, who searched for precise answers to theological questions. The scholastics insisted that individual believers accept and, indeed, memorize their doctrinal statements *verbatim.* Pietists, attacking this practice as dry and impersonal, avoided systematic theology, condemning intellectual gymnastics as irrelevant to Christian life. They believed that institutional rigidity and contentious debates over fine points of theology lulled believers into a drowsiness they often described as "dead." Pietists, instead, portrayed the church as a community of believers, whose polity, ritual, and fellowship they wanted to simplify, and they aimed to re-invigorate congregations with Bible studies, increased lay participation, and gospel gatherings, known

---

[1] August Hermann Francke, Hymn #346, *Geistreiches Gesangbuch*, in Peter C. Erb, ed., *The Pietists: Selected Writings* (Mahwah, N.J.: Paulist Press, 1983), 174-5.

as conventicles.[2]

Restoring life to the church required individual Christians to experience the Holy Spirit and to take steps that would bring them closer to God. According to Pietists, regeneration took "place in the heart" and was more spiritually meaningful than outward ceremonies and sacraments. A Lutheran periodical asserted that only a "thorough change of heart" could bring about salvation; baptism and communion were meaningless without renewal.[3] Without "an inward sprinkling," remarked one Mennonite, whose fellowship used this mode of baptism, the outward one by water meant little.[4] Likewise, good works had validity only if resulting from experience. When a young Lutheran pastor urged his parishioners to pledge in writing to abandon boozing, shooting, dancing, and horse-racing, a more experienced clergyman counseled him to "first lay a foundation of true Christianity in the hearts of the people and then build from the inside to the outside."[5] Besides the heart, Pietist metaphors often located spiritual experience in the digestive system. A reborn lay preacher, writing during Thomas Jefferson's Presidency, explained how difficult it was "to taste and feel

[2] Dale W. Brown, *Understanding Pietism* (Grand Rapids, Mich.: Eerdmans, 1978), 27-8, 32-4; Erb, *Pietists*, 2-9; Philipp Jacob Spener, *Pia Desideria*, ed., trans., and intro. by Theodore G. Tappert (Philadelphia: Fortress Press, 1964), 66-7, 87, 95-7, 99; and F. Ernest Stoeffler, *German Pietism During the Eighteenth Century* (Leiden: E. J. Brill, 1973), ix.

[3] "Sacramental Religion," *Lutheran Observer* (September 3, 1852): 781.

[4] Burkholder, "Third Address," in *Useful and Edifying Address to the Young on True Repentance, Saving Faith in Christ Jesus, Pure Love, etc.* (Lancaster, Pa.: n.p., 1857), 220. This book, written in 1792 and published in 1804, was signed by all or nearly all the ministers and deacons of the Lancaster Mennonites, indicating that it spoke for the denomination's leadership in that area. The book went through eight German and five English editions. See Martin H. Schrag, "The Impact of Pietism upon Early American Mennonites" (unpublished paper; Lancaster County Mennonite Historical Society), 6-7; and Robert Friedmann, *Mennonite Piety Through the Centuries: Its Genius and Its Literature* (Goshen, Ind.: Mennonite Historical Society, 1949), 238-42.

[5] Henry M. Muhlenberg, *Journals*, Theodore G. Tappert and John W. Doberstein, eds., 3 vols. (Philadelphia: Evangelical Lutheran Ministerium and the Muhlenberg Press, 1958), I, 267-8.

Christ until one comes to know him,"[6] and Philipp Spener, Pietism's founder, suggested that "it is not enough that your ear hears," but persons must let the Word of God "penetrate inwardly" into their hearts and "allow the heavenly food to be digested there."[7]

The internalization of Christ, possible through God's offer of grace, began with deep remorse over past sins and a determination to seek forgiveness. A "flame of God's voice" struck and "illumined inside" one convert, accusing him of never really knowing God.[8] Another observed that when penitents realized their sinfulness, they felt "something of a shock"; their "wounded and broken" hearts sighed over "the lost and troubled condition" of their souls. But, he maintained, God directed them to Christ, who cleansed them in body and soul and gave them "a new leader, the Holy Spirit."[9] Following this moment of the "new birth," an exceptionally joyous event, believers entered a new life that rejected their former, sinful existence and, according to a Pietist hymnal, exuded love and ethical concern, a "Godly walk leading to a proper fruit."[10] Thus, the 1771 discipline of a Lutheran congregation in Manheim, Pennsylvania, required its pastors to preach that salvation resulted from three sources: God's grace, confession, and "a living faith" in the new life.[11]

---

[6] Christian Longenecker, "On the True Conversion and New Birth," trans. Vernard Eller, *BLT* 7 (Spring 1962, originally published in 1806): 23. According to family tradition, Christian Longenecker is related to me, but the genealogical missing link remains to be discovered. He was stubborn, quarrelsome, and divisive, and so we are somewhat skeptical of the claim of ancestry. My wife, however, is more convinced of the relationship!

[7] Spener, *Pia Desideria*, 66-7.

[8] Lamech and Agrippa, *Chronicon Ephratense: A History of the Seventh Day Baptists at Ephrata*, trans. J. Max Hart (Lancaster, Pa.: 1889), 98-9. "Lamech and Agrippa" are probably Jacob Gast and Peter Miller, respectively. The *Chronicon*, first published in 1786, is generally accurate regarding early Pennsylvania German religion, especially the Dunkards, despite its strong pro-Ephrata bias.

[9] Ibid., 23-6. See also "Sermon by Peter Nead," January 3, 1836, in Benjamin Funk, *Life and Labors of Elder John Kline, the Martyr Missionary* (Elgin, Ill.: Brethren Publishing House, 1900), 43-4.

[10] Freylinghausen, "Preface," *Geistreiches Gesangbuch*, in Erb, *Pietists*, 169.

[11] *Church Book: Zion Evangelical Lutheran Church, Manheim, Lancaster County, Pennsylvania* (photocopy at the Lancaster Mennonite Historical Society), 5.

Pietists asserted that true hearts freely chose to confess, accept grace, and enter the new life. They rejected Calvinist beliefs in total depravity and divine predestination and instead underlined the response to God that brought salvation. Pietists believed that unrepentant souls preferred "darkness to the light," but that those who understood their "lost condition" sought God's "open arms." A popular Pietist hymnist in Europe prayed to be awakened "So that my path/ I might direct unchanged to you,"[12] and a German preacher in colonial Pennsylvania wrote,

> Yet might e'en the greatest sinner,
> If he would for love make place,
> Enable love to be the winner
> And give himself life's highest grace.[13]

Gone were church officials who held the keys to the kingdom; only Christ did that. The experience of saving faith could come to everyone, regardless of ecclesiastical or social rank, willing to make the choice.

Thus, early German immigrants to Pennsylvania wove the doctrine of inward religion tightly into the colony's religious fabric well before the famous awakenings of the 1740s. If, according to their teaching, God saves anyone who follows in obedience, He was willing to save all, not simply a predestined elite. Revelation 21:6, as translated in a hymnal popular among Pennsylvania Germans, urged all who heard God's voice to come and assured them that whoever would, might

---

[12] Johannes Braun, *Circular-Schreiben an die Deutschen Einwohner von Rockingham und Augusta, und den benachbarten Counties* (Harrisonburg, Va.: Laurentz Wartman, 1818), 17; Freylinghausen, "Preface," *Geistreiches Gesangbuch*, in Erb, *Pietists*, 168; and Freylinghausen, Hymn #66, in Erb, 172.

[13] Alexander Mack, Jr., "The Excellencies of Jesus," trans. Ora W. Garber, in Donald F. Durnbaugh, ed., *European Origins of the Brethren: A Source Book on the Beginnings of the Church of the Brethren in the Early Eighteenth Century* (Elgin, Ill.: The Brethren Press, 1958), 584-5.

"take the water of life without price." Anybody could become a saint.[14]

---

[14] The quote is from Christopher Sauer I's preface to *Das Kleine Davidische Psalterspiel der Kinder Zion*, published in 1744; see Durnbaugh, *The Brethren in Colonial America*, 555. For another citation of Revelation 21:6, see Peter Burkholder, "On Predestination," *Christian Spiritual Conversation on Saving Faith, for the Young in Questions and Answers, and A Confession of Faith, of the Mennonites*, trans. Joseph Funk (Lancaster, Pa.: John Baer and Sons, 1857), 295. Burkholder's work originally appeared in 1837 as a book printed in Winchester, Virginia; see *The Mennonite Encyclopedia: A Comprehensive Reference Work on the Anabaptist-Mennonite Movement*, 4 vols. (Hillsboro, Kan.: Mennonite Brethren Publishing House, 1955-59), I, 477-8.

CHAPTER 1

The Last Shall Be First:
The Socio-Economic Status
of German Anabaptists

In 1747 Henry M. Muhlenberg, the Lutheran missionary to Pennsylvania, complained that many of his fellow Lutherans were so poor that they could not properly clothe their children, "much less support churches, schools, preachers, and schoolmasters." In contrast, he noted, the Quakers, Mennonites, Dunkers, and "the like small denominations" had "enriched themselves" on the most productive farmland.[1]

Muhlenberg's lament reveals that the dominance enjoyed in Germany by the established denominations (Reformed and Lutherans) ended in William Penn's colony. The acceptance extended to Anabaptists in Pennsylvania created a socio-economic realignment because, as this chapter demonstrates, in Europe poverty was widespread among Mennonites and Dunkers,[2] tolerance was uncertain, and social rank low. The society created by Germans in Pennsylvania was much different than the one they left behind.

[1] Henry Melchior Muhlenberg, *The Journals of Henry Melchior Muhlenberg*, trans. Theodore G. Tappert and John W. Doberstein, 3 vols. (Philadelphia: Muhlenberg Press, 1924-58), I, 141-2, 145. Available evidence, though meager, supports Muhlenberg's observation about the Dunkards and Mennonites; see Richard K. MacMaster, *Land, Piety, Peoplehood: The Establishment of Mennonite Communities in America, 1683-1790* (Scottdale, Pa.: Herald Press, 1985), 79-110; and Chapter 4 of this work.

[2] In Europe Alexander Mack's followers often called themselves merely "the brethren" while outside observers employed terms like New Anabaptists or New Baptists. This chapter uses "Dunkers," the American term, to provide continuity throughout the book.

I

Most Germans had little understanding of and less sympathy for
Anabaptists. Arising first in Reformation-era Zürich from a movement
led by Conrad Grebel and Felix Mantz, Anabaptism spread quickly into
other parts of German- and Dutch-speaking Europe. Like many
reformers, Anabaptists called for a return to the New Testament
church, for them the golden age of Christendom, and they agreed with
Martin Luther, John Calvin, and Ulrich Zwingli that the church had
fallen into corruption. Anabaptists, however, dated the church's
demise from the moment that Constantine united it with the state, and
they faulted other reformers for confining their criticism to papal decadence of a much later period.

Anabaptists found Biblical inspiration in the story of Nehemiah,
who restored Jewish worship among the returned exiles, and they saw
themselves as modern Nehemiahs, reconstructing their church by restoring its emphasis on obedience and commitment to Jesus. Menno
Simons, an organizer of the Dutch Mennonites, was especially
captivated by this idea. He printed on the flyleaf of everything he
wrote a reference to I Corinthians 3:11: "For no other foundation can
man lay than that which is laid, which is Jesus Christ." Anabaptists
hoped to rebuild the church on its original foundation, Jesus Christ,
both savior and example.

Ceremonies in the reconstructed church, according to Anabaptists,
emphasized regeneration and obedience. Communion and baptism, instead of being sacraments, symbolized the inward experience of repentance and the new birth, or new life, that converts lead. They
refused to make their observation of the Lord's Supper become a
ceremony of hierarchical authority in which grace descended from
popes through the ecclesiastical ranks to the passive recipient. Instead,
they understood the bread and cup as tokens of their commitment to
Christian love. One early Anabaptist, Balthasar Hubmaier, described
the Last Supper as "a sign of brotherly love to which we are obliged."
Communion also taught them that obedience to Christ brought
suffering; they pointed out that Jesus instructed the disciples to drink
of his blood, that is, to experience His persecution. As the grapes
become communion wine, suggested a sixteenth-century Anabaptist, as
the grain is first ground into flour, then baked into bread, so the

believers through suffering in Christ become one loaf. Baptism was a voluntary covenant with the church, a public symbol of acceptance of the congregation's discipline, and a pledge to seek a righteous life, including simplicity and nonviolence. Anabaptists insisted that believers be baptized as adults, and they often opposed infant baptism with bitter ridicule.[3]

In fact, much of what the Anabaptists preached and practiced threatened to upend the social and political world. Because civic authorities in the Reformation era guided the spiritual life of citizens, rejecting their wisdom in matters of faith became political subversion. When Zürich's city council decided to retain infant baptism, Zwingli, an influential priest, yielded to them, but the Anabaptists refused to concede and consequently suffered persecution. Their unwillingness to bear arms--whether in time of military crisis, during routine patrolling of town walls, or guarding the town's flocks from wild animals--and the refusal to swear oaths tugged at political and social cohesion. Anabaptists felt little remorse over their assault on authority; government, they taught, was only for secular matters and should reserve its coercive powers only for use against the sinful. The state had God's blessing to restrain criminals but would eventually be condemned as evil.[4]

A few Anabaptist radicals rejected all government, even for non-Christians, and their rebellion at Münster confirmed the fears of those who considered Anabaptists as agents of anarchy. The movement at Münster, which predated the arrival of Anabaptist missionaries, arose from tensions within the city between common folk, the guilds, the council, and Bishop Franz of Waldeck, but believers' baptism arose as an effective symbol for reform. Millennial Anabaptists gained control, overthrowing the council and expelling adults who refused baptism. Oppressed Dutch Anabaptists, who believed that God had chosen

---

[3] Claus-Peter Clasen, *Anabaptism, A Social History, 1525-1618: Switzerland, Austria, Moravia, South and Central Germany* (Ithaca: Cornell University Press, 1972), 110-6; William R. Estep, *The Anabaptist Story* (Grand Rapids, Mich.: Eerdmans, 1975), Chapter 9 and 184-92; Franklin Hamlin Littell, *The Anabaptist View of the Church: A Study in the Origins of Sectarian Protestantism* (Boston: Starr King Press, 1958), 84-106.

[4] Clasen, *Anabaptism*, 99-102, 172-82; and MacMaster, *Land, Piety, Peoplehood*, 20-24.

Münster as the New Jerusalem that would usher in His kingdom, poured into the city. Münster's version of New Jerusalem included polygamy and, in imitation of the New Testament church, community of goods, but the reformers spurned nonviolence, never as strong among north German Anabaptists as it was in the south, and defended themselves from the Bishop's siege. Münster's enemies nevertheless pierced its walls and killed most of the male population. Authorities tortured three surviving leaders--Jan van Leyden, Bernhard Knipper-dolling, and Bernhard Krechting--and publicly exhibited them at various locations before their executions. The cages in which their bodies languished still hang from the tower of St. Lambert's church. Müns-ter's legacy tarred Anabaptism for centuries with the brush of fanati-cism, and even peaceful Anabaptists received the pejorative label, "Münsterie."[5] Typically viewed as seditious, then, Anabaptists often became the targets of oppression.

II

Because persecution was so prevalent, the desire for religious freedom often attracted Dunkers and Mennonites to areas that promised tolerance, but after arrival they frequently struggled in the sanctuaries. Typical was the German Palatinate of the late seventeenth century, which partially removed restrictions on Mennonite religious practice.

Prior to the Thirty Years' War, the Palatinate heavily persecuted religious dissent. In 1527 two prominent Anabaptists, Hans Denk and Ludwig Haetzer, published a German translation of Old Testament prophets there. The following year, however, Elector Ludwig V, citing an imperial mandate from Emperor Charles V that called for capital punishment for Anabaptists, issued a decree against them. Authorities in one locality, Alzey, executed numerous Anabaptists, the men by beheading and the women by drowning; estimates of the deaths ranged from 22 to 350. When Johann Odenbach, the preacher in Moschel, appealed in a sixteen-page letter to Ludwig for toleration for

---

[5] Clasen, *Anabaptists*, 174; and "Münster Anabaptists," *The Mennonite Encyclopedia: A Comprehensive Reference Work on the Anabaptist-Mennonite Movement*, 4 vols. (Hillsboro, Kan.: Mennonite-Brethren Publishing House), III, 777-9.

the arrested Anabaptists, officials imprisoned him as well. Ludwig, however, determined that Odenbach was harmless and released him, but only after the pastor promised not to publish anymore. Another minister, George Pistor at Zweibrücken, became an Anabaptist in 1532 and consequently suffered banishment.

Subsequent Electors continued to combat Anabaptists, employing a variety of tactics. Elector Friedrich II, a Lutheran, tried to recover the prodigal Anabaptists with kinder methods. He barred them from official positions and prohibited sermons and ringing bells at their funerals but tolerated their worship. Consistent with Friedrich's politics of persuasion, in 1557 he sponsored a disputation in which forty Anabaptists participated, including nineteen elders. In 1571 his successor, Friedrich III, held another debate at Frankenthal, but this one failed because most foreign Anabaptists, ignoring their safe conduct passes, stayed away; except for fifteen dissenters, the Elector's orthodox clerics preached to like-minded listeners. Friedrich's son, Ludwig VI, abandoned friendly persuasion by imprisoning and expelling Anabaptists and confiscating their property. Elector Johann Casimir (1583-91) proclaimed anew Ludwig's mandate against Anabaptists without strictly enforcing it.

Despite persecution, Anabaptism survived in the Palatinate. In 1558 an official visitation by Catholic authorities to Neukastel found both Schwenkfelders and Anabaptists there, and a delegation that year to Ilbesheim concluded that since Schwenkfelder and Anabaptist errors reigned, "the old pastor should be put away and a braver, more skilled man sent." In 1584 ecclesiastical visitations reported Anabaptists in three towns. By 1601 Anabaptists were growing. In Kriegsheim, where sixty-six Mennonites lived, the village pastor complained that although Hans Herstein had been instructed three times, he remained recalcitrant "and should be immediately fried in oil."[6]

Mennonite growth in the Palatinate proceeded more rapidly after the Thirty Years' War when they received greater toleration because of

---

[6] Gerhard Hein, "Die Herkunft der pfalzische Mennoniten," *Pfälzer-Palatines: Beitrage zur pfälzischen Ein- und Auswanderung sowie zur Volkskunde und Mundartforschung der Pfalz und der Zielländer pfalzischer Auswanderer im 18. und 19. Jahrhundert*, Karl Scherer, ed., (Kaiserslautern: Heimatstelle Pfalz, 1981), 208; Ernst Drumm, *Zur Geschichte der Mennoniten in Herzogtum Pfalz-Zweibrücken* (Zweibrücken: Veröffentlichungen der Stadtverwaltung, 1962), 12-23; "Palatinate," *The Mennonite Encyclopedia*, III, 106-9, "Pistor, George," ibid., 182; and "Odenbach," ibid., 17-8.

the extensive depopulation. The Electorate's loss may have been as high as sixty-five percent of the population. One district reported that fifty-eight of its sixty-two villages lost population during the war. In Oberamt Lautern residents deserted thirty of the sixty-two villages. By 1684 only ten of these had been rebuilt, and in the largest village, only six families who resided there when the war began remained. Intent upon repopulating his devastated domains, Elector Karl Ludwig extended toleration and other incentives to dissenters, including Mennonites, Hutterites,[7] and Polish Socinians.[8] He freed newcomers from the entry tax and other obligations and exempted immigrants, including Mennonites, from personal services, guard duty, and feudal obligations for one year if they farmed destroyed estates. He offered tax incentives for repairing old houses, building new ones, and farming overgrown or idle fields. Bounties for wolf scalps testified to the packs that roamed the region. Swiss farmers, refugees from an unsuccessful peasant uprising, were by far the largest group of newcomers; their numbers peaked in the early 1660s. Other large immigrant groups were Walloons from the Spanish Netherlands and French Huguenots.[9]

Though Palatine authorities eagerly invited dissenters to farm the war-torn countryside, they were more reluctant to allow them to practice their religion. As the area recovered, tolerance came grudgingly, and soon Elector Karl Ludwig imposed several restrictions on Mennonite immigrants. He permitted only two hundred of their families in the Electorate at any one time, forbad Mennonite meeting-houses, prohibited baptism, and limited their attendance at meetings to no more than twenty people. He ordered the Anabaptist congregations to provide the authorities with membership lists, to be updated

---

[7] Hutterites, founded by Jakob Hutter, were Tyrolean anabaptists who fled to Moravia where they established a communal economy. They migrated to Russia in 1622 to escape persecution and then to South Dakota in 1874.

[8] Socinians were rationalists who rejected the Trinity, the Fall, the divinity of Jesus, and the immortality of the soul.

[9] Günter Franz, *Der Dreissigjährige Krieg und das deutsche Volk: Untersuchung zur Bevölkerungs und Agrargeschichte* (Stuttgart: Gustav Fischer Verlag, 1961), 39-40, 85; Nuba M. Pletcher, "Some Chapters from the History of the Rhine Country" (Ph.D. diss.: Columbia University, 1907), in *History Chronological* 55 (n.d.): 78; and Volker Sellin, *Die Finanzpolitik Karl Ludwigs von der Pfalz: Staatswirtschaft in Wiederaufbau nach dem Dreissigjährigen Krieg* (Stuttgart: Klett-Cotta, 1978), 98-9, 107-8, 112-3.

whenever new arrivals appeared. Moreover, he denied them citizenship and required each immigrant family to pay three florins protection money (*Schutzgeld*) in its first year of residence and six florins thereafter.[10]

Tolerance, though incomplete, required renewal every time a new Elector ascended the throne, making coronations occasions of additional anxiety for Anabaptists. Karl Ludwig's Protestant successors confirmed the Mennonite privileges in 1682, 1686, and 1698, albeit lethargically, but the new Electors sometimes levied special taxes when they took the throne. In 1717 Mennonites protested one of these surcharges, claiming that it was unjust because authorities barred them from the trades. Their petition asserted that even Jews, who could become artisans if they paid the protection tax, enjoyed higher esteem. In 1742 Karl Theodor, a Catholic, demanded 10,000 guilders from Mennonites for his coronation expenses, but he also reversed a recent doubling of the annual protection fee and returned it to the traditional six guilders.[11]

Two incidents in Alzey illustrate the difficulties Mennonites faced with the Palatine counts. In 1726 Elector Karl Philip issued the "Law of Retraction" to permit the previous owners of Mennonite-held land to repurchase it for the original sale price. Because former owners could exercise this right at their pleasure, Mennonites who had cultivated dilapidated farms could years later suddenly lose the value of their improvements. Two Catholics invoked the law against a Mennonite named Landis, a Swiss immigrant who had resided in Alzey for twenty-five years. When local authorities refused to enforce the law against Landis, the plaintiffs appealed to Karl Philip. The Elector ruled that, concerning landholding, Mennonites had the same low status

---

[10] Harold S. Bender, *Mennonite Origins in Europe* (Akron, Pa.: Mennonite Central Committee, 1957), 61; Ernst H. Correll, *Das schweizerische Täufermennonitentum: Ein sozialogischer Bericht* (Tübingen: Verlag von J. C. B. Mohr, 1925), 85; John Horsch, *Mennonites in Europe* (Scottdale, Pa.: Mennonite Publishing House, 2nd ed., 1950), 266-7; and C. Henry Smith, "The Mennonite Immigration to Pennsylvania in the Eighteenth Century," *Proceedings and Addresses of the Pennsylvania German Society* (Norristown, Pa.: 1929), 31.

[11] Horsch, *Mennonites in Europe*, 268; "Palatinate," *Mennonite Encyclopedia*, III, 110; Smith, "Mennonite Immigration," 34, 37-8; and Marianne S. Wokeck, "A Tide of Alien Tongues: The Flow and Ebb of German Immigration to Pennsylvania, 1683-1776" (Ph.D. diss.: Temple University, 1982), 47-8.

as Jews and must give up the land. His officials then sent the decree to other localities where Mennonites resided. Mennonites protested the new law and declared that they had outdone all other Palatines in rebuilding "bare and destitute farm lands, and in bringing them back to a high state of productivity." They claimed that some had rented homes for eight decades and others had owned farms for as long as thirty years; they predicted hardships for their families if they lost them. The Count then exempted past purchases from the Right of Retraction and restricted it to future transactions with a three-year limitation. The unfortunate Landis, however, still somehow lost his farm. The Right of Retraction remained in force until 1801, when Mennonites acquired full citizenship from Maximilian Joseph, King of Bavaria, who also ruled the Palatinate.[12]

Burial services created another incident in Alzey. For fifty years Mennonite funerals had remained free from restrictions. In 1714, however, a Catholic priest in Spiesheim complained to the Elector that Chilis Hahn, a Mennonite, had held an open funeral service in a public cemetery. Again local authorities supported the Mennonites, but once more the plaintiff appealed to the ruler. The Elector learned that the priest's complaints about a lengthy public sermon were inaccurate-Hahn had merely remarked briefly on the uncertainty of life--and that he conducted the service only in the Reformed pastor's absence. The Elector, however, fined Hahn, paid the priest's court costs, prohibited Mennonite burials in public graveyards, and banned them from holding public funeral services.

Mennonites challenged this decision by reminding the Elector that they traditionally conducted their burials briefly and with the consent of either the Reformed preacher or village teacher. They offered to seek also the local priest's approval and noted their habitual willingness to contribute towards the state church, the parsonage, bells, and other public welfare taxes. The Elector thereupon conceded Mennonites a corner in the graveyard but remained opposed to public services. Later in the eighteenth century the Sulzbach family Electors prohibited even the Lutheran and Reformed clergy from burying Mennonite dead.[13]

---

[12] The petition is found in Horsch, *Mennonites in Europe*, 268. See also Bender, *Mennonite Origins in Europe*, 62; and Smith, "Mennonite Immigration," which also contains portions of the petition, 46-8.

[13] Smith, "Mennonite Immigration," 49-51.

Religious nonconformists in Wittgenstein, smaller and more isolated than the Palatinate, enjoyed more substantial toleration. A secluded territory in present-day Nordrhein-Westfalen, bounded by hills along the Eder River, this small state grew into a center for religious refugees and attracted dissenters from as far as Switzerland. The ruling count, Henrich Albrecht (1698-1723) of the Sayn-Wittgenstein-Hohenstein dynasty, was the son of a Huguenot and was himself Reformed. He felt attracted to Pietism, and his four younger sisters married Pietist commoners.

Wittgenstein, like the Palatinate, suffered devastation during the Thirty Years' War, and its Count also offered toleration as bait to attract settlers. Immigrants paid a yearly tax but enjoyed most of the benefits of citizenship plus exemption from many customary obligations. They farmed on lease. Many of the new settlers built crude houses and huts in hills above the village; one valley, in fact, became known as the Valley of Huts *(Hüttental)*. The town of Schwarzenau became the birthplace of Alexander Mack's Dunkers, a conventicle of eight who sought to add Pietistic enthusiasm to Anabaptist obedience, and it also accepted the Inspired, a sect of Radical Pietists, as well as separatists who disdained all organized religion.[14]

Wittgenstein, then, provided a variety of dissenters with a legal haven in an isolated rural setting. Ruled by sympathetic counts, it exhibited a uniquely high level of tolerance, dependant upon the commitment of the local nobility to resist pressure from other princes. Although neighboring rulers protested Wittgenstein's menagerie of dissenters to the imperial government, the sluggish machinery of imperial jurisprudence did not consider the complaints until 1720. By then, however, some of the dissenters, notably the Dunkers, had left. Although Wittgenstein was hospitable to Mack's Dunkers, their relatively quick departure and voluntary exposure to the difficulties, expense, and insecurity of emigration indicates their dissatisfaction with the little

---

[14] In 1736 a traveller, John Christopher Edelmann, a separatist, provided a firsthand description of Schwarzenau; his account is in Donald F. Durnbaugh, *European Origins of the Brethren: A Source Book on the Beginnings of the Church of the Brethren in the Early Eighteenth Century* (Elgin, Ill.: Brethren Press, 1958), 109. See also Hermann Guth, *The Amish-Mennonites of Waldeck and Wittgenstein* (Elverson, Pa.: Mennonite Family History, 1986), 6-7.

duchy.[15]

Tolerance in Krefeld was much wider than in the Palatinate and had a longer tradition than in Wittgenstein. Mennonites appeared in Krefeld as early as the sixteenth century, when scattered reports placed several in the town, including one "Wolter" with a long white beard. But an Anabaptist community did not emerge until the early seventeenth century when many Mennonites, along with other Dutch Protestants, migrated to the Krefeld area to flee persecution by the Spanish, who controlled the Netherlands.

In 1657 officials of Moers, a territory that ruled Krefeld, granted the Mennonite fellowship almost complete freedom of worship but imposed other burdens. Acknowledging Mennonite pacifism, authorities excused them from guard duty and watch in exchange for a contribution, and they permitted Mennonite ownership of houses and allowed full participation in commerce. On the other hand, officials denied citizenship to them and prohibited their growth through immigration. The agreement also admonished Mennonites not to give any offense. The only religious restriction was that their worship had to begin one hour after the Reformed service.[16] Verse, written in 1724, celebrated the variety of faiths that coexisted here:

> Lutheran and Mennonite,
> Catholic and Israelite,
> Calvinist and New Baptist
> All in Krefeld now exist.[17]

Nearby jurisdictions contrasted with Krefeld's tolerance. In 1654 the Duke of Jülich, reacting to complaints that Mennonites had illegally achieved a monopoly by purchasing flax still standing in the fields, expelled about seventy families from Gladbach. Most of them settled

---

[15] Durnbaugh, *European Origins of the Brethren*, 107-9.

[16] Herbert Kisch, "Prussian Mercantilism and the Rise of the Krefeld Silk Industry: Variations upon an Eighteenth-Century Theme," *Transactions of the American Philosophical Society* 58, pt. 7 (November 1968): 18; and Friedrich Nieper, *Die ersten deutschen Auswanderer von Krefeld nach Pennsylvanien: Ein Bild aus der religiosen Ideen geschichte des 17. und 18. Jahrhunderts* (Neukirchen, Kreis Moers: Buchhandlung des Erziehungsvereins, 1940), 15-22.

[17] Durnbaugh, "Relationships of the Brethren with the Mennonites and Quakers, 1708-1865," *CH* 35 (March 1966): 36.

in or around Krefeld, which was sufficiently close to Gladbach to allow retention of their business connections with flax-growers, spinners, and weavers in neighboring principalities. They generally resided in rural Krefeld, perhaps because of the town's housing shortage, but the traditionally hostile attitude of German towns towards newcomers may also have made the countryside more attractive.[18]

In 1694 another group of Mennonites, fleeing violent persecution in Rheydt, a nearby Catholic barony, arrived in Krefeld. Their difficulties began when a crowd of armed peasants, angry over Mennonite exemption from various services, duties, and taxes and resentful of Mennonite participation in the blossoming linen trade, broke into their homes. The mob, led by the baron and several priests, captured approximately forty persons and took them to the castle. Authorities then confiscated their property and held eighteen as hostages, demanding an 8000 Reichstaler ransom, sufficiently high that other Mennonite communities had to help. Four prisoners, however, raised their ransom promptly and pledged to a fund on behalf of the others, and Krefeld Mennonites assumed most of the remaining payments. Others received banishment after weeks of detention. The exiles benefitted greatly from intervention by William III, King of England, who as the Prince of Orange allowed them to keep their property until it was sold, a process that they drew out into the eighteenth century.[19]

The Dunkers, a much smaller group than the Mennonites, also found tolerance in Krefeld. They first appeared there in about 1710, and another group, eluding persecution in Marienborn, came five years later. After several of them left Krefeld in 1719, the Reformed Church Synod recommended that preachers "be very much on guard lest similar enthusiasts should insinuate themselves in the future."[20]

The rest of Germany offered little hope for Anabaptists. After the Münster disaster Mennonites generally refrained from missionary

---

[18] Kisch, "Prussian Mercantilism and the Rise of the Krefeld Silk Industry," 17-9.

[19] Smith, "The Mennonite Immigration," 34-5; Nieper, *Die ersten deutschen Auswanderer von Krefeld nach Pennsylvanien*, 23-30; and Kisch, "Prussian Mercantilism and the Rise of the Krefeld Silk Industry," 19-20.

[20] Minutes of the General Synod, July 13-21, 1719, found in Durnbaugh, *European Origins of the Brethren*, 283. See also Durnbaugh, 316-7; and Nieper, *Die ersten deutschen Auswanderer von Krefeld nach Pennsylvanien*, 122, 127.

activities, but Dunker evangelists in the eighteenth century who left
their refuge, either in Krefeld or Wittgenstein, often suffered persecution. When in 1717 three Dunkers from Krefeld conducted several
baptisms in the Rhine River at nearby Duisburg, the consistory warned
them "with all emphasis," but the reprimand went unheeded. The
authorities then prohibited the Dunker's from teaching and holding feet-
washings, love feasts, or communions,[21] but they still ignored the
consistory. Several months later the Kleve Synod complained that
Dunkers "refused to submit to any church or consistorial discipline"
and petitioned the King to put an end to this "disorder" and "irreg-
ularity."[22]

The Dunkers' evangelism similarly alarmed authorities in
Düsseldorf, and in 1717 they imprisoned six Brethren from Solingen.
During an examination in the Düsseldorf prison, the judges accused the
six of beginning a new doctrine, which they denied, and insisted that
they join one of the three established churches, which they refused to
do. Authorities placed the prisoners in solitary confinement with empty
cells between them because a Jesuit priest advised that if they conversed with each other, they would not convert. They suffered from
cold nights and a thieving jailer. Once when authorities tortured a
husband and wife, who were criminal suspects, the Dunkers heard
unbearable screams and shortly afterward were taken into the torture
chamber and, in these intimidating environs, urged to recant. But,
again, the dissenters resisted. The perplexed authorities consulted three
universities regarding the case--the Catholic scholars recommended
execution; the Lutherans, the galleys; and the Reformed, hard labor--
and then sentenced the Solingen six to labor for life at Jülich. For
nineteen months the prisoners lived in a windowless dungeon lit
primarily by candles. All became sick with scurvy. Their work included pulling grass from between stones in the town square during a
heat wave and shovelling muck while standing in a chilly, waste-deep
moat in October. A construction accident seriously injured one of
them. Eventually sympathetic Dutch officials obtained their release.[23]

---

[21] Duisburg consistory minutes, January 25, 1717, in Durnbaugh, *European Origins
of the Brethren*, 211-3.

[22] Minutes of the Kleve Synod, May 25-28, 1717, in ibid., 213.

[23] For the Dutch correspondence regarding the Solingen Brethren, see ibid., 277-80.

Two other well-known cases of individual persecution were John Naas and Christian Liebe. According to tradition, Friedrich Wilhelm I conscripted Naas, a Dunker preacher from Krefeld, into the army because of his height, but Naas refused to serve. He endured torture, but the King, impressed with Naas's faith, rewarded him with a gold coin and his release.[24] Liebe's persistent evangelism in Bern caused the angry town fathers to sell him to Italians as a galley slave.[25]

Thus, Anabaptists venturing outside their sanctuaries did so at their own risk, and even in the havens they often lost the rights of full citizens. Only in Krefeld was religious freedom, an important indicator of Anabaptist status, both widespread and secure, and in Wittgenstein the rights of dissenters rested on the count's personal commitment. Undoubtedly early Mennonites were thankful for the limited toleration and invitation to farm in the Palatinate, but they were less welcome as spiritual nonconformists and never achieved completely free exercise of their religion.

III

Economic fortune, like religious tolerance, smiled on some Anabaptists but frowned on most of them. Although the first Anabaptists in Zürich were townsfolk, the trend quickly changed, and by 1618 south German and Swiss Anabaptists were overwhelmingly rural and poor.[26]

This trend was less evident in Krefeld, where the range of wealth among Anabaptists was wider, according to the slim evidence available. So many of the early Krefeld immigrants to Pennsylvania were linenweavers, a lowly occupation, that the Germantown coat of arms

[24] Martin Grove Brumbaugh, *A History of the German Baptist Brethren in Europe and America* (Mount Morris, Ill.: Brethren Publishing House, 1899; reprinted in 1961 by L. W. Shultz and Carl A. Wagoner), 103-5.

[25] Minutes of the Bern City Council, January 6, 1714, and Secret Minutes of the Bern City Council, July 26, 1714, in Durnbaugh, *European Origins of the Brethren*, 218-9.

[26] Clasen, *Anabaptism*, 305-24, 330.

included a loom.[27] A Krefeld census identifies four Brethren who were too poor to purchase citizenship, including two "on relief," a button-maker, and a serge weaver. Of the 395 households enumerated, only thirteen received welfare, including two of the six Dunker residences.[28]

On the other hand, in this relatively tolerant setting some Krefeld Mennonites became wealthy and fully assimilated into the community, and the city recognized the value of their linen trade to the city's commerce. During a visit in 1738 King Friedrich Wilhelm I concluded that although the Mennonites would not become soldiers, he still needed subjects like them "who make me money," and he granted them relief from taxes to the Reformed Church. After touring a factory with one hundred employees, including Catholics, Reformed, Lutherans, and Mennonites, he pronounced, *"Das ist recht gut."*[29]

Several Mennonite families, who prospered from informal support mechanisms within their faith, helped give Krefeld prominence in silk manufacturing. The von der Leyen firm, founded by Heinrich around 1660, grew to a payroll of approximately four thousand. The Floh family owned one hundred velvet looms and a dye establishment. In 1763 the von Lingen concerns employed four hundred persons and paid forty thousand Reichstalers in annual wages. In 1775 the Preyers employed an estimated seven hundred at approximately thirty velvet looms and 309 velvet ribbon looms. These entrepreneurs developed channels of information among Mennonites and networks for the movement of goods and capital. Young men known for integrity found ample investment capital even if their ventures were questionable. Church discipline made blatant dishonesty by Mennonite businesspersons almost inconceivable, and those forced into bankruptcy tapped a fund that the congregation had established for this contingency, preserving the community's good name.

In the mid-eighteenth century, however, social bonds unraveled as warfare erupted among Mennonite potentates over trade privileges and

---

[27] Nieper, *Die ersten deutschen Auswanderer von Krefeld nach Pennsylvanien*, 90-1, 98-9.

[28] Boecken, "Early Brethren in Krefeld," 123; and Durnbaugh, *European Origins of the Brethren*, 214.

[29] Nieper, *Die ersten deutschen Auswanderer von Krefeld nach Pennsylvanien*, 36-7; and *The Mennonite Encyclopedia*, I, 734-5.

monopolies. Eventually the wealthy families assimilated into Krefeld's aristocracy, built mansions, entertained lavishly, and generally abandoned the traditional Mennonite style of life.[30]

Categorizations of poverty and wealth in Wittgenstein are more difficult because of its isolation. Lucas Vetter, a Dunker, sold a house in Schwarzenau but then joined the welfare roles in Krefeld. Mack, the son of a *Bürgermeister*, was once wealthy, but he probably lost heavily in serving his faith. Christopher Sauer I, who associated with the Dunkers but refused to become a member, owned his house and then migrated to Pennsylvania debt-free. A traveller through Wittgenstein in 1736 was surprised that the area's isolated but prosperous homes went undetected by robbers, a suggestion of material success that contradicts other references to huts. He noted, however, that when thieves learned that "wealthy people" occupied those homes, "the residents had a miserable time." (The Dunkers departed in 1720, so Edelmann's account did not describe them.)[31]

Palatine Mennonites, the largest Anabaptist community in Germany, exemplified the range in wealth among Anabaptists. The most informative extant tax listing that included them reported that a majority were poor. Over one-third of the propertied persons paid taxes comparable to the propertyless and another ten paid assessments only slightly higher.[32] Another Mennonite census points to a similar conclusion. This listing did not record tax assessments, but it categor-

---

[30] Kisch, "Prussian Mercantilism and the Rise of the Krefeld Silk Industry," 21-5, 29, 39-40.

[31] Durnbaugh reports that the Brethren themselves cited the area's poverty as a motive for emigration, but he provides no documentation. See *European Origins of the Brethren*, 289. Edelmann's account is in Durnbaugh, 109. See also "A Schwarzenau Census," June 4, 1721, ibid., 291-2; Charlotte Boecken, "Early Brethren in Krefeld--Lists and Documents: Some Supplements to Previous Research, Part I," *BLT* 35 (Spring 1990): 123; William G. Willoughby, *Counting the Cost: The Life of Alexander Mack, 1679-1735* (Elgin, Ill.: Brethren Press, 1979), 18, 23, 24; and Stephen L. Longenecker, *The Christopher Sauers* (Elgin, Ill.: The Brethren Press, 1981), 20-1.

[32] The census, taken in 1664, counted ninety-three Mennonites in the Alzey district; of eighty-three who owned property, thirty-two paid taxes similar to the propertyless, and another ten paid an only slightly higher rate. See George Frederick Newman and Clyde Lester Groff, "A Listing of Mennonites of the Main Office of Alzey," July 28, 1664, *Letters from Our Palatine Ancestors, 1644-1689* (Hershey, Pa.: Gary T. Hawbaker, 1984), 83-90.

ized residents as "wealthy" (*vermöglich*), "mediocre" (*mittel mässigen*), and "poor" (*schlechten*). Some Mennonites in this enumeration achieved prosperity, but slightly over half lived in poverty.[33] Their petition of 1726 against the Right of Retraction, which recalled that many of the Palatine Mennonites had owned their farms for "ten, twenty, and thirty years," only documented the success of some of them, while many others remained destitute.[34]

Although the economic picture of Anabaptists varied, poverty overshadowed it. Some Palatine Mennonites were well established and several of those from Krefeld became wealthy entrepreneurs. But that was scarcely typical in Wittgenstein, Krefeld, and the Palatinate.

IV

Citizenship and occupational prestige determined status for early modern Germans just as much as wealth did. Here, again, Anabaptists usually found themselves on the fringes of social respectability.

German social barriers normally were formidable, even in small towns. Citizenship conferred rights to vote and hold office and provided economic and physical protection from outsiders, who were carefully and sternly defined. Citizens used communal pastures and collected firewood and construction materials from communal forests. Citizenship, normally inherited, could be purchased, but it was difficult and expensive.[35]

Occasionally Anabaptists possessed this ticket to social respectability. In Krefeld both Mennonites and Dunkers became citizens; when Mennonites became eligible in 1670, twenty families applied at once. Many Wittgenstein Dunkers obtained most citizenship rights, such as

---

[33] This census, in 1724, found fourteen wealthy, eighteen mediocre, and thirty-three poor. See Harold S. Bender, "Palatinate Mennonite Census Lists, 1664-1774," *MQR* 14 (January 1940): 26-31.

[34] Horsch, *Mennonites in Europe*, 268.

[35] Eda Sagarra, *A Social History of Germany, 1648-1914* (New York: Holmes and Meier, 1977), 67-8; Mack Walker, *German Home Towns: Community, State, and General Estate, 1648-1871* (Ithaca and London: Cornell University Press, 1971), 136-8; and Wokeck, *A Tide of Alien Tongues*, 42.

home ownership. When forty families of approximately two hundred people left in 1720, a local official reported that they acted "quietly and devoutly in all things," and that no one "ever complained about them."[36] Palatine Mennonites, however, probably the largest group of Anabaptists, undoubtedly were not citizens. The Right of Retraction, the controversy over public burials, and the protection payments suggest that legally Mennonites were more analogous to despised Jews than to burghers. Sometimes local citizens respected them, as suggested by support of Alzey authorities for Mennonites in the contests over Retraction and burial services. Since in both cases the plaintiffs were Catholic, however, perhaps local authorities merely preferred Mennonite Protestants over Romanists.

In occupational status Anabaptists fared even more poorly, especially in the Palatinate. As predominately rural folk, they often found themselves near the bottom of the vocational Chain of Being, on which each occupation held an acknowledged social rank, that ruled German society. Especially in the seventeenth century, society brutally stereotyped peasants as stupid, lazy, coarse, crude, dirty, and boorish. After the Peasants' War gentlemen recited a popular little rhyme that reflected their attitude about rural folk:

Der Bauer ist an Ochsen statt,
Nur dass er keine Hörner hat.

The peasant could take the ox's place,
Had he but horns above his face.

In the 1680s one observer acknowledged that peasants were "indeed human beings, but somewhat more unpolished and coarser than others." Like dried fish, he suggested, peasants were at their best when "gently beaten and well pounded." A polite man was "easily distinguished" from a peasant, who had a "flail in his hand and a cudgel at his side, a mattock on his shoulder and a manure-fork at his door."

Most Palatine Mennonites had a manure-fork by their door. For example, a 1724 census contained twenty Mennonites who were tenants, eighteen weavers, including twelve linenweavers and one wool-

---

[36] Frederick Christian Lade, Schwarzenau, to Francis Erasmus von Emmerich, Imperial Solicitor, Wetzlar, June 24, 1720, in Durnbaugh, *European Origins of the Brethren*, 291, 316, 317.

spinner, eleven farmers, ten day workers, five stewards, five millers, one cow herdsman, one carter, and a blacksmith.[37] Occupations with minimal public esteem dominate this list. A wide majority of them, including the tenants and many day laborers, worked in agriculture. Linenweaving was a primitive trade with rural overtones. Herding ranked low. Middle class Germans distrusted millers as swindlers and unproductive middlemen; respectable people suspected that disreputable things happened in the lofts. On the other hand, absent from the census were the glue of German society--skilled craftsmen and artisans, such as butchers, shoemakers, locksmiths, coopers, tailors, and bakers--guild positions that brought high status.[38] And, of course, none of those mentioned were truly upper class.

A wider variety of occupations and prestigious trades marked the Wittgenstein Dunkers. They included a butcher, wealthy miller, sackmaker, tailor, and shoemaker as well as a pair of modest linenweavers. Michael Eckerlin was a citizen and a capmaker in Strassburg before being expelled. Prior to his baptism, Gottfried Neumann was a Lutheran theologian from Leipzig who taught at Halle; he later became an outstanding hymnist for the Moravians. It is uncertain, however, whether these refugee-artisans resumed their trades in Wittgenstein. Did George Grebe, who had been a wealthy court gunsmith in Kassel, practice gunsmithing in the Valley of Peace near Schwarzenau? Five of the Solingen six evidently were guildsmen, including two sword- or knifemakers, but according to a contemporary description, the sixth, a weaver, received different treatment because in his lower station, he "did not have to promise anything."[39]

Thus, the Solingen Dunkers and a few Mennonites, most notably in Krefeld, found a respectable position on the socio-economic ladder although the Solingen group relinquished it in the service of their faith. Most Anabaptists, nevertheless, especially in the Palatinate, remained

---

[37] The census also included a *Stiftschaffner*, who was probably a steward at a convent.

[38] Walker, *German Home Towns*, 98-9.

[39] "A faithful account of the seven persons imprisoned for the truth and for the sake of Christ," in Durnbaugh, *European Origins of the Brethren*, 266-7. The trades of several of the early Brethren are found in private letters and official reports included in the same, 81-2, 86, 87, 111, 123, 130-1, 147, 179-80. Among the Krefeld Brethren Johann Georg Schmidt was a band maker and day laborer, and Johannes Naas and Hans Jacob Preisz were stocking weavers; see Boecker, "Early Brethren in Krefeld," 123.

on the lower rungs, lacking citizenship privileges and prestigious occupations.

V

The relationship, therefore, between Anabaptists and church Germans in the three jurisdictions from which most Dunkers and Mennonites migrated changed in Pennsylvania. Although Anabaptists in the home country possessed nearly complete tolerance in Krefeld and Wittgenstein, authorities curtailed religious freedom in the Palatinate, and outside these few jurisdictions Anabaptists suffered heavily. Moreover, Dunkers and Mennonites tended to be employed in lowly occupations, and poverty was prevalent. Even in some of the principalities that gave them sanctuary, Dunkers and Mennonites felt persecution or economic disadvantage, and beyond the oases of toleration Anabaptists faced a desert of discrimination.

Many factors nourished the growth of tolerance in colonial Pennsylvania, but among the most significant were the new socio-economic relationships between German Anabaptists and Lutherans and Reformed. European Germans perceived Anabaptists as outcasts, but, as Henry M. Muhlenberg realized, these traditional, hierarchical relationships ended in Pennsylvania, enabling the last to become first.

CHAPTER 2

Testing the Limits of Tolerance: Radical Pietists in Early Pennsylvania

Among the first Germans to settle in Pennsylvania were those whose brand of Pietism led them further from the mainstream than most of their contemporaries had gone. Like other Pietists, they sought a direct and personal relationship with Christ, stripped of intermediaries, but these "Radical Pietists" differed by placing greater emphasis on mysticism and by having less use for formal church structure. Some sought to isolate themselves from society, and a few concluded that family ties impaired their spiritual life. They became extreme nonconformists, and, suffering oppression in Germany, many fled to the safety of Pennsylvania. Small in number, they became less prominent as the colony's population increased, but their standing in the early colonial era illustrates that Radical Pietists as well as Quakers and Mennonites added to Pennsylvania's pluralism and enjoyed its tolerance.[1]

I

Radical Pietism in William Penn's colony first grew from seeds planted by millennialists desiring to greet the returning Christ in the New World. The backers of this enterprise were a conventicle of Pietists in Frankfurt, who formed a company and bought fifteen thousand acres in Pennsylvania after Penn visited them during his 1677 trip through Germany. In 1683 they sent one of their members, Francis Daniel

[1] Dale R. Stoffer, *Background and Development of Brethren Doctrines, 1650-1987* (Philadelphia: Brethren Encyclopedia, 1989), 19-43.

Pastorius, to the colony as their agent.

Initially, they apparently considered Pennsylvania as hospitable to a new ecumenical ideal of universal brotherhood, but in 1685 several events, especially the Revocation of the Edict of Nantes, kindled intense millennial speculation. One of their number, Johann Jakob Zimmermann, concluded that the appearance of a comet in 1680, the French conquest of Strassburg in 1681, and the Turks' march on Vienna in 1683 meant that 1694 might bring the Second Coming. To greet the new age, Zimmermann organized a Chapter of Perfection.

The details of Zimmermann's fraternity of millennialists are hazy, except for the willingness of some members to move to the New World. However, none of the key German organizers besides Zimmermann attempted the journey, and he died en route in Rotterdam, leaving his widow and four children to continue on the trip. Johannes Kelpius, aged twenty, became leader, or "Magister," of the well-educated band and Bernhard Koester, a lawyer, linguist, and Biblical scholar, his deputy. The group interrupted its trip to spend six months in England with another group of millennialists, the Philadelphian Society. In 1694 Kelpius directed several dozen persons to found a settlement on the Wissahickon Creek, near Germantown, hoping that the purity of the wilderness would help ready them for the Christ's return.[2]

Despite Kelpius's unconventional millennialism, his testimony of conversion was typically Pietist. He confessed that before rebirth he "neglected to walk in the perfect light of Christ," and, like one of the "foolish virgins" of whom Jesus spoke, he found that when "the bridegroom entered, the gates [were] closed." Conversion, made available through God's grace, came after he had "chosen to imitate" Jesus, an acknowledgment of the role of humans in determining their salvation. He urged others similarly to "open" their hearts to the Holy Spirit and to "resign" themselves to God's direction. Those who did, he said, felt "a sweet Joyfull Gush of Tears" that initiated a new, intimate relationship with Christ. When the Holy Spirit dwelled within

---

[2] The Philadelphians desired to prepare society for the new age by promoting "universal peace and love." The quotation is from "The State of the Philadelphian Society" (1620), in Elizabeth W. Fisher, "'Prophecies and Revelations': German Cabbalists in Early Pennsylvania," *PMHB* 109 (July 1985): 320-1. See also Fisher., 316-9; *The Brethren Encyclopedia*, 3 vols. (Philadelphia: Brethren Encyclopedia, Inc., 1984), II, 1199-1200; and Julius Friedrich Sachse, *The German Pietists of Provincial Pennsylvania* (Philadelphia: published by the author, 1895), 60-2.

individuals, it inwardly prayed for them, making possible Paul's advice to pray without ceasing. This prayer came without awareness, "like breathing," and was possible for everyone, the "simple and unlearned" as well as the educated and sophisticated. Combining the new birth, free will, intimacy, and obedience, Kelpius compared Christ to a lover, "standing behind our Wall, showing himself through the Lattesse, saying Rise up my Love, my fair one, and come away."[3]

To be close to the "Beloved," Kelpius advocated spiritual and physical isolation. Keep the flesh in subjection, he advised; do not become "too busy with outward things." Only through denial of "inordinate inclinations," he said, could inward prayer proceed; "the affections of the mind and sense must be tamed."[4] Kelpius found in Revelation 6:12 Scriptural encouragement to subdue the flesh by escaping to the wilds: "And the woman fled into the wilderness, where she had a place prepared by God, in which to be nourished for one thousand, two hundred and sixty days." The woman, Kelpius assumed, was the Virgin Sophia, whom, many mystics believed, God created as an embodiment of divine truth. So as the millennium approached, the remnant of the true church would rejoin Sophia, their spiritual mother, in the wilderness and prepare for the Second Coming.[5]

Kelpius pictured this wilderness experience as having three aspects. The first and "barren" one he compared to the "Old Birth" and the second, the "fruitful wilderness," to the new. The first stage brought one "out of Egypt," as the enslaved Hebrews had been led, but only to die in the wilderness. (According to the Book of Exodus, some of the fleeing Hebrews regretted their decision and urged a return to

---

[3] Kelpius to Pallmer, in Sachse, *German Pietists*, 191; Kelpius to Rev. Magister Eric Biorck, *The Diarium of Magister Johannes Kelpius*, ed. Sachse, (Lancaster, Pa.: The Pennsylvania German Society, 1917), 62; Kelpius, *A Method of Prayer*, ed. and intro. E. Gordon Alderfer (New York: Harper and Brothers, 1951), 77-102, 125. Kelpius's work was first printed in English by Henry Miller in 1761 and by Christopher Sauer II in 1763.

[4] Kelpius, *Method of Prayer*, 106. See also ibid., 105-8; and Kelpius to Pallmer, in Sachse, *German Pietists*, 191.

[5] The quotation is from the Revised Standard Version. See also Fisher, "Prophecies and Revelations," 309, 322-3; and Samuel Whitaker Pennypacker, *The Settlement of Germantown Pennsylvania and the Beginning of German Immigration to North America* (Lancaster, Pa.: The Pennsylvania German Society, 1899), 269, 275-8.

Egypt: hence, their death in the wilderness.) The second stage, however, also born in Egypt, matured in the wilderness and was "set at Liberty" to enter the promised land. In addition, a few "chosen vessels," called to perform extraordinary tasks, entered what he called the third stage. Pointing to Elijah, David, Moses, John, Jesus, and Paul, Kelpius noted that God always prepared "his most eminent Instruments in the Wilderness." His close friend, Johann Seelig, thought Psalm 63 referred to such persons with the words: "My flesh longeth for thee in a dry and thirsty land." Kelpius granted that "one may arrive to the manhood in Christ" without attaining the third level of experience, but he confided that he kissed "the Father's hand" for leading him into the "desert."[6]

To make their sojourn in the Wissahickon wilderness a greater mortification of the flesh, the hermits slept on hard beds and wore homespun garments; Kelpius himself resided in a cave. Their "desert" included celibacy, which they probably adopted from Jacob Boehme, who taught that before the fall Adam was like God, genderless, "a man and also a women, a virgin, wholly pure in modesty." Kelpius hoped that through celibacy he could find pre-fall purity.[7]

Because Kelpius associated with Rosicrucians in Germany, many have considered the Kelpianites to be members of that fraternity. Rosicrucians believed that natural phenomena, such as eclipses and comets, and magical systems of mathematics revealed God's intent just as clearly as the Scriptures. They guarded these insights as secrets, which, they believed, enabled them to interpret God's revelations in nature. Sometimes Kelpius sounded like a Rosicrucian when he referred to mysterious events, including "Illuminations, Inspeakings, Prophesies, Apparitions, changings of Minds, Transfigurations, [and] Translations of their bodys," and he praised "wonderful Fastings for 11, 14, 27, 37 days, and Paradysical Representations by Voices, Melodies, and Sensations." But he spoke only rarely in such terms,

---

[6] Kelpius to Heinrich Johann Deichman (February 24, 1697), in Sachse, ed., *Diarium*, 30. See also Seelig to Deichman, May 12, 1699, in Sachse, ed., *Diarium*, 43; and Kelpius to Pallmer, in Sachse, *German Pietists*, 180-9.

[7] The Boehme quotation is in Fisher, "Prophecies and Revelations," 309-10. A nineteenth-century photograph of Kelpius's cave appears in Pennypacker, *Settlement of Germantown*, 274-5, and elsewhere. See also Kelpius to Dr. Johannes Fabricius, July 23, 1705, and Kelpius to Pallmer, in Sachse, *German Pietists*, 184, 199.

and more consistently emphasized an inner religious experience based upon self-denial.[8]

Despite their fondness for the "desert," the Society of the Woman in the Wilderness enthusiastically cooperated with other Protestants. Three Swedish Lutheran missionaries, who arrived in Pennsylvania in 1697 enjoyed a warm relationship with them. When the Swedes constructed their first church building, the Society chanted Psalms and other responses at the laying of the cornerstone. At the consecration of another Swedish church, *Gloria Dei*, in Philadelphia, the Wissahickon brothers performed instrumental music and chanted Psalms and responses before a large congregation of English, Germans, and Swedes and heard a sermon preached in both Swedish and English. Kelpius's fraternity also assisted in 1703 in the Swedish Lutheran ordination of Justus Falkner, formerly a member of their congregation.[9] Koester, Kelpius's assistant, conducted Lutheran worship in the Germantown home of Jacob Issacs Van Bebber, a wealthy Mennonite from Krefeld. These services attracted many English settlers, especially Keithian Quakers, who were drawn to a more doctrinal faith that taught Christ's physical as well as spiritual resurrection. Koester became an outspoken defender of the Keithians and left the Wissahickon community to establish his own settlement. Several German Quakers, angered over his support of Keith's schism, tried but failed to persuade Pastorius to disperse the mystical Pietists.[10]

In 1708 Kelpius died of a consumption that developed from a severe cold. According to tradition, he hoped for his body and soul to remain united in death, so as his end approached, he prayed for three

---

[8] Bernard Bailyn, *The Peopling of British North America: An Introduction* (New York: Alfred A. Knopf, 1986), 123-4; Jon Butler, "Magic, Astrology, and the Early American Religious Heritage, 1600-1760," *AHR* 84 (April 1979): 326-7; Delburn Carpenter, *The Radical Pietists: Celibate Communal Societies Established in the United States Before 1820* (New York: AMS Press, 1975), 307-9; Fisher, "Prophecies and Revelations," 307-10, 319-20; Kelpius to Steven Momfort, December, 11, 1699, in *Diarium*, 49; and Sachse, *German Pietists*, 6-7, 37-42, 69-77.

[9] Sachse, *German Pietists*, 144, 158.

[10] Sachse claims, with little documentation, that the Germans initially feared that the English were hostile Quakers attempting to pack the house in order to keep the Germans out. See *German Pietists*, 66-8, 85-7, 283. See also Fisher, "Prophecies and Revelations," 328.

days and nights to ascend as Elijah had. Eventually he gave up and in-structed a friend, Daniel Geisler, to throw a sealed but empty casket into a deep section of the Schuylkill River. At the river bank, howev-er, Geisler disobeyed instructions and hid the casket, intending to examine its contents after his master's imminent death. When Geisler returned, Kelpius sat up and said curtly, "Daniel, thou has not done as I bid thee. Thou hast not cast the casket into the river, but hast hid it by the shore." Geisler, convinced of Kelpius's occult powers, quickly retraced his steps and threw the casket into the waters, upon which lightning flashed and thunder crashed.[11]

The Wissahickon Society perished soon after its leader died. The Society's goal to ready the world for the millennium clashed with its vision of a perfectionist retreat.   Marriage caused defections, and Pennsylvania's labor shortage and attractive wages may have lured oth-ers away. By the end of its first decade in Pennsylvania, many fol-lowers of Kelpius, including Koester and Justus and Daniel Falkner, had re-emerged from the wilderness although remnants of the Kelpius group, as represented by Conrad Matthei and Christopher Witt, lived as Separatists into the 1730s.[12]

II

Several decades later and approximately sixty miles further west the Ephrata Cloister formed another counterculture commune. This group mixed the Pietist formula for salvation with a heavy dose of individual-ism and, paradoxically, rigid communal discipline.

Ephrata's spiritual and organizational life orbited tightly around the charismatic personality of Conrad Beissel. A baker's apprentice from the Palatinate, Beissel was born in 1690, two months after his alcoholic father died. In 1715 he was converted when, according to his followers, the "awakening-Spirit knocked loudly at his conscience." After his apprenticeship, his travels as a journeyman took him to

[11] Pennypacker, *Settlement of Germantown*, 279-80.

[12] Sachse, *German Pietists*, 176-7, 199; and Fisher, "Prophecies and Revelations," 332-3.

Heidelberg, where a baker named Kantebecker employed him and introduced him to secret meetings that Pietists held in the woods. Kantebecker and Beissel prospered, but their aggressive commercialism, which included a possibly illegal trade with Frankfurt, outraged the other master bakers, and Beissel's criticism of extravagant guild banquets further irritated them. The masters, therefore, arranged with the city council to arrest and jail the pious apprentice. He was acquitted at his trial, but an ecclesiastical court gave Beissel the choice of joining the Lutherans, Reformed, or Catholics or leaving. He departed only a few steps ahead of soldiers sent to arrest him. For a time he lived first with the Inspired at Marienborn and then near Alexander Mack's Brethren at Schwarzenau.[13]

Migrating to Pennsylvania in 1720, Beissel associated with the Dunkers. Peter Becker taught him weaving, and the following year Beissel assumed a hermit's life in the Conestoga country. There he became popular with other German Pietists and began to observe the Sabbath, or Saturday, rather than Sunday. In 1724 he attended a Dunker meeting led by Becker, who was itinerating in the backcountry, but resisted baptism because he feared losing his spiritual gifts and insights if someone with spiritual powers less than his baptized him. (Once, Beissel attempted to baptize himself.) But suddenly, Beissel's followers claimed, "a bright ray from the Gospel" revealed to him that Christ had been baptized by someone "less than himself." Seeing Becker, then, as his John the Baptist, Beissel entered the Pequea Creek and, following six others, was immersed.[14]

Before returning to Germantown, the Dunkers organized the Conestoga converts, who elected Beissel as their teacher and built a small house for him. Perhaps influenced by the Inspired, who prophesied during trances, Beissel preached extemporaneously with his eyes closed and without a Bible so that, according to his followers, his "testimony might not be weakened by written knowledge." In 1726 Anna and Maria Eicher, sisters, left their father to reside with him.

---

[13] Lamech and Agrippa, *Chronicon Ephratense: A History of the Community of Seventh Day Baptists at Ephrata, Lancaster County, Pennsylvania*, trans. J. Max Hart (Lancaster, Pa.: S. H. Zahn, 1889), 4-11.

[14] Ibid., 13, 15, 25; and "Life and Conduct of the Late Brother Ezechiel Sangmeister," trans. Barbara M. Schindler, *Historical Society of the Cocalico Valley, Ephrata, Pa.* (1986), I, 17-8.

Although Beissel maintained that he was only spiritually intimate with the women, this living arrangement understandably stimulated considerable comment in the neighborhood.[15]

Beissel's Conestoga Dunkers soon argued with their Germantown sponsors, especially over their leader's decision to worship on the Sabbath rather than Sunday. His statement that sin lay "hidden" in little children, who were not guaranteed salvation, also enraged many Germantowners, as did his advocacy of celibacy. Beissel had adopted sexual abstinence after determining that an employer's wife in Mannheim, Germany, was a "Jezebel"; he left that household, explaining that God's servants must "renounce Adam's generative work."[16] Many Dunker men feared that Beissel would break apart their marriages. One preacher reportedly embraced his wife and begged her "for God's sake" not to leave him. These disputes over the Sabbath and self-denial as well as over other matters became so intense that Beissel's followers "gave back" their baptism to the Germantown Brethren and baptized themselves anew. Then the congregations in Conestoga and Germantown banned each other.[17]

Soon, however, several controversies threatened Beissel's position within his own fellowship. Celibacy lost credibility when one of the oldest solitaries, Jan Meyle, suffered erysipelas in the head, an inflammation of the skin sometimes called St. Anthony's fire, and became a naked Peeping Tom. After standing unclothed, perhaps for relief from fever, by a cabin door, Meyle climbed into bed with the *Hausfrau*. He was seized, bound, and delivered to the justice of the peace. That officer sent him to the township's Poor Directors, who returned him to the congregation. Shortly thereafter, Meyle preached from the courthouse belfry in Philadelphia, attracting a crowd of the curious. Some of Beissel's followers blamed Meyle's actions on celibacy and contemplated resuming conjugal relations with their wives. Meyle subsequently returned to his senses, and he served the Society at Ephrata as chief baker until his death at the age of eighty-two.

At approximately the same time that Meyle's behavior raised

---

[15] *Chronicon*, 26-7, 33-4; and Sangmeister, "Life and Conduct," I, 19.

[16] The quotation is from the *Chronicon* and is not direct, 4-5. See also *Chronicon*, 44; and Sangmeister, "Life and Conduct," IV, 22.

[17] Sangmeister, "Life and Conduct," V, 103-4; and *Chronicon*, 36, 48-9.

doubts about celibacy, a jealous husband, enraged by his wife's lingering in Beissel's cabin, further embarrassed the preacher. Beissel's followers claimed that their leader had to permit this compromising situation "because of his vows to God." The husband, Hans Landis, brought his wife home from Beissel's residence several times, once employing the constable. Finally, Landis entered a love feast singing "on Babylon we've war declared," then tried to choke Beissel, refusing to release him until the Society permitted his wife to return home. After this, congregational leaders ordered Frau Landis to stay away. She obeyed, but once Landis bound her to prevent her attending a love feast. When Landis died, his widow returned to Ephrata, remaining there until her death in 1779.[18]

Battered by these conflicts, Beissel delivered a sermon to his assembled followers, appointed leaders in his place, and then resigned his office. He removed himself to an unsettled plot in the woods beside the Cocalico Creek, where he shared a cabin with Emmanuel Eckerlin. But soon his followers gathered around him again, forming the nucleus of the Ephrata Cloister.[19]

Under Beissel's dominance the Ephrata Society endorsed a theology that included Pietist free grace, an Anabaptist-like call for sacrifice, and an emphasis on both individual experience and conformity to the congregation. Much of what the Ephratites taught, of course, was indistinguishable from the teaching of many Pennsylvania German revivalists. Beissel believed that Christianity brought "glad tidings" that were attractive to the "free will of man." He confided that before conversion his conscience daily plunged into "greater misery," until God "awakened" him and taught him "denial and humility." He said that "through grace" he had kept "this covenant" and that his conduct after conversion was a work of the "new life of grace." George A. Martin, a sympathetic Dunker, recalled being seized by "inward emotion" that brought tears to his eyes during a hymn in Ephrata's prayer hall. The Cloister endorsed this experience as typical among those who were "truly born again." Likewise, when God "rapped on a new part" of one member's heart with instructions to "mend his

[18] I am grateful to William E. Longenecker, D.O., for his insights about erysipelas. See also *Chronicon*, 58-60; and Sangmeister, "Life and Conduct," 31.

[19] James E. Ernst, *Ephrata: A History*, ed. John Joseph Stoudt, (Allentown, Pa.: Pennsylvania German Folklore Society, 1963), 84-92; and *Chronicon*, 62-3, 65-6.

ways," the "internal joy and pleasure," made him feel as if he were "already in blissful eternity!"[20]

Beissel added, however, that conversion included "the cross and the severe disciplinary training" that humble a righteous person, and he gave his followers detailed instructions on how to bear their individual crosses. He organized the Society into three groups: Solitary Brothers and Spiritual Virgins, both celibate, and married Householders, who farmed in the neighborhood. Although the householders lived as families, some of them also may have practiced celibacy. Ezechiel Sangmeister, a Beissel convert, condemned men who, when God tests them with "poverty, drought, and cold," found "no consolation other than the flesh of a woman." Other followers said that those who married "dragged the gifts of the Spirit into the flesh."[21] The solitaries, on the other hand, occasionally broke their vows, as in the case of a Spiritual Virgin who in 1752 delivered triplets. The celibates dressed in simple, white cowls. The Householders initially wore gray but eventually resumed worldly dress; the men grew beards. Early Cloister residents lived in barren cells and slept on narrow benches with wooden blocks for pillows, but as the Society aged, it relaxed its austerity somewhat and allowed members to sleep in beds. The solitaries did without horses and cows and tilled the ground only with hoes. Midnight watches, initially lasting four hours, which the Cloister admitted was "a sore crucifixion of the flesh," were routine because they anticipated "the advent of the Judge" at that hour; eventually the Cloister halved their length. During these midnight services a curtain concealed the women. Ezechiel Sangmeister, who typified Ephrata's spirituality, expressed a desire only to "live in" God forever and to "forget everything else." "Away with people," he admonished, "away

[20] Beissel to Peter Becker (April 12, 1755, and May 20, 1756), Donald F. Durnbaugh, ed., *The Brethren in Colonial America: A Source Book on the Transplantation and Development of the Church of the Brethren in the Eighteenth Century* (Elgin, Ill.: The Brethren Press, 1967), 104-8; *Chronicon*, 255-6; and Sangmeister, "Life and Conduct," IV, 67.

[21] Sangmeister, "Life and Conduct," V, 104; and *Chronicon*, 35.

with money, away with land, everything brings only pain. "[22]

Beissel's appeals for celibacy especially attracted women, who perhaps used it as a morally acceptable form of divorce or simply to escape the dangers of bearing children. When Beissel visited one family whose daughter was betrothed, he converted her so quickly that she departed for Ephrata without her groom's knowledge and took vows of celibacy. This speedy conversion suggests that she used Ephrata as an escape from an arranged or otherwise undesirable marriage. Another woman, the wife of Christopher Sauer I, Maria Christine, mother of a twelve-year-old son, probably left an unhappy marriage to live at Ephrata.[23]

Beissel carefully preserved his authority. According to Sangmeister, he taught that those who followed him could not "go wrong" and that his followers were "in a fair way" if their goodness combined equalled his. Furthermore, Sangmeister alleged, Beissel warned that those who left the community would not enter heaven, even if they led "an angelic life," because everyone's "goodness" came from the fellowship.[24]

When commercialism briefly surfaced in the Cloister's communal economy and threatened Beissel's "severe disciplinary training," he crushed it. Under the influence of the Eckerlin brothers--Emmanuel, Gabriel, Israel, and Samuel--who managed the businesses, the Ephrata Cloister bought grain from neighboring farmers and stored it in granaries until the price rose. Meanwhile, wagons continually delivered flour and other goods to Philadelphia markets. But Beissel determined that such fervent entrepreneurialism might corrupt the Cloister, and he convinced the community to abandon aggressive capitalism. He drove the Eckerlin brothers away, a mill mysteriously burned, and the community uprooted its profitable orchard. They sold

---

[22] E. G. Alderfer, *The Ephrata Commune: An Early American Counterculture* (Pittsburgh: University of Pittsburgh Press, 1985), 65-6; *Chronicon*, 35, 77-8, 92-3; "Letter to the Editor," in Durnbaugh, *Brethren in Colonial America*, 137-8; Stephen Koch to Johann Lobach (November 13, 1738), ibid., 98; Morgan Edwards, *Materials towards a History of the American Baptists* (Philadelphia: Joseph Crukshank and Isaac Collins, 1770), 74-79; and Sangmeister, "Life and Conduct," VI, 52, 104.

[23] *Chronicon*, 56, 68-9; and Stephen L. Longenecker, *The Christopher Sauers* (Elgin, Ill.: The Brethren Press, 1981), 30-4.

[24] Sangmeister, "Life and Conduct," IV, 83, 84.

to the Lutherans of Lancaster a bell that the Eckerlins had ordered from England. Only the printing press survived Beissel's housecleaning, although the mill was rebuilt. (By 1770, after Beissel's death, several other mills were in operation, and Ephrata had begun selling vegetables in Lancaster.)[25]

Despite strenuous efforts to separate their fellowship from the larger society, the Ephrata Cloister enjoyed cordial relations with many outsiders. Beissel's insistence on working on Sunday violated Pennsylvania law, but after several court appearances and fines, the authorities ignored his behavior. Peter Miller, a scholar, corresponded with Benjamin Franklin, and Charles Thomson nominated him to membership in the American Philosophical Society for studies on the Hessian fly.[26] Neighbors, who mostly belonged to "the great religious denominations," as the Cloister put it, quickly helped to rebuild the burned-out mill, and the Brothers reciprocated by joining in the construction of a church building. When George Martin asked Peter Miller if he "did not still owe something" to the Reformed, his former denomination, Miller responded, "not only to the Reformed but to all men, whatever I have and can."[27]

Frequently, visitors to Ephrata were impressed. Morgan Edwards expected "sour aspects and rough manners" but found "a smiling innocence and meekness." He recalled that members of the Cloister spoke with "a softness of tone and accent" and their behavior "was gentle." Guests often marveled at the choir, which Edwards described as "charming, partly owing to the pleasantness of their voices, the variety of parts they carry on together, and the devout manner of performance." Another visitor compared a solo he heard to the lute-stop of an organ, but he saw the soloist when the curtain was pulled back. He also noticed the neatness and cleanliness of the homes and furniture and marveled that in a fly and insect-infested country Ephrata had none. He explained that all Germans in America used a repellent that

---

[25] Alderfer, *Ephrata Commune*, 86-122, 163-96; and Ernst, *Ephrata*, 211-34, 249-82; Edwards, *Materials towards the History of American Baptists*, 74-79; and "Letter to the Editor," *Monthly Review* (February 1778), in Durnbaugh, *Brethren in Colonial America*, 138.

[26] Alderfer, *Ephrata Commune*, 159, 162.

[27] *Chronicon*, 44-5, 197, 210-2, 254.

they made by mixing a little sugar in a plate of water, then adding a substance called fly-stone and hanging the poisonous mixture from the ceiling.[28]

Others viewed Ephrata less sympathetically. In the settlement's early days, the Cloister accused local residents of trying to drive them away. The locals allegedly set fire to the woods, hoping to burn out the community, but the fire turned. Thereafter hostile neighbors resorted to rumor and, the Cloister complained, "began everywhere to warn one another against seduction."[29]

In fact, Beissel made enemies easily. Besides the Dunkers, he repudiated Christopher Sauer I, Matthias Baumann of the "New Born," and Count Nicholas Ludwig von Zinzendorf, the Moravian's leader. (Sauer, however, later enjoyed a rapproachment with Ephrata.) Stephen Koch, who moved to Ephrata in 1738, easily endorsed the running battles with the Dunkers because "awakened" souls must earnestly witness against worthless "outward ceremonies" that had neither spirit nor "inner life." This, he said, "often causes much dispute and trouble within a congregation"; Christ, he said, came to "bring peace, but not for the old life."[30]

Symbolic of both the tension and tolerance between Ephrata and the outside world is a well-known tale that celebrates Peter Miller's walk to Valley Forge during the American Revolution to save Michael Widman, a Reformed deacon and the local tavern keeper. Widman, who detested the Cloister and once spat upon Miller, had been court-martialed for treason and was destined for the gallows, but Miller's extraordinary journey to plead for his enemy moved George Washington to issue a pardon. Miller delivered the pardon to the hangman as Widman approached the scaffold. Upon spotting Miller in the crowd, Widman at first assumed that he had come to relish the execution but after his release embraced his rescuer.[31]

Under Miller, who assumed leadership of Ephrata after Beissel's death in 1768, the Cloister dwindled. In 1770 Morgan Edwards found

[28] Edwards, *Materials towards the History of American Baptists*, 74-9; and "Letter to the Editor," in Durnbaugh, *Brethren in Colonial America*, 138-9.

[29] *Chronicon*, 66.

[30] Koch to Lobach, in Durnbaugh, *Brethren in Colonial America*, 97.

[31] Alderfer, *Ephrata Commune*, 166-7; and Ernst, *Ephrata*, 349-51.

only fourteen Solitary Brothers, forty-two Spiritual Virgins, and ninety-nine in the lay congregation.[32] After the Battle of Brandywine in 1777 George Washington directed Ephrata to care for approximately five hundred wounded, transforming it into an overcrowded hospital. During the winter, camp fever took the lives of scores of soldiers and ten Ephrata residents, now an elderly group less resistant to disease. Two Mennonite neighbors who helped care for the wounded, John Baer and his wife, also fell victim to the epidemic. When the soldiers departed, Ephrata decontaminated itself by destroying its two largest buildings. An officer who regained his health there "left with regret," he said, because at Ephrata he saw "pure and practical Christianity" in action.[33]

Only a skeleton of the Cloister survived into the nineteenth century. In approximately 1810 a visiting British diplomat, Sir Augustus J. Foster, found two Brothers and eight Sisters in the congregation, but only five of them, ranging in age from sixty-five to eighty, still lived at the Cloister.[34]

[32] Alderfer, *Ephrata Commune*, 159, 162.

[33] Ibid., 164-6.

[34] Two spin-off congregations, founded near the end of the eighteenth century, Snow Hill in Franklin County and Enterprise, near Bedford, survived Ephrata's collapse. George Martin's Dunker congregation, called Antietam, evolved into the Snow Hill Cloister, attracting a total of forty-three people. The congregation, stimulated by Peter Miller's visits, gradually adopted Beissel's system, beginning in about 1775 with sabbatarianism and establishing a celibate commune in 1798. Working on Sunday conflicted with Pennsylvania statutes, and Snow Hill members, unlike Ephrata, regularly paid fines. In 1846 they unsuccessfully went to court, employing Thaddeus Stevens as their attorney. Several members lost property and were imprisoned, but after this the authorities overlooked the infractions. Communalism at Snow Hill lasted until 1889.

In the late 1980s two congregations of Seventh Day German Baptists, both moderately fundamentalist, persisted: one at Snow Hill, now called Quincy, and the other at Enterprise. Members return semi-annually to the Ephrata Cloister, operated by the Pennsylvania State Museum Commission, for a covered dish love feast and feetwashing in the chapel. See ibid., 174, 184.

III

Besides the Ephrata and the Wissahickon societies, smaller fellowships of Radical Pietists and individual nonconformists further illustrate the religious diversity among Pennsylvania Germans. Typical were Matthias Baumann and his followers, the New Born. After a serious illness and apparent death in 1701, Baumann, a poor day laborer in the Palatinate, experienced visions, for which authorities examined and imprisoned him. He fled to Berks County, Pennsylvania, and itinerated extensively before organizing the New Born. Unlike many other Pietists, Baumann and his followers claimed that their second birth made them perfectly and literally free from sin. Baumann asserted that he was "even firmer" than Adam before the fall. To prove the divine inspiration of his beliefs, he offered to walk across the Delaware River.

The New Born received little support from other communions. According to the Lutheran leader, Henry M. Muhlenberg, the New Born condemned the sacraments as "ridiculous" and "of the devil," like the ministry, churches, and schools. He accused them of using the Bible out of context to justify their position. George Michael Weiss, a Reformed minister, published a booklet to expose their errors, and when Baumann visited Ephrata, Beissel mocked his perfectionist teachings by suggesting that Baumann "smell his own filth and then consider whether this belonged to the new birth."[35]

Other Radical Pietists, like Johann Adam Gruber, never joined a religious organization in Pennsylvania. Gruber's spiritual roots lay among the Inspired, German Pietists who worshipped with emotion and prophesied during convulsions. They assumed that, just as in the primitive Christian church, a still-active God communicated "hidden things through visions, dreams, and revelations" and provided "present-day inspiration" as powerful as Scripture. Scribes recorded the sayings of their prophets, or "instruments" (*Werkzeuge*), because the speakers often forgot what they said during their trances. Among

---

[35] Baumann is quoted in *Chronicon*, 17. See also *Chronicon*, 16, 17n4; *The Brethren Encyclopedia*, II, 925; Henry Melchior Muhlenberg, *The Journals of Henry Melchior Muhlenberg*, ed. and trans. Theodore G. Tappert and John W. Doberstein, 3 vols. (Philadelphia: Muhlenberg Press, 1942-58), I, 149, 357-8; and George Michael Weiss, *Der in der americanischen Wildnusz unter Menschen von verschiedenenen Nationen und Religionen hin und wieder herum Wandelte und verschiedentlich angesochtene Prediger* (Philadelphia: Andrew Bradford, 1729).

later generations of Inspired, the volumes of recorded testimonies received authority equal to that of the Bible. The Inspired also refused to take an oath of allegiance to political authorities or to perform military service.[36]

Although Gruber's conversion to this group was typically Pietist, the accompanying emotion was not. Turmoil and rebellion plagued his boyhood. Although his conscience "punished" him, he recalled that no "serious awakening" came to him until he and his family met the Inspired. He wept for several days when his father joined them and at the next meeting felt a trembling that lasted all night, the following day, and into the evening. Then came his first prophecy, a two-hour stem-winder. The Grubers quickly assumed leadership in the small sect; Gruber's father, a former Lutheran minister, became its head. Johann Adam's charismatically delivered "Twenty-Four Rules of True Godliness" was their doctrinal cornerstone until well into the twentieth century.

The Grubers and the Inspired lived in Büdingen-Ysenburg, a German haven for dissenters, ruled by the Wittgenstein dynasty, but after they prophesied judgment against the local count, the authorities lost patience with them. One official complained that despite a warning the Inspired still met in homes "with shaking, leaping, raging, crying, and shouting 'Woe! Woe!' and prophesying the most alarming judgement of God on town and country." On one visit this official ordered them to emigrate in twenty-four hours and then quickly left after observing that the younger Gruber "appeared to be about to have one of their usual paroxysms."[37]

In 1715 the Inspired moved to Wittgenstein, but the Grubers began to argue. In 1720 Johann Adam married and six years later took his family to Pennsylvania; both actions defied the guidance of his communion and his father. He lost his children at sea, lamenting that he "had to watch them perish and, so to speak, die of thirst." Nevertheless, Gruber encouraged his parents to follow him to Pennsylvania

---

[36] The quotations are from Eberhard Ludwig Gruber in Bertha M. H. Shambaugh, *Amana That Was and Amana That Is* (Iowa City, Iowa: State Historical Society of Iowa, 1932), 23-4. See also ibid., 24-5, 28; and Diane L. Barthel, *Amana: From Pietist Sect to American Community* (Lincoln, Neb.: University of Nebraska Press, 1984), 4-6.

[37] See Donald F. Durnbaugh, "Johann Adam Gruber: Pennsylvania German Prophet and Poet," *PMHB* 83 (October 1959): 386-7.

because of its fertility and its "freedom."[38]

In Pennsylvania Gruber remained aloof from all communions except the tiny Associated Brethren of the Skippack, a short-lived gathering of separatists for whom he authored a manuscript. This little fellowship excited him, and he tried often to persuade his nearest neighbor, Christopher Sauer I, to join them. Sauer remembered that the conversations "worked on" him "violently," and he believed that joining Gruber's communion "would have certainly disturbed [his] brain." Gruber never joined another denomination but corresponded regularly with his former co-religionists in Germany, who published at least seven of his writings. Sauer and others in colonial Pennsylvania also printed many of his essays.[39]

Although Gruber's physical isolation from the Inspired prompted him to separatism, Sauer I was a separatist in both theory and in practice. He condemned the Mennonites, Dunkers, and Quakers for being too exclusive and proclaimed that he would "curse the day" when he should join or "help build a congregation, sect, or circle," which always created oppressive regulations and creeds. According to tradition, he met often with the Germantown Dunkers, even offering his home for worship, but never became a member.[40]

Sauer also had a warm relationship with George Whitefield, the famed Anglican revivalist who attracted listeners from many denominations. Sauer published several of Whitefield's sermons in German, and Whitefield appealed to the *Societaet Charitatis* in London, unsuccessfully seeking a donation of paper for the edition of the Bible published by Sauer. In 1754 Sauer prominently reported the great evangelist's preaching tour, noting especially the crowds that Whitefield attracted to the large, new Presbyterian church in Philadelphia--so great that the listeners outside the church equalled those inside. Sauer's newspaper followed closely the accounts of Whitefield's subsequent tour to New

---

[38] Quoted from Gruber's letter of December 14, 1726, in ibid., 391. See also ibid., 390-1.

[39] Sauer is quoted in ibid., 393-4. See also ibid., 382-91. The Amana Community in Iowa is an American transplantation of the Inspired.

[40] Longenecker, *The Christopher Sauers*, 99-100; and Durnbaugh, "Was Christopher Sauer a Dunker?" *PMHB* 93 (July 1969): 384-9.

York and Boston.[41]

Another separatist, Peter Schaeffer, a Finn, was even further outside the mainstream than Sauer or Gruber yet also freely witnessed his faith. When Schaeffer arrived with several Pietists from Halle in 1690, the Wissahickon Society welcomed him. Schaeffer, however, argued with Kelpius over the sacraments, on which he insisted, and left. Kelpius offered to place him as a tutor with several families, but Schaeffer instead confronted Edward Shippen, a wealthy Anglican, in Philadelphia, saying that God wanted him to live with Shippen for forty days and nights and to subsist on bread and water. Remarkably, Shippen accepted him. Early in 1700 Schaeffer briefly taught school for the Swedes but soon began a death fast in New Jersey, during which he received a revelation to wander randomly. He returned to the Wissahickon; then, after refusing an offer to pastor certain Swedes, he joined a missionary tour among Indians in the Conestoga country. After this Schaeffer claimed that a vision instructed him to return to Europe. Later, he received another revelation during a forty-day fast and returned to his old home in Finland and reprimanded the authorities. For his impudence they imprisoned him in a fortress, after which he lost his sanity and died.[42]

IV

Pennsylvania's attitude towards Peter Schaeffer and other Radical Pietists contrasts with the status of iconoclasts in other colonies. In Connecticut, for example, the Rogerenes stubbornly resisted persistent official persecution. Named for their founders John and James Rogers, the Rogerenes evolved from Seventh Day Baptists in neighboring

[41] Copies of the *Pensylvanische Berichte* are not extant for the 1739 and 1740 Whitefield visits. Sauer printed three volumes of Whitefield's early sermons: *Von Georg Weitfields Predigten* (Germantown: 1740). See also Christopher Sauer to Dr. Henry Ehrenfried Luther, September, 1740, and October 11, 1740, in Edward W. Hocker, *The Founding of the Sower Press* (Philadelphia, Pa.: Germantown Historical Society), 150, 152; and *Pensylvanische Berichte*, August 16, September 1, November 16, and December 1, 1754.

[42] Sachse, *German Pietists*, 141-2.

Rhode Island, and in 1677 they added Quaker ideas, including paci-fism, unpaid preachers, and abstinence from oaths. They also adopted faith-healing and anointing with oil, at which point the Baptist congregation in Westerly disassociated from them. In 1744, the group warmly welcomed Conrad Beissel and several of his followers, though on their return New York authorities nearly arrested the Ephrata monks, suspecting them of being Jesuits.

The Rogerenes were bold; they baptized by immersion publicly and traveled and worked openly on Sunday. Once, John Rogers, a shoemaker, pushed a wheelbarrow full of shoes into a Congregational worship and began hawking his wares. Never amounting to more than one hundred members, they confirmed the widespread notion that without strict control, religion would degenerate into infidelity and fanaticism. Authorities imposed fines, imprisonment, and other harassments and punished attendance at an unauthorized service with a whipping. The Rogerenes refused to pay the fines, and John Rogers spent a total of fifteen years in jail.[43]

New England authorities condemned as insane another extreme nonconformist, James Davenport. After briefly itinerating with Gilbert Tennant, a "New Side" Presbyterian, and George Whitefield, Daven-port began evangelizing on his own in eastern Connecticut in 1741. By preaching for up to twelve hours, he waged a verbal war of attrition on his hearers, stressing radical conversion, recounting his personal experience, naming individual sinners from the pulpit, and urging the repentant to separate completely from evil relationships. He stayed at Groton, Connecticut, four or five days, preaching repeatedly; one meeting with a thousand worshippers lasted until 2:00 a.m. A modern historian has termed Davenport a "crazy extremist," but his intense, spontaneous, and unorthodox tactics worked. In 1742 Hartford officials arrested him for disturbing the public peace and expelled him from Connecticut, declaring him to be "disturbed in the rational Faculties of his Mind." One year later at New London he led his followers in burning "symbols of worldliness," such as "wigs, cloaks, hoods, gowns, rings, necklaces," and books authored by "unregenerate theologians." The New Light Congregationalist ministers then formally

[43] William G. McLoughlin, *New England Dissent, 1630-1833: The Baptists and the Separation of Church and State*, 2 vols. (Cambridge, Mass.: Harvard University Press, 1971), I, 250-3; and *Chronicon*, 175-7.

censured him. Later the Supreme Court of Massachusetts tried Davenport for slander but found him not guilty due to insanity, and banished him.[44]

Radical Pietists similarly taxed the patience of more conventional fellowships in Pennsylvania, including Anabaptists and moderate Pietists, but without suffering persecution. Kelpianites, the Ephrata Cloister, the New Born, and separatists pushed the levelling theology of freewill conversion much further than other Pietists, professing to remove all intermediaries between themselves and God; their unconventionality probed the boundaries of tolerance. Although the interdenominationalism popular with moderate Pietists was occasionally visible among the Radicals, other times they tested the limits of early Pennsylvania's tolerance.

The Radical Pietists were a small minority, even in the early days, but tolerance is measured by how a society treats those who are atypical. Such persons enjoyed security in Pennsylvania. They were free to evangelize, grow, or decline according to their ability to win converts. These fellowships demonstrate the diversity of early Pennsylvania and testify to the presence there of German religious radicalism many decades prior to the mid-eighteenth-century awakenings.

---

[44] Davenport is quoted in Stephen A. Marini, *Radical Sects of Revolutionary New England* (Cambridge, Mass.: Harvard University Press, 1982), 18. See also Marini, 17-9; Patricia U. Bonomi, *Under the Cope of Heaven: Religion, Society, and Politics in Colonial America* (New York: Oxford University Press, 1986), 150; and David S. Lovejoy, *Religious Enthusiasm in the New World: Heresy to Revolution* (Cambridge, Mass.: Harvard University Press, 1985), 183, 186-7.

CHAPTER 3

Keeping the Commandments:
The Anabaptists

"If you love me, you will keep my commandments."--John 14:15.

Mennonites, Dunkers, and Amish, like the Radical Pietists, occupied a distinctive position in Pennsylvania religion. Both within the fellowship of believers and outside the meetinghouse they reflected in unique ways the egalitarianism within Pietism, but the Anabaptists' strong commitment to obedience, which particularly stressed separation from the larger society, sometimes discouraged tolerance of other communions.

I

Inward religion became vital for Anabaptists in colonial Pennsylvania, and the colony's earliest recorded revival may be the awakening that accompanied the American reorganization of the Dunkers.[1]

During their first three years in Pennsylvania the Dunkers,

---

[1] The Dunkers first crossed the Atlantic in the second decade of the eighteenth century and by the 1740s had transplanted their entire sect to North America. A 1770 study of them counted fifteen congregations with 763 communicants and an estimated faith community of 2095, including children and unbaptized adults. The Dunkers enjoyed influence greater than their numbers suggest, however, because two of their worshippers, Christopher Sauer I and II, operated a printing enterprise that served a large number of the Pennsylvania Germans. See Morgan Edwards, *Materials towards a History of the American Baptists* (Philadelphia: Joseph Crukshank and Isaac Collins, 1770), 90.

whether struggling to survive in a new land or divided by an internal dispute, failed to meet, but in 1719 Peter Becker sparked a renewal by instituting house meetings aimed at uniting the dispersed communion.[2] While engaged in revitalization, they met Pietists, who lived along the Schuylkill River and had come to Philadelphia to hear Christian Liebe, a well-known European Dunker. Liebe never appeared, and some of the "newly awakened" Pietists, as a contemporary described them, instead attended Dunker services in Germantown. They came again, and then the Germantowners reciprocated the visit. The relationship grew until six of the "newly awakened ones" asked the Germantown Dunkers for baptism. On Christmas, 1723, the Dunkers finalized their reorganization with a love feast, and later that day they baptized the six in the Wissahickon Creek, no doubt an icy date for trine immersion.[3]

Soon the Dunkers' revival intensified, appealing especially to their young people, but other persons also participated until the crowds overflowed the room that held their worship. An eighteenth-century history, the *Chronicon Ephratense*, written by the Ephrata Cloister, uses "awakened" and "awakening" twelve times in five pages to describe the Dunker enthusiasm. Evangelists spread their revival by visiting Brethren in the backcountry, especially in the Conestoga area, which was heavily peopled by Mennonites and separatists who were particularly receptive to these early itinerants. One meeting in Novem-

---

[2] Timothy L. Smith argues that the anxieties of migration and frontier life as well as experiential religion account for the "exaggerated emotions which characterized congregational life." In the midst of the "threatening wilderness," he says, a newly forming congregation filled the desires of immigrants to find the security and relationships left behind in the "long lost community." See Smith, "Congregation, State, and Denomination: The Forming of the American Religious Structure," *WMQ* 25 (April 1968): 155-60.

[3] The quotations are from Lamech and Agrippa, *Chronicon Ephratense: A History of the Seventh Day Baptists at Ephrata*, trans. J. Max Hart (Lancaster, Pa.: 1889), 20-3. See also Donald F. Durnbaugh, *The Brethren in Colonial America: A Source Book on the Transplantation and Development of the Church of the Brethren in the Eighteenth Century* (Elgin, Ill.: The Brethren Press, 1967), 61. A detailed and exuberant but undocumented account of the early Brethren is Martin Grove Brumbaugh, *A History of the German Baptist Brethren in Europe and America* (Mount Morris, Ill.: Brethren Publishing House, 1899; reprinted in 1961 by L. W. Shultz and Carl A. Wagoner), 155-65; and a modern study is Dale R. Stoffer, *Background and Development of Brethren Doctrines, 1650-1987* (Philadelphia: Brethren Encyclopedia, 1989), 19-43. Carl Bowman's forthcoming book, tentatively titled *Brethren Society*, will be the definitive study of that denomination.

ber, according to the Ephrata book, induced "extraordinary revival powers," and following the sermon, the Brethren baptized five persons in the Pequea Creek.[4] Such enthusiasm continued among Dunkers for at least a decade. In 1730 a German Reformed preacher complained that Dunkers were "constantly traveling through the whole country trying to recruit as many as they possibly can."[5] Their revivalism preceded Jonathan Edwards' famous 1734 meetings in Northampton, Massachusetts, and roughly coincided with the awakenings Theodore Freylinghuysen led among the Dutch of New Jersey and Gilbert Tennant inspired among English-speaking Presbyterians in the Delaware Valley.

Revivalism remained important for the next generation of Dunkers, as suggested by Catherine Hummer's visions, which became the focal point of an awakening in Lancaster County. According to her account in the *Chronicon*, which must have relished her suggestion that love had "grown cold" among the Dunkers, her experience came when an angel knocked at her door, and Johann Adam Gruber related that she saw hundreds of "persons baptizing in eternity" in heaven. Hummer's insights always came when she was alone or in the company of one young man, and when she married him, the visions ended. Because of the suspicious circumstances of these experiences, Hummer's congregation quarreled over their legitimacy, and she complained to Alexander Mack, Jr., a denominational leader, that her critics persecuted her. Yearly Meeting considered the matter, was unable to agree, and appealed for tolerance. It did, however, criticize Hummer's father, a preacher, for creating discord by bringing "too much of his human nature" into the affair and advised him to apologize. Moreover, undoubtedly casting a wary eye towards Sister Hummer, it urged that "all unnecessary and too-frequent visiting cease." On the other hand, the Brethren refused to denounce the visions and urged that rumors about Hummer end.[6]

Although Catherine Hummer alleged that love had cooled among

---

[4] Durnbaugh, *Brethren in Colonial America*, 66; and *Chronicon*, 20-5.

[5] Boehm to the Classis of Amsterdam, November 12, 1730, in William J. Hinke, ed., *Life and Letters of the Rev. John Philip Boehm, Founder of the Reformed Church in Pennsylvania, 1683-1749* (1916; reprinted, New York: Arno Press, 1972), 202-3.

[6] Durnbaugh, *Brethren in Colonial America*, 259-60, 265.

the Dunkers, no one claimed that their lively worship style changed. One cynic suggested that their motto should be "We sing and preach with great outcry;/ If only the Spirit could be thereby." He remarked that "one hymn chases another" and that praying and preaching came with "great clamor, as if their God were hard of hearing."[7]

For Mennonites Pietism became increasingly intertwined with their faith in America until it grew nearly as prominent among them as with the Dunkers.[8] Anabaptism was over one century older than Pietism, but Mennonite households in Pennsylvania frequently owned devotional literature written by European Pietists, often Gerhard Tersteegen's prayerbook, *Geistliches Blumengärtlein* (Little Spiritual Flower-Garden) and sermon books by Jacob Denner. Pietist catechisms, especially those by Christopher Dock, a Germantown schoolteacher, and Gerrit Roosen, a West Prussian Mennonite, were popular.[9] By the 1760s Mennonites frequented interdenominational revival meetings, and the number of Mennonite Pietists cited throughout this book testifies to the importance of the doctrine of new birth in Mennonite theology. Thus Pietism, whether absorbed gradually and informally by the Mennonites

---

[7] The description comes from a travel account, *The Alert Traveller Through Europe and America*, written by "J. B. S.," the anonymous and scholarly leader of a Pietistic sect, *Die Stillen im Lande* (Quiet Ones in the Land), which settled in Pennsylvania in the 1750s but returned to Germany due to financial failure. See Durnbaugh, *Brethren in Colonial America*, 122-4. For another example of Dunkers praying loudly see Durnbaugh, 88.

[8] The first Mennonites in Pennsylvania, a small band from the Netherlands, arrived in the 1680s, and early in the next century a wave of Swiss Mennonite immigration hit the colony, cresting in the 1740s. Many of the Swiss had settled earlier in the German Palatinate (see Chapter 2) but left after several decades for the greater promise of Pennsylvania. By the mid-eighteenth-century revivals, approximately 6000 Mennonites resided in the colony with conferences of preachers and elders in the Lancaster and Franconia, or Montgomery County, areas. Statistics on the sectarians are few and unreliable because they believed that counting their members contributed to excessive pride; see "Statistics," *The Brethren Encyclopedia* (Philadelphia and Oak Brook, Ill.: The Brethren Encyclopedia, Inc., 1983), 1219. See also John B. Frantz, "The Awakening of Religion among the German Settlers in the Middle Colonies," *WMQ* 33 (April 1976): 270n19; and Richard K. MacMaster, *Land, Piety, Peoplehood: The Establishment of Mennonite Communities in America, 1683-1790* (Scottdale, Pa.: Herald Press, 1985), 202-3.

[9] MacMaster says that eighteenth-century inventories often listed a "Mennonist Catechism," which, he concludes, "was probably Roosen's book"; see *Land, Piety, Peoplehood*, 167. See also MacMaster, 170-2.

or at denominational birth by the Dunkers, became just as important for Anabaptists as for other German Christians.

II

While having much in common with other Pietists, Dunkers, Mennonites, and Amish differed from them in the interpretation they gave to Biblical commandments on the fellowship of believers and nonconformity. Still, much of what Anabaptists taught about obedience and separation echoed Pietism's stress on the inner faith; only through spiritual renewal could Anabaptists avoid sins of the flesh. Faith and works were like two brothers, wrote Peter Burkholder, a Mennonite from the Shenandoah Valley, "born of the same parents; both gifts of God." Those who are "born again," he said, bear their crosses daily. Another Mennonite, emphasizing that the Apostle Paul "laid the first emphasis on a new creature in Christ," cited inward faith to caution against legalism, warning that "inner pride in plain clothing" was much more dangerous than "outward glitter." Dunkers linked conversion with the new life by declaring that as newly baptized Christians climb out of the water, they also "rise up into a new life."[10] Inner experience also accompanied compassion for the downtrodden, according to a hymn in the Dunkers' first English songbook (1791):

> Blest is the man whose bowels move,
> And melt with pity to the poor;
> Whose soul, by sympathizing love,
> Feels what his fellow saints endure.[11]

Inward religion, Alexander Mack, Sr., asserted, gave believers strength

---

[10] Peter Bowman, *A Testimony of Baptism, as Practiced by the Primitive Christians, from the Time of the Apostles* (Baltimore: Benjamin Edes, 1831; originally published in German in 1817), in Roger Sappington, ed., *The Brethren in the New Nation: A Source Book on the Development of the Church of the Brethren, 1785-1865* (Elgin, Ill.: Brethren Press, 1976), 137.

[11] *The Christian's Duty, Exhibited in a Series of Hymns, Collected from Various Authors, Designed for the Worship of God, and for the Edification of Christians, Recommended to the Serious of All Denominations, By the Fraternity of Baptists* (Philadelphia: Peter Leibert, 1813; originally published in 1791), 28.

"even in outward matters." The Holy Spirit, Mack claimed, wrote God's laws in every believer's heart just like God placed the tablets inside the Old Testament's Ark of the Covenant. This inner law was identical to the one "written outwardly" in the New Testament.[12]

The decision to obey the inner law was conscious. A newly regenerate person, claimed a Dunker preacher, "searches diligently to discover what God's will for him is." He underscored that no command of the Lord was "too petty or too small" for a real Christian and thereupon penned a lengthy criticism of interest-bearing loans and a defense of wearing beards.[13] Christopher Dock, a schoolteacher and probably the most popular American hymn-writer among eighteenth-century Mennonites, listed "many nets, stumbling blocks and snares" for his students to avoid, including fame, sensuality, success, wealth, vanity, avarice, deceit, guile, lying, hypocrisy, hatred, jealousy, envy, enmity, war, and murder. He counseled against unrestrained eating, drinking, dancing, carousing, swearing, cursing, and "singing frivolous, vulgar, wicked songs." To this dark admonition, however, Dock added the Pietist promise that Christ would clothe the repentant sinner "with the wedding garment" that brought "a rapture the heart cannot control."[14] Likewise, when in 1711 Alexander Mack, Sr., baptized several people who knelt in a German stream, he asked them to

---

[12] Peter Burkholder, *The Confession of Faith of the Christians Known by the Name of Mennonites, in Thirty-Three Articles; with a Short Extract from Their Catechism*, trans. Joseph Funk (Winchester, Va.: Robinson and Hollis, 1837), 316-8; and Alexander Mack, Sr., *Rites and Ordinances: A Brief and Simple Exposition of the Outward but Yet Sacred Rights and Ordinances of the House of God*, in Donald F. Durnbaugh, ed., *European Origins of the Brethren: A Source Book on the Beginnings of the Church of the Brethren in the Early Eighteenth Century* (Elgin, Ill.: The Brethren Press, 1958), 385-6. Durnbaugh translates "Rechte" as "rights" but a more accurate word is "laws." See also Carl Frederick Bowman, "Beyond Plainness: Cultural Transformation in the Church of the Brethren from 1850 to the Present" (Ph.D. diss.: University of Virginia, 1989), 804n28.

[13] Christian Longenecker, "On the True Conversion and New Birth," ed. and trans. Vernard Eller, *BLT* 7 (Spring 1963): 25-6, 33.

[14] Gerald C. Studer, *Christopher Dock: Colonial Schoolmaster* (Scottdale, Pa.: Herald Press, 1967), 336, 360-3, 336. See also Ada Kadelbach, "Hymns Written by American Mennonites," trans. Elizabeth Bender, *MQR* 44 (July 1974): 345-9.

renounce "the world and the devil and [their] own flesh."[15] Later, Mack's son in Pennsylvania proclaimed that pious persons made it "their duty" to obey God's commands.[16] Anabaptists urged Christians to remain faithful to God's law even in the face of persecution, or as Freylinghausen wrote, "even if covered with blood."[17] Similarly, Peter Becker declared to his fellow-believers, "Thy Savior's likeness thou shoulds't gain,/ And suffer gladly every pain."[18] Such a commitment and resulting exhilaration flowed from voluntary decision rather than coercion and was available to all persons.

Those who made the freewill decision to obey the inner and outer commands of God were to avoid those who did not. Separation from the "unclean," as Mack termed the rest of the world--Christians and nonbelievers alike--was indispensable, and Peter Burkholder warned that God wanted "a perfect renunciation of the world." Mack cited the Biblical metaphor that depicts a field with good seeds, which become God's followers, and bad seeds, planted by the devil, which sprout into weeds that God will burn "with everlasting fire" at harvest time. The Dunkers, according to Sauer I's observation, "erected a fence around themselves" and became "jealous and quarrelsome" with outsiders. Mennonites agreed that the "whole world lieth in wickedness," and Burkholder concluded that too many Christians ignored the difference between "light and darkness," especially in dress. He criticized those who accepted "fleeting fashions" and decorated their "vile" bodies to

---

[15] An eyewitness account of the service in Heinz Renkewitz, *Hochmann von Hochenau (1670-1721): Quellenstudien zur Geschichte des Pietismus* (Luther-Verlag Witten, 1969), 277; and translated in Durnbaugh, *European Origins of the Brethren*, 160-1.

[16] Alexander Mack, Jr., "The Excellencies of Jesus," trans. Vernard Eller, in Donald F. Durnbaugh, *The Brethren in Colonial America: A Source Book on the Transplantation and Development of the Church of the Brethren in the Eighteenth Century* (Elgin, Ill.: Brethren Press, 1967), 586.

[17] Freylinghausen, Hymn #732, *Geistreiches Gesangbuch* in Peter C. Erb, *Pietists: Selected Writings* (Mahwah, N.J.: Paulist Press, 1983), 179-80. For other examples see Michael Schlatter, "When Christ with His Teaching True," *Ausbund*, in Beulah Stauffer Hostetler, *American Mennonites and Protestant Movements: A Community Paradigm* (Scottdale, Pa.: Herald Press, 1987), 56; and Hans Tschantz quoted in MacMaster, *Land, Piety, Peoplehood*, 175.

[18] Peter Becker, "Patience," trans. John S. Flory, ibid., 551.

avoid being "laughed or pointed at."[19]

Dunkers and Mennonites who struggled to steer clear of Satan and the world found guidance from the fellowship of believers. Deacons usually conducted visits prior to communion to determine if members were at peace with each other and the church, and communion was open only to members in good standing. Mennonites warned baptismal candidates that the faith community observed its members and, if necessary, reprimanded those who appeared too worldly, and Dunkers required converts to take a vow promising to submit to the congregation. Mack underscored the necessity for backsliders to allow themselves to be "disciplined in love." If two individuals committed the same sin, Mack suggested that the transgressor who willingly accepted the congregation's correction and repented would be saved, but the one who remained in "arrogance and selfishness [would] be lost." According to Mack, God conducted "a ban like this" with most of the world.[20]

Because Anabaptists believed that Jesus wanted the church as well as individual Christians to separate from the world, they tried to purge their fellowships of those who conformed to the darkness. Mack urged believers to "cut off all sinful and offensive members, lest the entire body be spoiled." He proposed that, like the Jewish temple of the Old Testament, which barred entrance to lepers, the uncircumcised, and the unclean, the New Testament church should expel members who indulged in "works of flesh." It was only fair, he said, because their sin jeopardized the purity of the entire fellowship. Similarly, Christian Burkholder, a Lancaster County Mennonite, denounced as "despisers of true religion" those who spoke against excommunication, which he praised as "the rule of the church." He told Mennonites to avoid company with notorious sinners and to withdraw from those who created disorder by spurning Mennonite practices. "If there come any

---

[19] Bowman, "Beyond Plainness," 79; Burkholder, *Confession of Faith*, 314-5, 431; Abraham Godschalk, *A Description of the New Creature* (Doylestown, Pa.: William M. Large, 1838), 54, 59; Mack, Sr., *Rights and Ordinances*, in Durnbaugh, *European Origins*, 363; MacMaster, *Land, Piety, Peoplehood*, 193-4; and Christopher Sauer I to "all good friends and acquaintances at Schwarzenous, Berleburg, Laasphe, and Christainseck," August 1, 1725, in Durnbaugh, *Brethren in Colonial America*, 36.

[20] Bowman, "Beyond Plainness," 105-6; Christian Burkholder, *Useful and Edifying Address to the Young on True Repentance, Saving Faith in Christ Jesus, Pure Love, etc.* (Lancaster, Pa.: n.p., 1857), 238; Peter Burkholder, *Confession of Faith*, 431; and Mack, *Rights and Ordinances*, in Durnbaugh, *European Origins*, 363, 372-4

unto you" who threaten the tradition, he advised, "receive him not into your house, neither bid him God speed."[21]

Dunkers and Amish used a harsh form of excommunication, the ban, or sometimes called the shun, that prohibited worship, social intercourse, or even eating with the excommunicated until they had repented. Many Mennonites, on the other hand, merely withheld communion from those who had lapsed into sin. For decades persecution, rather than church discipline, had removed lukewarm Mennonites from the fellowship, and by 1690 few Mennonites held to Menno Simon's strict teaching regarding the ban.[22] Their reluctance to shun excommunicated members contributed significantly to the schism in Europe that created the Amish, whose founder, Jacob Ammann, criticized the growing laxness of many Mennonite congregations in enforcing the ban. In Pennsylvania the Amish continued to ban those who joined other denominations, and Amish who violated sanctions against former members were themselves shunned if they did not ask the congregation for forgiveness.[23] Early Dunkers employed the ban with little restraint, and Alexander Mack's first theological writing, *Rites and Ordinances*, which deals primarily with church discipline, urged it. In 1727 they shunned Jacob Stuntz for marrying a close relation, and when two itinerating preachers lifted Stuntz's ban on their own initiative, the congregation disciplined them, too. The previous chapter describes the bans that the Conestoga and Germantown congregations placed on each other. Christopher Sauer I thought that the Dunkers expelled members too frequently, and George Adam Martin, who suffered the shun for fraternizing with Ephrata, complained about the zealousness of the Dunkers' "European ban-branch."[24]

[21] Christian Burkholder, *Useful and Edifying Address*, 250-1; and Mack, *Rights and Ordinances*, in Durnbaugh, *European Origins*, 367-71, 381.

[22] Peter Burkholder, *Confession of Faith*, 433; and MacMaster, *Land, Piety, Peoplehood*, 194.

[23] MacMaster, *Land, Piety, Peoplehood*, 161; and John A. Hostetler, ed., *Amish Roots: A Treasury of History, Wisdom, and Lore* (Baltimore: The Johns Hopkins University Press, 1989), 85-6.

[24] Bowman, "Beyond Plainness," 29-34, 106-9, 804n28; *Chronicon*, 36, 48-9, 250; Mack, *Eberhard Louis Gruber's Basic Questions*, in Durnbaugh, *European Origins*, 336-7; Mack, *Rights and Ordnances*, ibid., 371-6; "Life and Conduct of the Late Brother Ezechiel Sangmeister," trans. Barbara M. Schindler, *Historical Society of the Cocalico*

In fact, the intensity with which first-generation Dunkers pursued separation suggests that a psychological attraction to nonconformity reinforced their interpretation of the Scriptures. The Dunkers were so far outside the mainstream that survival--institutional and psychological--required supreme certainty in their standard of righteousness. Having abandoned family ties and social standing, early Brethren stood alone, like the Kelpianites and Reformation-era Anabaptists, apart from society, bearing abuse. Only those who could believe that everybody else was wrong and they were right could persist. Being a social outcast brought fulfillment, and being correct was more important than organizational unity. Despite Anabaptist preaching about the importance of submissiveness to the congregation, the movement attracted only the strongest nonconformists who quickly followed their own conscience.

Pietism fortified confidence in the individual's gift for determining truth. As the Kelpianites, separatists, and other Radical Pietists discovered, individual conversion carried to its logical extreme eliminated the need for earthly authority. Because believers had an individual relationship with God, their conscience ruled devoid of intermediaries. If individuals could feel guilt over sin, repent, and enter into a new life through direct communication with God, then they required no further assistance from preachers or even the faith community in matters of conscience or interpretation.

The Dunker's high rate of movement illustrates their willingness to be outside the mainstream. So eager were the first Brethren to follow Mack's admonition to segregate themselves from all "false sects and religion" that they became a generation of transients. Their entire membership in Wittgenstein had probably relocated there from some other part of Germany. In 1720 they migrated to Friesland, where they denounced ice-skating, which they had never seen before, as the work of the devil,[25] and at the end of the decade they crossed the Atlantic. In 1719 Peter Becker's contingent, who formed the Germantown congregation, left Krefeld. After arrival in Pennsylvania many Brethren quickly moved into the backcountry, often for farmland, and

---

Valley, Ephrata, Pa., vol. V (1986): 103-4; and Christopher Sauer I to "all good friends," in Durnbaugh, Brethren in Colonial America, 33-38.

[25] Stephen Blaupot ten Cate, History of the Mennonites in Friesland (1839), in Durnbaugh, European Origins, 292-3.

Philadelphia was Alexander Mack's fourth homeland.

Undoubtedly a variety of motivations, including competition from rival sects, particularly the Inspired in Wittgenstein, prompted the Dunker's emigration, and other Anabaptists also found Pennsylvania's tolerance attractive.   Furthermore, economic opportunity proved appealing. Nevertheless, the considerable mobility of the Dunkers and its semi-voluntary nature suggest that the Brethren possessed the souls of mavericks.[26]

This willful defiance of the world as a tiny minority--a mark of courage that intensified denominational identity--became devastating when Dunkers employed their individual standard of righteousness within the fellowship. Finding no other communion suitable, including already existing dissenter groups, each of the first Brethren had already withdrawn from a religious body when they created their little eight-person organization, and internal quarrels nearly destroyed the fledgling sect. George Grebe, one of the founders at Schwarzenau, later publicly denounced Mack, telling him that he and his followers were spiritually "dead."[27]   In Krefeld that flourishing congregation effectively ended when a member, named Häcker, married the daughter of a merchant, who also was a member but still received payment from his former Mennonite congregation to preach. Both Krefeld preachers, Christian Liebe and John Naas, recognized that Häcker required discipline for marrying outside the faith, but Liebe insisted on the ban while Naas only wanted to suspend Häcker from communion. The feud deeply divided the congregation and persisted for years. Naas claimed that over one hundred persons, who had agreed to baptism, left the fellowship.[28] Either this controversy or new arguments that developed during the journey may have delayed for several years Peter Becker's re-organization of the Krefelders who migrated to Pennsylvania. Naas later withdrew from the Brethren and migrated alone to Pennsylvania, where he returned to the fellowship after a conciliatory visit from

[26] Sauer to "all good friends," in Durnbaugh, *Brethren in Colonial America*, 33-8; and Durnbaugh, *European Origins*, 289.

[27] Miller in *Chronicon*, 246-7.

[28] George Adam Martin's account in ibid., 249; and Durnbaugh, *European Origins of the Brethren*, 281. Martin was not in Krefeld and probably received his information from John Naas.

Mack. No sooner did the Pennsylvania Brethren recover their unity than Conrad Beissel, preacher of one of their three congregations, created another split taking with him, according to one claim, seventeen brothers and sisters from the Germantown congregation, including Henry Kalckglasser, who was a preacher, and Alexander Mack, Jr., who subsequently returned.[29] Thus, despite sharing general consensus on Pietism and Anabaptism, early Dunkers continually bickered over details.

The Dunkers, therefore, struggled with the dilemma of the supremacy of the conscience within a close-knit community of believers. They created a denomination out of free spirits who labored with difficulty to observe their teachings about accepting guidance from the fellowship of believers.

Radical Pietists and Mennonites also may have drawn persons peculiarly attracted to nonconformity, but in Pennsylvania only the Dunkers attempted to construct a new fellowship entirely out of them. Radicals disdained formal organization, making irrelevant tension between the conscience and direction from the congregation, and Mennonites, who shared with Dunkers the burden of being social and economic outcasts, relied on an identity that dated to the Reformation. Many Mennonites in the early eighteenth century were born into the faith, whereas all of the first-generation Dunkers abandoned the tradition of their birth.

Not until after the Dunkers inhabited Pennsylvania for several decades did the turbulence within their denomination subside. Perhaps Pennsylvania's live-and-let-live atmosphere drew less attention to nonconformists, appealing to fewer who thrived on being unconventional. Later generations tended to be born into the faith, and evolving denominational traditions brought stability. Yet, the Dunkers, and all Anabaptists, preserved their conviction that the community of believers needed to separate from the rest of society, a doctrine that discouraged cooperation with other communions.

III

[29] *Chronicon*, 15, 22, 101; Miller's account in *Chronicon*, 247; and Durnbaugh, *Brethren in Colonial America*, 90.

Anabaptists, then, particularly the Dunkers, were not especially interdenominational, but they expressed the tolerance within Pietism in other ways. Because Anabaptists agreed with other Pietists that true Christians were not those with rank or status but those who experienced Christ in their hearts and deliberately chose a new life of obedience, they were convinced that being close to God was more important than how far one had climbed on the social ladder. This often led them to defy traditional patterns of rank.

The Mennonite and Dunker practice of calling pastors from among the laymen of a congregation, for example, contrasted with standards of rank that usually prevailed for ministerial candidates in the German Reformed and Lutheran churches and most English-speaking communions, who established schools to train clergy and created formal structures to control their selection. As early as 1632 New England Puritans founded Harvard, and by 1700 clergy-dominated "consociations" in each county exercised considerable influence over ministerial appointments. German Lutherans and the Reformed tried to match European norms, and as they became better organized in Pennsylvania, ordination was said to require university training although in fact many clergymen failed to meet that requirement. Pennsylvania Presbyteries controlled the assignment of preachers to congregations of that faith, and the London-based Society for the Propagation of the Gospel in Foreign Parts named most of the Anglican preachers who filled pulpits for the Church of England in Pennsylvania.[30]

In contrast, the German Anabaptists required of their preachers neither a university degree nor a hierarchy's blessing. Rather, the selection of spiritual leaders strengthened egalitarian attitudes and gave rank and file members a major voice. Mennonites made their final choice of leaders through the casting of lots, which theoretically allowed God, rather than worldly forces, to speak. Each nominee

---

[30] Martin E. Lodge, "The Crisis of the Churches in the Middle Colonies, 1720-1750," *PMHB* 95 (April 1974): 195-220; Richard L. Bushman, *From Puritan to Yankee: Character and the Social Order in Connecticut, 1690-1765* (Cambridge: Harvard University Press, 1967), 149-51, 215-7; Jon Butler, "Power, Authority, and the Origins of American Denominational Order: The English Churches in the Delaware Valley, 1680-1730," *Transactions of the American Philosophical Society* 68 (February 1978), 52-64, 71; and David D. Hall, *The Faithful Shepherd: A History of the New England Ministry in the Seventeenth Century* (Chapel Hill: University of North Carolina Press, 1972), 220-2.

received a book, and the one who found a slip of paper hidden inside was elected. Hans Tschantz, a bishop in Lancaster County, suggested three Scriptures to use in ordination services, each referring to the lot (Proverbs 16:33, Acts 1:15-26, and Acts 6:1-8), indicating its usage among Lancaster conference congregations. Morgan Edwards observed that Mennonites began with a congregational ballot, but he added that "when two or more are nominated they leave it to the decision of the lot." Those who considered themselves undeserving of the honor rarely rejected this calling, believing it divine, although they had that right.[31]

After selecting their leaders from among themselves, Mennonites helped them avoid the temptation of authoritarianism by assigning several preachers to each congregation, which also allowed novices to learn the ropes. A typical service featured a lengthy sermon by an elder, a shorter comment by an assistant, called an "exhorter," and testimonies from others seated on the "preachers' bench." Newly-elected ministers did not actually preach a full-blown sermon until they moved up through the ranks of preacher and exhorter to elder. Because a single congregation had several meetinghouses, the ministry team served several groups in a given district. Rather than one flock having a single shepherd, several shepherds watched over several flocks. Mennonites further insured popular control over their pastors by occasionally revoking the right to preach. Henry Funck the younger was "benched" (it is not clear by whom) in 1781 for expecting the congregation "to be subject to him" and for horse swapping.[32]

Mennonite congregations also appointed deacons, sometimes referred to as "elders," but their duties, aside from administering the poor fund, were vague. Deacons made some decisions without consulting the membership, but the lines of authority often became blurred. From 1756 to 1783 Christian Moyer administered the alms of the Franconia congregation, yet his name did not appear on a list of those ordained. However, in 1773 he was one of the leaders who met to restore peace with Christian Funk before the fellowship gathered around the Lord's Table. Also, Moyer conducted the council meeting for a local meetinghouse that year. The three offices of elder, preacher, and deacon were obviously unequal, but Mennonites did not assign them a

---

[31] MacMaster, *Land, Piety, Peoplehood*, 196-7.

[32] Ibid., 201-2.

strict hierarchy.[33]

Social rank contributed little to the creation of status among Anabaptists, particularly for the Dunkers. The Brethren distributed offices broadly on the theory that the Holy Spirit dispersed gifts throughout the body of believers. Alexander Mack, Sr., suggested that modern Christians imitate the early church's custom choosing "men from among them" who were filled with the Holy Spirit and practiced obedience.[34] The Dunkers, therefore, elected their preachers and ordained them by the ceremony of laying on of hands; ministers received no compensation for their labors because the Brethren believed that preaching for pay spawned self-centeredness and evil. Christopher Sauer II's description of his rise to the pulpit of the Germantown congregation was typical:

In May, 1747, the brethren made me overseer of the poor.

On June 1, 1748, I was among the four brethren elected to minister to the congregation.

On June 7, 1748, Sander Mack and I were given the supervision of the congregation, on trial.

On June 10, 1753, Brother Sander Mack, Brother Henry Schling-luff and I were ordained by the laying on of hands.[35]

Dunkers were certain that God did not call to the pulpit only those who had succeeded in the marketplace. Occasionally, Dunker congregations chose the richest communicant to be their leader, but often they by-passed the wealthiest men and selected members with

---

[33] The list of ordained ministers is in Andreas Ziegler, Isaac Kolb, and Christian Funk to Holland Mennonites, March 1, 1773, in John C. Wenger, *History of the Mennonites of the Franconia Conference* (Scottdale, Pa.: Mennonite Publishing House, 1938), 402-4. See also Robert Levers to William Moore, October 31, 1781, in MacMaster, Samuel L. Horst, and Robert F. Ulle, *Conscience in Crisis: Mennonites and Other Peace Churches in America, 1739-1789, Interpretations and Documents* (Scottdale, Pa.: Herald Press, 1979), 338-9; and MacMaster, *Land, Piety, Peoplehood*, 199-204.

[34] Mack, *Rites and Ordinances*, in Durnbaugh, *European Origins of the Brethren*, 356-7.

[35] Durnbaugh, *Brethren in Colonial America*, 221.

smaller holdings.   Congregations usually (but not consistently) overlooked persons at the lower end of the economic scale, frequently selecting preachers who were economically established; no congregation chose tenants.   Possibly they assumed that low economic status disqualified persons for spiritual leadership, but it seems just as reasonable that poorer members could not afford to donate the time that the ministry required.   Wealth did not eliminate a candidate for the ministry, then, but neither did it guarantee election.

Consequently, Dunker leaders exhibited a wide range of wealth, as exemplified by the Germantown congregation.   In 1770 the group's preacher was Alexander Mack, Jr., a weaver of modest means, frequently indebted for small sums.   Of the twelve men listed in the congregational rolls who appear on the tax lists, six paid more taxes than Mack, and three of them paid twice as much.   Assisting Mack was exhorter Christopher Sauer II, a wealthy printer and one of Mack's creditors; Sauer's tax, four times greater than Mack's assessment, was the highest of any Germantown Dunker.[36]

Elsewhere, similar variety appeared. In the Cocalico congregation elder Jacob Sonday, the preacher, owned twenty acres and paid a tax of three shillings; his assistant, exhorter John Landis, owned 130 acres and paid sixteen shillings.   Twenty-three members of the Cocalico congregation appear on the tax lists, but Sonday outranked only the four tenants in acreage and assessment, while seven landholders outranked Landis.   The Coventry congregation named as its preacher Martin Urner, whose 230 acres made him one of the largest landowners among Pennsylvania Dunkers.   But its exhorter, Peter Reinhart, was listed only as a "freeman" with no assessment.   In the Codorus congregation Jacob Spitler, who did not hold a congregational office, possessed 280 acres and was assessed sixty-one pounds, five shillings, and Peter Brilharth, Sr., owned 200 acres and paid an eighty pound tax; but the exhorter, Henry Neff, held a more modest 100 acres and paid a paltry tax of twelve pounds, ten shillings.   In the White Oak congregation the preacher, Christian Longenecker, ranked eighth in acreage and tied for sixth in tax assessment among eighteen men identified in the tax lists.   In two congregations, however, the weightiest brothers were those with the heaviest purses.   Exhorters George Miller and Adam Hammaker at Great Swatara owned 225 and

---

[36] Mack's will and ledger in ibid., 224-7.

200 acres, respectively, and at Little Swatara exhorter Peter Hackman was the largest landholder with 237 acres. But the three largest landholders among all the Pennsylvania Dunkers, Abraham Stauffer, who owned 400 acres, Henry Raudibush, who held 300, and John Light, who owned 300 and a servant, occupied no offices.

The selection of Dunker preachers and exhorters seems especially egalitarian compared to secular leaders in colonial Pennsylvania. Deference to wealth was commonplace in the colony and elites controlled office-holding. Justices of the Peace, assemblymen, sheriffs, county commissioners, and assessors tended to be among the wealthiest members of the community. By contrast several of the Dunker preachers and elders came from the lower ranks of their membership, whereas between 1729 and 1755, for example, none of the Chester County assemblymen or justices of the peace were among the lower half of taxpayers.[37] A comparison of Mennonite leaders with their followers is difficult because membership lists are not extant. But apparently Mennonites selected leaders who were well-established economically.[38]

IV

Perhaps the most radically levelling practice of the Anabaptists was feetwashing, an act of servanthood in a time when owning servants, not being one, was the mark of status. Moravians, Amish, and Dunkers as well as the Lancaster Mennonite conference included it in the Lord's Supper.

Moravians, who were not Anabaptists, washed feet at large gath-

---

[37] Tax lists contain several problems, including underestimation of capital wealth, tax evasion, and assessment rates. The statistical samples are small, but my investigation includes the entire Dunker membership appearing on the tax lists. For further data on Dunker preachers see Stephen L. Longenecker, "Democracy's Pulpit: Pietism and Egalitarianism among Early Pennsylvania Germans" (Ph.D. diss.: Johns Hopkins University, 1989). See also Alan Tully, *William Penn's Legacy: Politics and Social Structure in Provincial Pennsylvania, 1726-1755* (Baltimore and London: The Johns Hopkins University Press, 1977), 73, 79, 83, 111, 114.

[38] MacMaster, *Land, Piety, Peoplehood*, 198-9.

erings as well as at observances of the Lord's Supper. While they used the basin and the towel, a leader sang hymns that emphasized Christ's example, such as "As I, your Lord, have washed your feet,/ So each shall wash his brother."[39]

Feetwashing for Mennonites may have occurred at a service largely given over to it; Hans Tschantz prepared a meditation for such a service. In the early 1780s Lancaster-area Mennonite ministers asserted that feetwashing was "humility founded upon Christ, because by his power he has washed our souls." Feetwashing was not a universal Mennonite practice, however. Those in the Lancaster area made it a custom, but only three Franconia congregations did, and Jacob Ammann complained that Swiss and south German Mennonite congregations erred when they dropped the ceremony from communion. Several Lancaster conference meetings gradually drifted away from the practice in the late eighteenth and early nineteenth centuries, but feetwashing was such a strong tradition among other Mennonites that later Methodist and United Brethren congregations containing many former Mennonites continued the rite.[40]

Feetwashing was more central to the religious life of the Dunkers. They were conscious that this custom placed them at odds with many of their Protestant neighbors, acknowledging that it seemed "outwardly mean and suspicious in the eyes of carnal reason." Dunkers nevertheless fervently defended the rite, noting that the New Testament commanded its observance (John 13: 1-14). Brethren wondered if those who did not wash feet considered themselves to have "progressed farther than did Peter, to whom Jesus said, 'If I do not wash you, you have no part in me.'" Brethren especially prized the "inward humility" signified by the service as worshippers humbled themselves before others. Those motivated by love and "an inward, fervent obedience," wrote William Knepper, received "an inward blesing."[41]

---

[39] John Jacob Sessler, *Communal Pietism Among Early American Moravians* (New York: Henry Holt and Company, 1933), 133.

[40] MacMaster, *Land, Piety, Peoplehood*, 195-6, 200; and Sem C. Sutter, "Mennonites and the Pennsylvania German Revival," *MQR* 50 (January 1976): 49-50.

[41] "The Testament of William Knepper" (1755; reprinted 1880) in Durnbaugh, *The Brethren in Colonial America*, 560, 567; and *Ein Geringer Schein des Verachteten Lichtleins, der Wahrheit die in Christo ist...*, author unknown (Germantown: Christopher Sauer, 1747), in Durnbaugh, 443-4. Some speculate that Alexander Mack, Jr., wrote

By the nineteenth century two methods, or "modes," of washing feet became popular among Dunkers, and because early Brethren left no description of the ceremony, later Dunkers argued incessantly over which form was authentic. Single-mode advocates had one brother or sister wash and dry the feet of another believer (of the same gender), who then washed and dried the feet of the next person. The ceremony continued around the circle until everyone had participated. Those favoring the double mode performed the ceremony with two Brethren serving six to ten others, one washing and the other drying. Then, two others acquired the towel and basin. Both sides agreed that all members should have their feet washed and also perform the task; the argument was primarily over historical accuracy.[42]

By washing feet Amish, Brethren, Mennonites, and Moravians put their egalitarian beliefs into practice. Prosperous farmers washed the feet of tenants, and established artisans washed the feet of freemen, journeymen, and indentured servants. As they knelt before each other to perform this religious service, they abandoned conceptions of rank within the group and demonstrated that in God's kingdom all believing followers are equal.

V

The zeal of the Anabaptists for Scriptural obedience, particularly their devotion to simplicity, had egalitarian side effects outside the meeting-house, as well. Their devotion to simplicity, for example, caused them to condemn the accumulation of goods that eighteenth-century Pennsylvanians usually thought defined social status.

---

this treatise, which answered a Quaker essay that Dunkers perceived as a threat. Knepper wrote his Testament while on his deathbed; his family preserved and printed it in an English translation in the nineteenth century. Another strong Dunker defense of feetwashing is Alexander Mack, Sr., "Beylage. Eine Brief wegen dem Fuzwaschen," in "Grundforschende Fragen" (Germantown: Christopher Sauer, 1774), in Durnbaugh, 463.

[42] "Proceedings of a Council-Meeting [Adams County, Ill.]," *Gospel-Visiter* 1 (February 1852): 179-80; "Letter from Illinois," ibid., 2 (October 1852): 115-8, and continued in ibid., 2 (June 1852): 11-12; and (August 1852): 68-71. See also Bowman, "Beyond Plainness," 75.

Material goods became increasingly plentiful in Pennsylvania as a consumer revolution spilled over from England into the American colonies. The New World aristocracy spent itself into debt through the accumulation of mirrors, silver, furniture, fine gardens, and clothing. Fashion often changed yearly. The middle classes did their best to imitate social pacesetters and acquire the badges of status--so much so that in England status based on clothing became increasingly difficult to recognize. Consumption in Pennsylvania, also robust, generally decreased as distance from the seaboard increased, and so commonplace goods in towns--chests, clocks, looking glasses, spice boxes, leather chairs, and silver--became luxuries in rural areas, but ear rings, lace, ribbons, silver shoe buckles, expensive riding whips, wigs, and expensive fabric remained readily available to most Pennsylvanians with extra cash. Goods tended to be more expensive in Pennsylvania, but incomes were higher.[43]

The Dunkers, Mennonites, and Amish generally avoided and opposed such acquisitiveness. During the Protestant Reformation, Menno Simons commented that lovers of possessions

> say that they believe [in Christ], and yet, alas, there are no limits nor bounds to their accursed haughtiness, foolish pride and pomp; they parade in silks, velvet, costly clothes, gold rings, chains, silver belts, pins and buttons, curiously adorned shirts, shawls, collars, veils, aprons, velvet shoes, slippers, and such like foolish finery.... Everyone has as much finery as he can afford and sometimes more than that.

He quoted the Apostle Paul's observation that "all that is in the world, the lust of the flesh, and the lust of the eyes, and the pride of life, is not of the Father, but is of the world," and he warned believers to follow the pattern of the early church and not to adorn themselves with gold, silver, costly pearls, embroidered hair, and expensive or unusual dress. Females, he said, should wear clothing that "becomes women

---

[43] Neil McKendrick, John Brewer, and J. H. Plumb, *The Birth of a Consumer Society: The Commercialization of Eighteenth-Century England* (Bloomington: Indiana University Press, 1982), 10-1, 51-5; Jack Michel, "In a Manner and Fashion Suitable to the Degree: A Preliminary Investigation of the Material Culture of Early Pennsylvania," *Working Papers from the Regional Economic Research Center* 5 (1981): 25; Gottlieb Mittelberger, *Journey to Pennsylvania* (Cambridge, Mass.: Harvard University Press, 1960), 37, 50-1, 88-90; and Carole Shammas, "Consumer Behavior in Colonial America" (paper presented at the Capitol Historical Society Symposium, Washington, D.C., 1986).

professing godliness" and was suitable to their occupations.[44]

Although protected somewhat by the Atlantic Ocean from European consumerism and sheltered from Philadelphia customs by a belt of fertile farmland, pious Anabaptists in Pennsylvania concurred with Menno and consistently warned of the sins of personal indulgence. As Mennonites in Pennsylvania experienced increasing tolerance and prosperity, their historic emphasis on suffering, so appropriate among persecuted believers in Europe, seemed an awkward transplant. Accordingly, they gradually replaced their stress on suffering with an emphasis on humility. Given the spreading eighteenth-century passion for demonstrating status with outward shows of luxury, this transition appears credible. In 1782 a Franconia-area Mennonite, Christian Holdeman, remarked in a sermon that true Christians are "not avaricious" and do not seek "honor or high places or offices in the world" but rather "yield themselves willingly under the banner of the cross of Christ." Another preacher complained that although Jesus showed the way of meekness and humility, modern Christians often say "Joseph had a coat of many colors, and Job was also rich, and Solomon, too," despite Jesus' clear command, "If you love me, keep my commandments." Mennonites broke with Christ, he said, when they "daily live like the rich man" and clothe themselves "in purple and costly linen, with all kinds of forbidden ornamental decorations, with cutting the hair and curling the hair and so many other things."[45] A Dunker poet agreed that wealth promoted pride, writing "And many a man conceited is/ Because of all the wealth that's his."[46]

Although it was somewhat easy for Dunkers and Mennonite farmers in the backcountry to avoid "coats of many colors," the valuable estate of Christopher Sauer II in Germantown also shows noticeable restraint. Conspicuous by their absence from his possessions were typical eighteenth-century luxuries, such as tea services, candlesticks, ceramic and china ware, silver of any kind, and a carriage.

[44] "True Christian Faith," 1541, in *The Complete Writings of Menno Simons, c. 1496-1561*, ed. John Christian Wenger, trans. Leonard Verduin (Scottdale, Pa.: Herald Press, 1956), 377, 386.

[45] MacMaster, *Land, Piety, Peoplehood*, 176-82.

[46] John Preisz, "Man, Like a Flower," trans. Ora Garber, in Durnbaugh, *The Brethren in Colonial America*, 553.

Curiously, Sauer had no horse.   Eighty-four households owned
carriages in Philadelphia, including thirty-three Quakers, but not Sauer.
He did enjoy several items that marked his achievement: many beds
(but evidently without expensive bed curtains) and numerous chests,
chairs, an eight-day clock and case, a thirty-hour clock, and a watch.
Unlike wealthy Quaker merchants in Philadelphia, however, he owned
no silver tankards, braziers, porringers, salvers, or teapots, no exotic
woods like mahogany, and no Turkish carpets.   Many of the more
valuable items in Sauer's estate were utilitarian, such as the beds and
timepieces, while the items he shunned, such as silver and tea services,
had less practical use.[47]

Clothing was the most conspicuous application of Anabaptist
simplicity. Christopher Sauer I sharply denounced powdered wigs and
caps on shaven heads as "a silly European custom"--this in a century
when wigs in over 150 styles were a major sign of rank. (Occupations
with the highest prestige called for the most ornate wigs, giving rise to
the expression "bigwigs.") Sauer also condemned expensive New England funerals for the large amounts of money spent on black mourning
clothes.   In contrast, the dress of the Brethren was *"bürgerlich"*
(middle-class), according to one observer, and Morgan Edwards
reported that Dunkers generally used "great plainness of language and
dress." Most of the men grew beards; Mennonite men likewise wore
beards, dressed plainly, and prohibited "proud colors."   In 1780 a
British prisoner of war billeted in Lancaster attended a Mennonite wedding and noticed that the faithful never wore "buckles or metal but-
tons"; the wedding feast, on the other hand, "was a profusion of soups,
meats, pies, &c, enough for a Regt of soldiers." In the same period
Hugh Kelly, a Maryland Loyalist, passed safely through Pennsylvania
to the British in New York by fooling the authorities into thinking he
was a Dunker; he grew a long beard and wore characteristically Brethren garb.   While Dunkers did not codify plain dress or specify
hairstyles, cut of the coat, colors, etc., until the nineteenth century and

---

[47] Frederick B. Tolles, *Meeting House and Counting House: The Quaker Merchants
of Colonial Philadelphia 1682-1763* (Chapel Hill: University of North Carolina Press,
1948), 128-31; and "An Inventory of the Personal Estate Belonging to Christopher Sauer
Senr. (July 27th, 1778)," *PA*, Series VI, Vol. 12, 865-72. The estate was again inven-
toried two days later and the sale proceeds are also recorded in the *Pennsylvania
Archives*. All three records are in agreement on the worth of the Sauer estate.

Mennonites waited until the early twentieth, Anabaptists in colonial Pennsylvania evidently dressed distinctively.[48]

Although these Anabaptists practiced plainness for religious reasons rather than for social levelling, their avoidance of luxury nevertheless rejected the methods by which the eighteenth century displayed status. Fernand Braudel has written that "Costume is a language. It is no more misleading than the graphs drawn by demographers and price historians."[49] The sartorial language spoken by the German Anabaptists accented simplicity.

VI

As the Anabaptists practiced their interpretation of Biblical obedience, they inadvertently promoted the egalitarianism with Pietism. They washed feet and dressed simply to further humility and to obey to the commands of Jesus but nonetheless provided a democratic contrast to hierarchical ideas. It is hard to imagine an eighteenth-century custom that moved more directly against the prevailing currents of elitism than feetwashing. Lay ordination similarly derived more from loyalty to the Scriptures than to social levelling.

On the other hand, the priority the Anabaptists placed on separation and, especially, their determination to preserve the purity of the church created tension with other denominations. About the Amish little documentation exists, but mid-eighteenth century Dunkers, who embraced the ban and were only a generation or two removed from their founders' legacy of self-confident nonconformity, responded cautiously to the coming interdenominational awakenings, avoided the popular Wesleyan movement later in the century, and opposed camp

---

[48] Durnbaugh, *Brethren in Colonial America*, 174; "J.B.S.," *The Alert Traveler*, in ibid., 122; Durnbaugh, "Religion and Revolution: Options in 1776," *PMH* 1 (July 1978): 8; Thomas Hughes, June 27, 1780, *A Journal by Thos. Hughes: For his Amusement, and Designed only for his Perusal by the time he attains the Age of 50 if he lives so long (1778-1789)* (Port Washington, N.Y.: Kennikat Press, 1947, reissued 1970), 88-9; and *Pensylvanische Berichte*, August 1, 1749, and May 1, 1752.

[49] Fernand Braudel, *Capitalism and Material Life, 1400-1800*, trans. Miriam Kochan (New York: Harper and Row, 1973), 235.

meeting revivalism in the 1800s. They would contribute little to the growing cooperation in early Pennsylvania, but the acceptance accorded to them confirms Pennsylvania's growing tolerance. Mennonites, with their larger size and a looser denominational organization, refrained from strict sanctions--perhaps their rich heritage and lengthier history gave them greater confidence--and participated more fully in the rising tolerance and continued evolution of Pietism.

CHAPTER 4

Wachet auf:
The Pennsylvania German Awakening

In late November 1739, six thousand people stood for two hours beneath a Germantown balcony to hear George Whitefield, the young but already famous Anglican revivalist. His words, somehow overcoming the difficulties that Germans had in understanding English, moved many to tears. Whitefield recalled with satisfaction that afterwards Germantowners shook his hand and invited him into their homes and that one of them "most kindly entertained me." Especially impressing him were colonists who had fled religious persecution in Germany that stemmed from their "preaching Christ." At about four o'clock--with the late November sun low in the sky--Whitefield, presumably in powdered wig and vestments, hiked down to the Wissahickon Creek with his sizeable entourage to visit an aged Kelpianite. The great evangelist especially praised the settlement's harmony; he counted "no less than fifteen denominations" yet found that all agreed "to hold Jesus Christ as their head, and to worship Him in spirit and in truth." In Germantown, Whitefield concluded, he "felt a blessed union and communion with many souls, though of different nations and professions."[1]

Six months later Whitefield returned to Pennsylvania and preached to almost four thousand in Germantown, three thousand at Henry Antes' farm in Skippack, and two thousand at another Skippack location. Both Skippack services were bilingual. Following Whitefield's sermon, a Moravian minister, George Boehler, preached in

---

[1] John Frantz uses the phrase "German awakening" in "The Awakening of Religion among the German Settlers in the Middle Colonies," *WMQ* 33 (April 1976): 266-88. See also *George Whitefield's Journals (1737-1741): To Which Is Prefixed His "Short Account" (1746) and "Further Account" (1747)*, intro. William V. Davis (Gainesville, Fla.: Scholars' Facsimiles and Reprints, 1969), 354-5.

German. Then the Germans "prayed and sung in their language," after
which, Whitefield recalled, "God enlarged my heart to pray in ours."
He praised "the order, seriousness, and devotion of these people" and
thought their common life "most worthy of imitation."[2]

Aside from Whitefield's status as a celebrity, his experiences
among Pennsylvania Germans were not extraordinary. If Whitefield
articulated the aspiration for spiritual awakening in an unfamiliar
tongue, his theme was familiar, and many of those who crowded under
Whitefield's Germantown balcony considered this Anglican sojourner
in America to be a kindred spirit.

I

The large and enthusiastic turnout for Whitefield suggests that for the
church Germans--Lutherans and Reformed--Pietism became just as vital
to their spiritual life as for the Anabaptists.[3] The most prominent
German Reformed Pietist was Michael Schlatter, an enthusiastic
denominational organizer, but years before his arrival in 1746 other
Pietist preachers, probably a majority of their few clergymen, labored
among the Reformed. Samuel Guldin, who preached to the early
Germantown Reformed congregation, asserted that he had a Pietistic
conversion experience "on the 4th of August, 1693, between nine and
ten o'clock in the forenoon, [when] the light of faith arose, and was
born within" him. Guldin, or, as a colleague called him, "the old
Gulde," had lost his last two pastorates in Germany because civil authorities disliked his Pietism. In 1710 he immigrated to Philadelphia
with Swiss Mennonites.[4] The timing of Johann Bechtel's awakening is
less certain, but he preached for the Reformed for approximately ten

---

[2] *Whitefield's Journal*, 406, 409-10; and Beulah Stauffer Hostetler, *American
Mennonites and Protestant Movements: A Community Paradigm* (Scottdale, Pa.: Herald
Press, 1987), 23.

[3] Joseph Henry Dubbs, *The Reformed Church in Pennsylvania* (Lancaster, Pa.: The
Pennsylvania German Society, 1902), 78-9.

[4] Ibid., 68-70. See also Charles H. Glatfelter, *Pastors and People: German Lutheran
and Reformed Churches in the Pennsylvania Field, 1717-1793* (Breinigsville, Pa.: The
Pennsylvania German Society, 1980), 49-50.

years, then worshipped with the Pietistic separatists at Skippack, and later became a Moravian.[5] Peter Miller, who served several Reformed congregations in the early 1730s, vigorously defended lay authority in pastoral placement, an indication of Pietist influence before joining the Ephrata Cloister.[6]

Henry Dorsius, who in 1737 immigrated to America, instilled Pietism in several protégés, including the sons of Theodore Freyling-huysen, the Dutch Reformed revivalist in Raritan, New Jersey. Freylinghuysen commended Dorsius as a "learned, gifted, graciously-endowed and faithful minister." In 1748 Dorsius's ministry in Pennsylvania ended when his wife left him for several reasons, in-cluding allegations of drunkenness, and he returned to Europe.[7] Henry Goetschi, aged eighteen, arrived from Zürich with his family in 1735 and, though unlicensed and unordained, preached to Reformed congregations almost immediately. Two years later the Presbytery of Philadelphia licensed him but refused ordination until he studied with another clergyman. So Dorsius tutored Goetschi for a year, then joined Freylinghuysen and Gilbert Tennant, the "New Side" Presbyterian, in ordaining him. Henry M. Muhlenberg endorsed Goetschi's "upright heart and godly life," despite the young minister's preoccupation with absolute grace, which caused his "ailing" wife to cry "bitterly" because she could not say with certainty that she had been saved; she "felt in herself nothing but darkness, wrath and death."[8]

Apparently, then, most Reformed preachers before the mid-century awakenings were Pietists, but only one of them, Bartholomew Rieger, accepted that all adults might achieve salvation by exercising their God-given free will. Rieger dissented with "some scruples" from a Pennsylvania coetus statement that endorsed the strongly predestinari-an Canons of Dort. Rieger's stance hardly disturbed his colleagues,

---

[5] Glatfelter, *Pastors and People*, 18; and Henry Harbaugh, *The Life of Rev. Michael Schlatter* (Philadelphia: S. R. Fisher, 1857), 39-40.

[6] Glatfelter, *Pastors and People*, 91.

[7] Dubbs, *Reformed Church in Pennsylvania*, 92-3; and Glatfelter, *Pastors and People*, 31.

[8] Glatfelter, *Pastors and People*, 46-7; and Henry Mechior Muhlenberg, *The Journals of Henry Melchior Muhlenberg*, ed. Theodore G. Tappert, 4 vols. (Philadelphia: Muhlenberg Press, 1942-1958) I, 298.

who elected him president of the next coetus, and he delivered its opening sermon.[9]

Only one of these early Reformed preachers, Johann Philip Boehm, the most prominent cleric among them, openly opposed Pietism. Boehm, a schoolteacher who spearheaded early efforts to organize the Reformed diaspora in Pennsylvania, had served first as a sermon reader and later submitted to his congregation's call to preach. The shortage of ministers, which prompted Boehm's ordination, delayed matters because there were no other local preachers to perform the ordination ceremony. The nearest clergy were Freylinghuysen and his associates in New Jersey, but their revivalism repelled him. So in 1729 Boehm travelled to New York to be ordained by more traditional Dutch Calvinists. By the early 1740s he filled five pulpits simultaneously while itinerating to outlying congregations.[10]

Another organizer, Conrad Templeman, left little record regarding his beliefs although his encouragement of lay-centered practices, whether resulting from convictions or the pressure of circumstances, was typical of Pietists. Templeman, a tailor, led devotions in private Conestoga-area houses, reading sermons and conducting hymns and prayers. He did not baptize or preside at communion, however, since only ordained ministers might administer the sacraments. Beginning in 1725, these house meetings developed into several congregations. According to Boehm, Templeman's Lancaster communion was "pretty strong" although led by "irregular men [who] never cared for church

---

[9] Rieger pastored several congregations from 1731 until 1743, then returned to Europe to study medicine. Soon he reappeared and combined his ministry with medical practice. See *Minutes and Letters of the Coetus of the German Reformed Congregations in Pennsylvania, 1747-1792* (Philadelphia: Reformed Church Board, 1903), 40-1, 45, 53; and Glatfelter, *Pastors and People*, 108-9.

[10] Boehm to Classis of Amsterdam, April 4, 1740, in William J. Hinke, ed., *Life and Letters of the Rev. John Philip Boehm, Founder of the Reformed Church in Pennsylvania, 1683-1749* (New York: Arno Press, 1972), 302; Boehm to Classis of Amsterdam, July 25, 1741, id., 325; the Consistories of the German Reformed Churches of Falkner Swamp, Skippack, and Whitemarsh to the Classis of Amsterdam, July 1728, id., 156-9; the Classis of Amsterdam to the Ministers at New York, June 20, 1729, id., 177; and Glatfelter, *Pastors and People*, 21-2.

order." He later followed Boehm's example and agreed to ordination.[11]

Pietism's influence among early Lutherans is more difficult to measure. They had almost no clergy and were even more disorganized than the German Reformed, but Pietist practices among the Lutherans similarly preceded their landmark organizer, Muhlenberg. The first German Lutheran Pietists in Pennsylvania were with Johannes Kelpius's small group of mystics along the Wissahickon Creek. One of their number, Heinrich Bernhard Koster, conducted Lutheran services but took no steps to form a congregation. Two other of these Wissahickon mystics, Daniel and Justus Falckner, sons of a Lutheran clergyman in Saxony, had studied theology in German universities: Justus at the Pietist institute at Halle and Daniel at Erfurt. In 1703 Swedish Lutherans ordained Justus, the first Lutheran ordination in America, but he immediately moved to New York. Daniel Falckner, yet unordained, pastored the New Hannover congregation until 1708, when the Frankfurt Land Company, for whom he was an agent, dismissed him for fraud. He probably led a congregation in New Jersey's Raritan Valley from 1724 to 1734.

During the first decade of the eighteenth century, therefore, no ordained German Lutheran clergyperson lived in Pennsylvania, only Swedish ones, a situation that improved very little in the next several decades. In 1717 Andrew Jacob Henkel appeared from Germany and functioned as the Lutheran counterpart to Boehm, organizing and visiting scattered congregations until he died from a fall off his horse in 1728. We know little about his position on Pietism. Caspar Stoever, Jr., though unordained, preached for many years after 1733 from his base in Lancaster County, sixty miles west of Philadelphia. He travelled to New Jersey on one occasion, hoping to persuade Daniel Falckner to ordain him, but Falckner refused. Stoever toiled in Pennsylvania until his death in 1779 but always suffered strained relations with Pietist ministers, which may explain Falckner's refusal to ordain him. In 1732 a recently arrived minister, Christian Schulze, organized several congregations, but he quickly persuaded them to commission him as a fund-raiser in Europe, whereupon he left Pennsyl-

---

[11] Glatfelter, *Pastors and People*, 317; Report of Mr. Boehm to the Classis of Amsterdam, January 14, 1739, *Life and Letters of Boehm*, 275-6; and [Conrad] Templeman to Synods of North and South Holland, February 13, 1733, in Dubbs, *Reformed Church in Pennsylvania*, 82-3.

vania forever. To tend the flocks in his absence, he ordained Stoever
and his father, Caspar Stoever, Sr. The latter took a congregation in
Hebron, Virginia, in the Shenandoah Valley, leaving his son as
probably the only German Lutheran minister in Pennsylvania. In 1742
another cleric, Valentine Kraft, claimed to be commissioned by the
Consistory of Hesse-Darmstadt to organize Pennsylvania Lutherans.
Although Kraft's ordination was indeed valid, his commission from the
Consistory was not.[12] The severe shortage of preachers, the opposition
of the younger Stoever, and the lack of information regarding Kraft,
Henkel, and others, makes the influence of Pietism less certain among
the early Lutherans in Pennsylvania than among the German Reformed.

   Thus, although the thin ranks of German Reformed and Lutheran
preachers had by no means closed around Pietism, certainly a majority,
including unordained ministers, embraced the doctrine of the new birth,
even before Muhlenberg and Schlatter. Their early accent on the
importance of free will in conversion placed princes and paupers alike
on equal footing before God, thus preparing the way for tolerance and
the mid-century awakenings in early Pennsylvania.

                                II

The tendency of Pietism to promote cooperation became more explicit
with the proposal of Count Nicholas Ludwig von Zinzendorf in 1742
to unite all German religious movements under one banner. Zinzendorf
assumed leadership of the Moravians after he invited these spiritual
descendants of the fifteenth-century Hussite movement, a persecuted
fellowship following the Counter-Reformation, to live on his estate in

---

[12] Muhlenberg, *Journals*, III, 377; Glatfelter, *Pastors and People*, 59-61, 70-2, 126,
138-43; Leonhard R. Riforgiato, *Missionary of Moderation: Henry Melchior Muhlenberg
and the Lutheran Church in English America* (Lewisburg, Pa.: Bucknell University
Press, 1980), 51, 63-5, 70; Julius Friedrich Sachse, *The German Pietists of Provincial
Pennsylvania, 1694-1708* (1895; repr., New York: AMS Press, 1970), 251-89, 299-322;
Theodore G. Tappert, "The Influence of Pietism in Colonial American Lutheranism," F.
Ernest Stoeffler, ed., *Continental Pietism and Early American Christianity* (Grand
Rapids, Mich.: William B. Eerdmans Publishing Company, 1976), 15; and Abdel Ross
Wentz, *A Basic History of Lutheranism in America* (Philadelphia: Muhlenberg Press,
1955), 15-7.

Saxony. In 1740 they first came to Pennsylvania, hired by George Whitefield to build a school for blacks in Nazareth. Although Whitefield and the Moravians quickly parted company, Zinzendorf's followers established a permanent settlement nearby, Bethlehem, along the Lehigh River. Because Moravians believed that peers--boys, girls, single men, single women, married persons, etc.--had special capability to assist each another in spiritual growth, they created a unique system of communal living in which "Choirs" of like age, gender, and marital status became the center of worship, work, and daily living.[13]

Zinzendorf's unification effort originated with the monthly meetings of the separatists at Skippack. August A. Spangenberg, a Moravian missionary, attended their gatherings and wrote to Zinzendorf that perhaps the Skippack concept could be enlarged to include all Pennsylvania German Christians. Zinzendorf promptly embraced the suggestion and in 1742 came to Pennsylvania with his daughter, Benigna, to unify awakened Germans. He also hoped to find new areas for Moravian settlements and to convert both Indians and whites to Christian faith.[14]

Zinzendorf envisioned a spiritual confederation of all German Christians that would undermine denominational identities. When asked why he participated in Moravian love feasts if he was German Reformed, Henry Antes replied, "I am Reformed; I am also a Lutheran; I am also a Mennonite. A Christian is everything."[15] Members of the invisible church of God's true followers--"The Church of God in the Spirit"--would, however, remain in their denominations, called "tropes," because these organizations were uniquely suited to train and appeal to their own adherents. Moravians believed that each denomination possessed God's protection, or as Zinzendorf remarked

---

[13] Beverly Prior Smaby, *The Transformation of Moravian Bethlehem: From Communal Mission to Family Economy* (Philadelphia: University of Pennsylvania Press, 1988), 1-12.

[14] Jacob John Sessler, *Communal Pietism Among Early American Moravians* (New York: Henry Holt, 1933), 28-9; John Joseph Stout, "Count Zinzendorf and the Pennsylvania Congregation of God in the Spirit: The First American Oecumenical Movement," *CH* 9 (December 1940): 370; and John R. Weinlick, *Count Zinzendorf* (New York and Nashville, Tenn.: Abingdon Press, 1956), 161.

[15] Boehm attributes this statement to Antes in his "Second Faithful Warning and Admonition," May 19, 1743, *Life and Letters of Boehm*, 378.

later, "each sect should retain its good salt, lest it lose its savor."[16] The tropes, therefore, were to respect each other; a Lutheran visiting the Reformed trope would abide by its rules, for example, and Lutheran and Reformed ordinations would remain valid. This scheme allowed Zinzendorf to maintain his own Lutheran ordination and thus be identified in Pennsylvania only as Dominie de Thurnstein, a Lutheran pastor. He hoped that this would enable Lutherans to accept him more readily and also permit him to retain affiliation with the Prussian state church.[17]

Moravians began their unification efforts with a letter that Henry Antes addressed to all German communions, urging them to discover their common beliefs by attending an interdenominational gathering in Germantown on New Year's Day, 1742. He explained that his intent was

> not to wrangle about opinions, but to treat with each other
> in love on the most important articles of faith, in order to
> ascertain how closely we can approach each other fundamen-
> tally, and bear with one another in love on opinions which
> do not subvert the ground of salvation.

Antes confidently predicted that the gathering would be large, but he implored his readers not to let this deter their attendance.[18]

Approximately one hundred persons from nearly all German communions--Lutherans, Reformed, Moravians, Mennonites, Dunkers, the Ephrata Society, and Schwenkfelders--plus several separatists accepted Antes' invitation and participated in the first assembly, strong evidence of the growing interdenominationalism that had preceded it. Between New Year's and June 1742, Moravians hosted six other such ecumenical events, called "synods." Attendance averaged above one

---

[16] The quotations are from Sessler, *Communal Pietism*, 31-2; and Count Zinzendorf to Joseph Muller [undated but probably 1742], in Donald F. Durnbaugh, ed., *The Brethren in Colonial America: A Source Book on the Transportation and Development of the Church of the Brethren in the Eighteenth Century* (Elgin, Ill.: The Brethren Press, 1967), 291.

[17] Sessler, *Communal Pietism*, 20-2; and Weinlick, *Zinzendorf*, 158-64.

[18] Henry Antes' letter of December 15, 1741, is in Sessler, *Communal Pietism*, 29, and many other sources.

hundred for these other synods, about half of that number being accredited delegates. Visitors included Anglicans, Presbyterians, and Quakers.[19]

The synods, however, became increasingly disputatious and did not evoke the spiritual brotherhood that Zinzendorf envisioned. Zinzendorf's authoritarian personality and a Moravian tendency to dominate affairs contributed as much to the plan's failure as doctrinal differences. The gatherings frequently employed Moravian practices such as the lot, sang Moravian hymns, heard Moravian readings, and obeyed Dominie de Thurnstein, which was how the Count instructed the synods to address him. Observers criticized Zinzendorf's "anger and fiery spirit," one noting that "this is a free country. The people here are not much interested in counts." Dropouts increased until only Moravians remained.

Divisions in several congregations mirrored those of Zinzendorf's synods. At Philadelphia, where Lutherans and Reformed shared a building, a Lutheran deacon closed the church to Lutheran Moravians. Zinzendorf's followers broke the lock to enter, but anti-Moravians interrupted the service and, amidst shouting, pushing, and elbowing, carried assistant pastor John Pyrlaeus out of the pulpit. The opponents then took the Moravians to court on charges of illegal entry. A mediator, who attempted to reconcile Johann Philip Boehm, the Reformed leader, with Zinzendorf's adherents, recalled that his effort ended when someone mentioned this incident, upon which Boehm's "eyes perfectly struck fire, and he declared with great passion he would as soon agree with ye devil as with ye Count."[20] In Lancaster, rival factions came to church armed after the newly arrived Swedish Lutheran pastor, Laurentius Thorstonsen Nyberg, who had developed Moravian sympathies while in Europe, openly declared for the Zinzen-

[19] Letter of [anonymous] Brethren to Germany Concerning Zinzendorf and Mueller, in Durnbaugh, *Brethren in Colonial America,* 303; it is possible that the authors were not Brethren but Mennonite. See also Sessler, *Communal Pietism,* 30-9, 44, 49-53; and Weinlick, *Zinzendorf,* 164.

[20] Richard Peters to Proprietors, January 15, 1743, *Life and Letters of Boehm,* 365-6,n237a.

dorfers.[21]

Opposition to the Moravians became extensive in Pennsylvania. Calvinists, such as Gilbert Tennant, Boehm, and Whitefield, argued with Zinzendorf over predestination because Moravians taught "free grace in the blood of the Lamb," that is, that Christ's atonement made everyone's salvation possible.   According to Tennant, Moravians neglected the struggle with sin that precedes the new birth and, thereby, incorrectly viewed regeneration as a joyful experience. Tennant further accused Zinzendorf of preaching that believers could free themselves from sin in the earthly life (perfectionism) and that eventually all would be saved (universalism), and he repeated in a New York pulpit the vicious rumor that Benigna was not really Zinzendorf's daughter but the child of a naval officer.[22] Boehm, the most influential Reformed critic, concentrated his anger on ministers, such as Jacob Lischy and Johann Bechtel, whom he considered Moravian wolves hiding in Reformed vestments. He attacked Bechtel for calling himself a Reformed minister but "proudly [boasting] of the publication of a Pietist book." He criticized Lischy for preaching the universalist doctrine that "people should not worry, all men would be saved, none should be lost." According to Boehm, parishioners stopped listening to Lischy after he acknowledged attending a Zinzendorf love feast.[23]

Separatists joined the fray. Johann Adam Gruber of Germantown, who probably corresponded with Old World opponents of Zinzendorf, challenged the stipulation that only members of denominations could enter the Church of God in the Spirit. Gruber boycotted the first

[21] "Faithful Letter of Warning addressed to The High German Evangelical Reformed Congregations and All their Members in Pennsylvania for their Faithful Warning against the People who are known as Herrn Huters...." (Philadelphia, Pa.: Andrew Bradford, 1742), ibid., 364-6; "Report of John Adam Gruber," ibid., 366-7; "A Protestation of the Several Members of the Protestant Lutheran and Reformed Religions in the City of Philadelphia," ibid., 368-9; Glatfelter, *Pastors and People*, 100-1; Muhlenberg, *Journals*, I, 75-6, 109, 111-2; and Weinlick, *Zinzendorf*, 162.

[22] Sessler, *Communal Pietism*, 67-8; and Milton J. Coalter, Jr., "The Radical Pietism of Count Nicholas Zinzendorf as a Conservative Influence on the Awakener, Gilbert Tennant," *CH* 49 (March 1980): 43-4.

[23] Boehm's "Faithful Letter of Warning," 358-9, and his "Second Faithful Warning," in *Life and Letters of Boehm*, 377. See also "Second Fiathful Warning," 360-1, 364, 375-8.

synod, although it met in his Germantown neighborhood, and he authored anti-Moravian reports, poems, and polemics. Another separatist, Christopher Sauer I, printed a collection of hymns for the Moravians, *Hirten Lieder von Bethlehem* (Shepherd's Songs from Bethlehem), but soon after its publication, he quarreled with the Moravians over Zinzendorf's creation of yet another religious organization. Sauer then refused to publish Antes' Moravian tract because he considered it malicious, especially the suggestion that the Dunkers were worse than "a pack invented by the devil." In 1746 Sauer charged that Zinzendorf, like the Roman Catholics, only let commoners read the Bible if they already agreed with him. Four years later Sauer placed in his newspapers an advertisement for a sermon attacking Moravians just beneath King George II's proclamation against them.[24]

Zinzendorf's relations with Lutheran leaders were no better. The one brief colloquy Muhlenberg held with Zinzendorf widened the gulf between Lutheran Pietists and the Moravian leader. Muhlenberg described the debate as having taken place before "a large gathering of [Zinzendorf's] generals and corporals, the Count presiding at a small table." The conversation became heated and uncivil. Although Muhlenberg had arrived in Pennsylvania only weeks before Zinzendorf left, his leadership effectively ended Moravian hopes of recruiting large numbers of Lutherans.[25]

Dunkers also rejected Moravianism. George Adam Martin, who attended Zinzendorf's third synod, described the conferences as snares intended to bring "simple-minded and inexperienced converts back to infant baptism," thus "erecting the old Babel again."[26] In 1750 leading Dunkers, including Alexander Mack, Jr., and Peter Becker, rebuked a Moravian preacher who was formerly with the Brethren. They found

---

[24] Durnbaugh, "Johann Adam Gruber: Pennsylvania German Prophet and Poet," *PMHB* 83 (October 1959): 393-402; and the correspondence between Sauer and Antes in Durnbaugh, *Brethren in Colonial America*, 315-9. See also *Pensylvanische Berichte*, June 16, 1746, and December 16, 1750; and Stephen L. Longenecker, *The Christopher Sauers* (Elgin, Ill.: Brethren Press, 1981), 111-3.

[25] Muhlenberg, *Journals*, I, 76-80.

[26] Martin's account is in Lamech and Agrippa, *Chronicon Ephratense: A History of the Community of Seventh Day Baptists at Ephrata, Lancaster County, Pennsylvania*, trans. J. Max Hart (Lancaster, Pa.: S. H. Zahn, 1884), 245; and in Durnbaugh, *Brethren in Colonial America*, 287.

that the Moravians' use of "fiddles, organs, flutes, oboes, bass-fiddles, bagpipes, and such nonsence," together with infant baptism, was "so suspicious" that they considered the "whole affair an abominable soup" from which they desired "to taste [not] a single drop."[27]   Others suspected that the Church of God in the Spirit was a front for Moravianism and that Zinzendorf, as one Dunker wrote, "wanted to be the head of the separatists, Brethren, Sabbatarians, Mennonites, Schwenkfelders, Quakers, Reformed, and Lutherans."[28]

To be anti-Moravian was not necessarily to oppose interdenominationalism, but Zinzendorf's version of cooperation alarmed church leaders, who perceived his restructuring as a threat to their frail institutions. The Count provoked sectarian reactions and managed only to unite Pennsylvania Christians in opposition to his plan. Although many Germans never fully comprehended the Church of God in the Spirit, a difficult concept at best, broad participation in the early synods indicates some initial receptiveness to Zinzendorf's ideas.

III

As Zinzendorf's vision of an ecumenical confederation evaporated, denominational loyalties intensified, fueled by a burst of Pietistic enthusiasm, but also by sectarian rivalries. Zinzendorf's followers gradually came to concentrate on the development of the Moravian church. Energetic, ordained Pietist missionaries--Michael Schlatter of the Reformed and Henry M. Muhlenberg of the Lutherans--itinerated to stir the hearts of their people to support the traditional denominational structures. Mennonites and Dunkers, whose congregations possessed the power to ordain, relied less on ecclesiastical structures and demonstrated their denominational vitality in more modest ways.

A burst of Mennonite publishing activity reveals their renewed ardor. Before 1742 their only American imprint was an English translation of the *Dordrecht Confession of Faith*, issued in Philadelphia

---

[27] Henry Jacobs, *et al.*, Brethren reply to Johannes Muller, Canantacken, February 12, 1750, in Durnbaugh, *Brethren in Colonial America*, 312-5.

[28] Letter of a Brethren to Germany, November 15, 1744, ibid., 302-3. The identity of the writer is unknown.

in 1727. But in the 1740s Mennonites issued a group of publications that reinforced their heritage and doctrine. In 1742 they produced a new edition of their hymnal, the *Ausbund*. Shortly afterward, Skippack-area Mennonites arranged for the Ephrata Cloister to print a German-language edition of the *Martyr's Mirror*, a chronicle of Anabaptist saints (originally in Dutch) running to fifteen-hundred pages, one of the largest books produced in colonial America. In 1744 Sauer printed Heinrich Funk's *Ein Spiegel der Tauffe, mit Geist mit Wasser und mit Blut* (A Mirror of Baptism, of the Spirit, with Water, and with Blood), which explained the Mennonite concept of discipleship, including baptism "with blood," that is, obedience and suffering. Funk's book rejected baptism by total immersion, and many Mennonites boycotted copies of the *Martyr's Mirror* that contained a frontispiece showing John immersing Jesus in baptism. (Eighteenth-century binderies often offered buyers a choice of covers, and Ephrata's *Martyr's Mirror* edition contained several frontispieces.) A posthumous 1763 edition of *Ein Spiegel der Tauffe* was more conciliatory and suggested that Christians not argue over differences of "understanding and form in the matter of things ceremonial." The Mennonites also published at Ephrata *Die Ersthafte Christenpflicht* (Earnest Christian Duty), a prayerbook compiled by Palatine Mennonites, and *Guldene Aepffel in Silbern Schalen* (Golden Apples in Silver Vessels), a Swiss Mennonite devotional.[29]

Dunkers tightened an already flourishing denominational structure by instituting yearly meetings in direct response to the Moravians. As one Brethren leader put it, because some of their members had become "smitten with this vain doctrine" of Moravianism, they "agreed to get ahead of this danger" by holding a "great meeting."[30]

Moravians clung to their ecumenical self-perception but denominational evolution continued. In 1744 Spangenberg, now a Moravian bishop, returned from Germany to administer Bethlehem and other Moravian projects in British North America. By 1748 missionaries had organized thirty Moravian settlements, including seventeen in Pennsyl-

---

[29] Richard K. MacMaster, *Land, Piety, Peoplehood: The Establishment of Mennonite Communities in America, 1683-1790* (Scottdale, Pa.: Herald Press, 1985), 143-6.

[30] *Chronicon*, 245.

vania, which became the nuclei for the emerging denomination.[31]

The continued progress of the smaller, nonconformist communions helped motivate the Lutherans and Reformed to solidify denominational structures. According to one traveler, dissenter criticism was responsible for a popular saying that Pennsylvania was "heaven for farmers" but "hell for officials and preachers." Schlatter decried "all kinds of sects and erring spirits" in Pennsylvania, and Muhlenberg fretted that innumerable sectarians along with excessive worldliness threatened to extinguish the weak Lutheran spark in Penn's Woods. He complained that Anabaptists generally ridiculed Lutherans and Reformed, especially if the "church people" were both "unenlightened and unconverted." But when piety grew, Muhlenberg suspected that Mennonites, Dunkers, and Moravians attempted chicanery to capture members from among such people, and Schlatter suggested that before the revival in his denomination, the "seductive doctrines" of the "crafty Herrnhuters" threatened to win over many Reformed and Lutherans. Boehm penned especially bitter words about competition from the sects; he lamented that "the 'Tumplers' [i.e., Dunkers], Seventh-day people, Mennonites" and others had won over a number so large as to produce tears.[32] Leaders of the older denominations were eager to return their flocks to the fold.

The interaction between Pietism and denomination building was especially evident among Lutherans. In the dying days of Zinzendorf's Church of God in the Spirit, Muhlenberg, a Halle Pietist, came to Pennsylvania bent on unifying his communion. The Lutheran missionary preached regularly to several congregations, travelled from Maryland to New York and the Carolinas, sought pastors both in

---

[31] Weinlick, "Moravianism in the American Colonies," F. Ernest Stoeffler, ed., *Continental Pietism and Early American Christianity* (Grand Rapids, Mich.: William B. Eerdmans Publishing Company, 1976), 144-5, 149-51.

[32] Mr. Boehm and the Philadelphia Consistory to Deputy Velingius, October 28, 1734, *Life and Letters of Boehm*, 239; Gottlieb Mittelberger, *Journey to Pennsylvania*, ed. and trans. Oscar Handlin and John Clive (Cambridge, Mass.: Harvard University Press, 1960), 48; Muhlenberg, *Journals*, I, 144; Muhlenberg to J. M. Boltzius, January-March 1750, *Die Korrespondenz Heinrich Melchior Muhlenbergs: Aus der Anfangszeit des deutschen Luthertums in Nordamerika*, 3 vols. (Berlin and New York: Walter de Gruyter, 1986), I, 363; and Michael Schlatter, "Journal," in Henry Harbaugh, *The Life of Rev. Michael Schlatter: With a Full Account of His Travels and Labors among the Germans--1716-1790* (Philadelphia: S. R. Fisher, 1857), 144-5.

Europe and America to assign and install in New World pulpits, and organized synods everywhere.

To expedite these essentially sectarian ends, Muhlenberg encouraged revivalism and rejoiced over emotional and tearful "awakenings." He told how an eighteen-year-old boy "like a new-born child, drank in the sincere milk of the Gospel" and "amid many tears and great emotion renewed his baptismal covenant." An elderly couple, he recorded, "promised in tears to be obedient to the invitation with God's help." On another occasion he testified that God had "awakened" an old man.[33] Other Lutherans similarly stressed emotional aspects of the new birth. At the first synod in Pennsylvania a preacher admonished elders that to be effective they must "be converted from the heart" because he suspected that some "were not entirely converted." At another synod one repentant insisted that the preacher, Johann Friedrich Handschuh, ask the congregation to pardon his "former scandalous life." After Handschuh did this, the sinner then tearfully spoke to the congregation on his own behalf.[34]

Lutherans experienced emotional renewal in groups as well as individually. At Conewago, where the crowd's size forced services into a large barn, Muhlenberg reported that "they wept loudly at hearing God's Word." A large gathering of German and English settlers in Frederick, Maryland, was "very attentive and hungry and drank in the Word of God as parched earth drinks in the warm rain." At another service there several days later some worshippers said they had travelled as much as twenty miles--Germans often journeyed long distances to attend church--and many had to stand outside the building. Muhlenberg suggested that faithful Lutherans often endured great hardship and tolerated difficult weather to attend his services.[35]

---

[33] Muhlenberg, *Journals*, I, 145, 151. See other examples of tearful confessions in *Journals*, I, 119, 196, 204, 228.

[34] The quotation is in A. Spaeth, H. E. Jacobs, and G. F. Spieker, eds., *Documentary History of the Evangelical Lutheran Ministerium of Pennsylvania and Adjacent States: Proceedings of the Annual Conventions from 1748 to 1821* [hereafter cited as *Lutheran Ministerium*] (Philadelphia: The Evangelical Lutheran Church, 1898), 12; see Handschuh's "diary" in Spaeth, 25.

[35] Mittelberger, *Journey to Pennsylvania*, 43; Muhlenberg an Boltzius, *Die Korrespondenz Muhlenbergs*, 364; and Muhlenberg, *Journals*, I, 155-6, 162. See other examples in *Journals*, I, 152, 158, 167.

The Lutheran revival grew with the arrival of other Pietist preachers, who soon dominated Pennsylvania's Lutheran clergy. By 1770 twelve Pietist pastors from the University of Halle had followed Muhlenberg to Pennsylvania, many in response to calls for volunteers from G. A. Franke, the son of the August Hermann Francke, the Halle patriarch. When the Tulpehocken Lutherans expressed appreciation for the assistance of Europeans in finding them a minister, they singled out the recommendations from Halle, which they called "a city set upon a hill." They were so pleased with their pastor, Johann Nicolas Kurtz, that they agreed to build a stone meetinghouse and parsonage. If the receptions of Kurtz and Muhlenberg were typical, Lutheran settlers welcomed their Pietist clergymen.[36]

Michael Schlatter, the German Reformed organizer, shared Muhlenberg's enthusiasm for bringing order to his denomination. A thirty-year-old Swiss, Schlatter came to Philadelphia in 1746 with a commission from Reformed church officials in Amsterdam to organize its Pennsylvania congregations. Schlatter, who fled a scandal in Switzerland, undoubtedly had more complex motives for immigration than Muhlenberg. While serving as a vicar, or assistant, to a village pastor, the future missionary had conceived a child with the preacher's daughter, a married woman, who was the mother of eight other children but estranged from her husband. Several days after the birth Schlatter fled, leaving behind his lover, his newborn son, and his parents, who told authorities they felt "offended and betrayed." His parents also publicly complained that their son had squandered a sizeable portion of his inheritance on travel and books, but they nevertheless secured a favorable reference for him to take to Holland.[37]

On arrival in Pennsylvania, Schlatter began work immediately. He promptly journeyed sixteen miles to pay his respects to Boehm, who despite his opposition to Pietism, promised full support. The next day

[36] Muhlenberg an G. A. Francke und F. M. Ziegenhagen, May 24, 1747, *Die Korrespondenz Muhlenbergs*, I, 287; and *Lutheran Ministerium*, 21. See also Glatfelter, *Pastors and People*, 23, 47, 50, 52, 55, 57, 71, 73, 76, 115, 119, 124, 152.

[37] Marthi Pritzker-Ehrlich, "Michael Schlatter von St. Gallen (1716-1790), Eine Biographische Untersuchung zur Schweizerischen Amerika-Auswanderung des 18. Jahrhunderts" (Ph.D. diss.: Universität Zürich, 1981), 25-32, 36-7, 169-70; and Pritzker-Ehrlich, "Michael Schlatter: A Man in Between," *Swiss American Historical Society Newsletter* 19 (1983): 5-6.

he went eight miles further to visit Jacob Reiff, a controversial lay leader, and then he returned to Philadelphia looking for 130 missing German Bibles that the Dutch had sent years ago. (He found them, and most Reformed congregations received several.) Soon the Philadelphia congregation heard Schlatter's first sermon in Pennsylvania, then listened to his explanation of his commission to set German Reformed congregations in order. Under Schlatter's leadership the Philadelphia congregation grew remarkably, forcing a move into their unfinished building, *sans* windows and pulpit, where Schlatter administered communion on Easter, 1748, to 171 souls.[38]

Boehm described Schlatter's ministry in much less flattering terms. The former schoolteacher reported to Dutch authorities that the young missionary had alientated many through lackluster leadership and that his extravagances during worship, such as lifting high the bread and cup, gave offense. Boehm, however, spoke critically of all but the most orthodox Reformed preachers, and perhaps his reports best demonstrate that both he and Schlatter were self-promoters.[39]

Like Muhlenberg, Schlatter lubricated the mechanics of organization with expressions of religious emotion that resembled revivalism. He believed that his first sermon "awakened" and "inspired new life" among the Philadelphia worshippers. They responded emotionally, Schlatter wrote, and "thanked God, with tears of joy, because He had awakened the hearts" of Dutch Reformed officials to care for their souls. After reading his instructions to other congregations, he often saw "tears of joy flow richly down the cheeks of most of the hearers." In a partially completed Frederick, Maryland, church building Schlatter observed weeping and then fell to his knees, whereupon the congregation spontaneously followed him. A few days later at Conewago, Adams County, Pennsylvania, Schlatter administered communion to ninety-seven, baptized several aged persons and children, married three betrothed couples, and installed new elders and deacons; all, he reported, with the "greatest propriety of deportment, deep reverence, [and] much enlivening of the hearts."[40]

---

[38] Schlatter, "Journal," 124-30, 169.

[39] Pritzker-Ehrlich, "Michael Schlatter," 99-100; and Boehm to a Classical Commissioner, December 1748, in *Life and Letters of Boehm*, 442-63.

[40] Schlatter, "Journal," 130, 143, 176-7.

In Lancaster, another German Reformed Pietist clergyman, Philip William Otterbein, similarly emphasized spiritual renewal, especially by insisting on examination prior to communion. Later, at Tulpehocken, he introduced such revivalistic strategies as extemporaneous preaching and evening gatherings in homes featuring Scripture readings, exhortations, hymns, and an invitation to kneel in prayer. On the first of several such invitations Otterbein knelt alone, but later others joined him.[41]

Large turnouts everywhere demonstrated enthusiasm to win souls among the Reformed. Schlatter travelled thirty-nine miles to baptize Dr. John Miller's wife and his eight living children--a ninth had died only a few days earlier--before an audience of several hundred persons. On another occasion he baptized twenty-one children outdoors because, he wrote, "the house could not contain the multitude." In Lancaster Schlatter led communion for a large, joyous crowd of 205. At Tulpehocken, one Sunday, Schlatter and two assisting pastors led in worship six hundred persons who, he said, "listened to God's holy word with great devotion and attention." "The old and young together shed tears of joy," he said, when, to "their exceeding joy and surprise," they saw three ministers together, a circumstance they had never witnessed before.[42]

Mid-century Pennsylvania Germans, therefore, intensified devotion to revivalism, Pietism, and their denominations. Emotional religion, a vital part of all German communions, was especially integral to Lutheran and Reformed efforts to build a denominational structure.[43]

---

[41] Henry G. Spayth, *History of the Church of the United Brethren in Christ* (Circleville, Ohio: Conference Office the United Brethren Church, 1851), 22-4, based on the memories of Otterbein's contemporaries; "Rules of Order at Lancaster German Reformed Church, 1757," in Arthur C. Core, *Philip William Otterbein: Pastor, Ecumenist* (Dayton, Ohio: Board of Publication of the Evangelical United Brethren Church, 1968), 109; J. Steven O'Malley, *Pilgrimage of Faith: The Legacy of the Otterbeins* (Metuchen, N.J.: Scarecrow Press, 1973), 171-5; and A. W. Drury, *The Life of Philip William Otterbein: Founder of the Church of the United Brethren in Christ* (Dayton, Ohio: United Brethren Publishing House, 1890), 77-82, 93-5.

[42] Schlatter, "Journal," 133-5, 150, 153-4, 154, 158.

[43] In 1943 the German Reformed Church merged with the Evangelical Synod of North America, a denomination comprised primarily of mid-westerners of German descent, to create the Evangelical and Reformed Church, and this fellowship, then, in 1957 joined with the Congregational Church and the Christian Church to form the United Church of

As Schlatter noted, forty-nine heads of family at Monocacy, Maryland, "anxious after spiritual food," pledged financial support for a pastor after shedding "tears of joy" during his sermon.[44]

IV

As denominationalism strengthened in Pennsylvania, the models of church polity Schlatter and Muhlenberg imported from Europe underwent democratic modifications. American conditions, especially the shortage of clergy, encouraged an active role for the laity, and Muhlenberg deplored congregations who declared that "they would rather have something than nothing" and then elected schoolteachers to the ministry. He doubted the competence of brevet preachers, who often raised foolish disputes, such as whether to begin the Lord's Prayer with "*Vater Unser* or *Unser Vater.*" They were, he complained, "not only ignorant, but unconverted besides," and he charged that their contentiousness damaged many congregations. Many congregations held together for years without leadership from a minister, and later, when ordained preachers arrived in significant numbers, Lutheran and Reformed leaders could not assign them to congregations without local approval. A small gathering at Donegal pleased Schlatter because they "cheerfully promised" to support a pastor. Pondering where to place Handschuh, Muhlenberg mused that "one cannot use force in this country, but must proceed with discretion" and cited Judges 17:6, "In those days there was no king in Israel, but every man did that which was right in his own eyes." In Pennsylvania, Muhlenberg discovered, neither deacons, elders, nor government influenced religious behavior. Each person "has the right to do what he pleases," Muhlenberg observed, and "everything depends upon the vote of the majority."[45]

Christ.

[44] Schlatter, "Journal," 154.

[45] Patricia U. Bonomi, *Under the Cope of Heaven: Religion, Society, and Politics in Colonial America* (New York: Oxford University Press, 1986), 82-4; and Muhlenberg, *Journals*, I, 67, 151-2, 188, 211-12; Die Vorsteher von Augusta County an Muhlenberg,

Others, however, defended the power of Pennsylvania's laity to elect and dismiss pastors. While still with the Reformed, Peter Miller praised the "glorious liberty" that strengthened congregational authority in the New World. He believed that Christians had no need of episcopal supervision anywhere, Christ alone being "their head in heaven," and he argued that church authorities should not be able to force ministers upon congregations. Another Pietist, claiming to be "living in a free land," surreptitiously inserted in a Dutch church official's letter four out-of-context paragraphs asserting "the divine right" of congregational authority.[46]

Once accepted, many ministers experienced financial pressure from their parishioners. Sauer I reminded Germans of Penn's wish and law that no one need give "one penny" to support a preacher of a denomination to which he or she did not belong. Instead of regular salaries or tithes, which were customary in Europe, the clergy received annual contributions plus occasional gifts and fees for baptisms, weddings, and funerals. One critic noted that Pennsylvanians hired preachers for the year "like cowherds in Germany," and those who failed to please were "given notice."[47]

Further evidence of the new status of laypersons was the increased efforts the clergy made to communicate with them. Bilingualism, discussed below, sharply contrasted with the Roman Catholic insistence on Latin, and emphasis on the spoken word over the written showed interest in reaching a wide audience. Muhlenberg encouraged his colleagues to keep sermons simple and not to "enter the pulpit unprepared and shake something out of your sleeve *ex tempore.*" Sermons, Muhlenberg believed, should emphasize the new birth and subordinate other details of doctrine and behavior. These, he said, were "outward husks" that did not help "poor, simple people" but only taught them to "find fault with other sects and parties," while their own

February 2, 1766, *Die Korrespondenz Muhlenbergs*, III, 365, Muhlenberg an die Gemeinden in Culpeper und Augusta County, June 10, 1766, id., 390; and Schlatter, "Journal," 158.

[46] Boehm to the Classis of Amsterdam, November 12, 1730, in *Life and Letters of Boehm*, 200. Also see Letter of the Rev. Dr. John Wilhelmius of Rotterdam to the Reformed Brethren in Pennsylvania, December 31, 1730, id., 304-5.

[47] Mittelberger, *Journey to Pennsylvania*, 46-8; and *Pensylvanische Berichte*, August 16, 1747.

hearts remained unconverted and their lives ungodly.[48]

Even Zinzendorf's rank brought little respect. Antes apologized to the Count for addressing him with the familiar (*du*) form but explained that "many simple souls" had objected to pronouns that acknowledged Zinzendorf's superior rank. Antes mollified such critics by claiming habitually to use formal pronouns with persons whom he "did not know very well," but he implied to the Count that his utilization of the informal (*du*) would continue.[49]

Despite dwindling deference towards the clergy, many Pennsylvania Germans still thirsted for spiritual leaders. Muhlenberg complained that he felt like a bird that children tormented and loved to death and then wondered why the dead bird stopped chirping. One German innkeeper treated Muhlenberg royally, ordering the other guests to "walk on tiptoe" to avoid disturbing the honored guest. So eager were the colonists for preaching that young Heinrich Goetschi, barely out of his boyhood, found several pulpits open to him.[50]

The great demand for preachers and decentralized denominational polity encouraged charlatans, with whom New World congregations dealt largely alone, unlike in Europe. The Sauer newspaper warned, often aggressively, against certain notorious men of the cloth. One item described a preacher who cheated in horse trading, seduced daughters, and performed marriage services for people as often as they wished. Another alarm denounced Caspar Ludwig Schnorr, a Reformed preacher in Lancaster, as "not only lewd as any knave, but as filthy and obscene as a slut." According to Sauer, Schnorr's parishioners verified that the drunken divine often fell from his horse. When Schnorr found another congregation, Sauer's newspaper followed him, alleging excessive drinking and printing the pastor's complaint that a

---

[48] Bonomi, *Under the Cope of Heaven*, 124; and Muhlenberg to Caspar Stoever, January 20, 1747, in Theodore G. Tappert, "John Caspar Stoever and the Ministerium of Pennsylvania," *LCQ* 21 (April 1948): 181. Muhlenberg cited August Hermann Francke, "A Letter to a Friend Concerning the Most Useful Way of Preaching"; see Peter C. Erb, ed., *The Pietists: Selected Writings* (New York: Paulist Press, 1983), 117-27.

[49] Antes to Zinzendorf, December 18, 1741, in Durnbaugh, *Brethren in Colonial America*, 283.

[50] Bonomi, *Under the Cope of Heaven*, 77; and Muhlenberg, *Journals*, I, 721, and II, 440.

prostitute had taken money from his pants pocket. Sauer claimed that
being God's servant obligated him to alert unsuspecting neighbors of
prowling scoundrels, but Schnorr's fierce criticism of Sauer's edition
of the Bible may have sharpened the printer's pen.[51] Charletans plus
the dearth of clergy and the power of the laity thus kept denominational
order among the Lutheran and Reformed unstable.

Reconstructing a European-style polity especially interested Johann
Philip Boehm, so he felt particularly frustrated. Boehm complained
that the Germantown congregation never willingly submitted to his
vision of church order. "Some arose even among ourselves who
wanted to be ministers," he said. "Nothing can be done here," he
fretted to Dutch ecclesiastical officials; "everything passes," he
continued, "because of this liberty." Boehm urged them to consider
how to restrain "the excessive liberty in this country, so harmful to the
true Church," blaming it upon the "pernicious sects" driven to America
"from all parts of the world." Gottlieb Mittelberger, a Lutheran
schoolteacher and organist, agreed with Boehm; "Liberty in Pennsylvania," he asserted, "does more harm than good." After enduring "great
confusion" for four years in Penn's Woods, Mittelberger returned to his
home in Württemberg and the security of European order.[52]

In practice, then, power in the Lutheran and Reformed traditions
moved towards the laity, just as it did in the Pietist conversion process.
By accepting a greater local role in pastoral placement and by emphasizing communication with worshippers, Muhlenberg and Schlatter
shrank the differences between so-called "church Germans" and
"sectarians," although their preference for university-trained clerics still
sharply distinguished them from Mennonites, Dunkers, Amish, and
Moravians.

[51] *Pensylvanische Berichte*, May 16, 1746, June 16, 1750, and May 16, 1753; Bonomi,
Under the Cope of Heaven, 77; Glatfelter, *Pastors and People*, 121-2; and Longenecker,
The Christopher Sauers, 56, 101-2.

[52] Report of Mr. Boehm to the Classis of Amsterdam, January 14, 1739, *in Life and
Letters of Boehm*, 273-4; Mr. Boehm and the Philadelphia Consistory to Deputy
Velingius, October 28, 1734, id., 239; Mr. Boehm to the Classis of Amsterdam,
November 12, 1730, id., 202-3, 206; Certified Pledges of the Reformed Congregations
Towards Ministers' Salaries, February-March 1740, id., 292; and Mittelberger, *Journey
to Pennsylvania*, xiii-xiv, 48, 80.

V

As Pietists reduced distinctions between clergy and laity, they also brought denominations closer together. Pietism provided a unifying thread by minimizing doctrinal differences and explicitly encouraging unity among Christians. But sectarian rivalries continued, especially between groups with major doctrinal differences, such as those dividing Anabaptists from Lutherans and Reformed. Tolerance and cooperation, however, are more meaningful when groups differ because ecumenism is almost irrelevant in a homogeneous society. Thus, it is significant that German Christians, committed to their own denominations, learned to accept and sometimes work with other communions.

Contemporary Virginia, Connecticut, and Massachusetts were striking contrasts to colonial Pennsylvania. As late as 1771 Virginia Baptist preachers suffered physical abuse, including whippings. In 1774 James Madison lamented that in Virginia the "diabolical, Hell--conceived principle of persecution" still raged.[53] Connecticut enacted a Toleration Act in 1708 and in 1729 exempted Anglicans, Quakers, and Baptists from church taxes, but authorities interpreted this legislation so narrowly that few congregations qualified for the exemptions. A 1742 law, aimed at New Lights (that is, revivalist Congregationalists and their itinerants), prohibited uninvited ministers, whether lay or ordained, from preaching in parishes not their own. Other contemporary laws similarly discriminated against revivalists. Near mid-century compromise and the passage of time eased Connecticut's religious wars, but for years religion remained a major political issue. In 1754, for example, over one thousand persons signed a petition to the King claiming that Connecticut violated the Toleration Act.

Massachusetts, as well, enacted general exemption laws but failed to live up to them. In 1768 the Assembly passed the "Ashfield Laws," requiring all residents of that town to support the Congregationalist "Standing Order" despite the exemption statutes. When Ashfield Baptists refused to pay the taxes those laws required, constables sold their land. Other Baptists in the colony complained that authorities administered the exemption laws unjustly and that when cases came to trial,

---

[53] Rhys Isaac, *The Transformation of Virginia, 1740-1790* (Williamsburg, Va.: Institute of Early American History and Culture, 1982), 161-3, 201-2.

Congregationalists, who were biased against Baptists, filled the jury boxes.

Religious persecution in New England so annoyed Baptists that it influenced their response to the Revolutionary movement. Massachusetts Baptists remained aloof from the Patriots' cause until 1775, when they expressed their presumption that the new order would bring greater tolerance. A few of them, however, held out for neutrality. As late as 1780 a Baptist congregation in Connecticut found "little heart to hold the sword against the British invader" because of the Assembly's past measures restricting their "liberty and conscience."[54]

Certainly Pennsylvanians were not immune from such conflicts. Moravians endured considerable antagonism, as we have seen, and Anabaptists and separatists often battled the professional clergy of the church Germans. According to Muhlenberg, Anabaptists assumed that Lutheran and Reformed ministers could not be "religious" in their office, but if a particular clergyman nevertheless struck them as pious, they observed what a shame it was that such a devout person was a preacher. In an essay entitled, "On Preachers," Sauer I repeated William Penn's statement that it was unjust for a minister, who preached for an hour or two, to receive the same wages as a wood chopper, who labored hard all day.[55]

Sauer especially irritated the professional clergy. During a war scare, he ripped into Gilbert Tennant for permitting a militia drill on his church grounds, something that never happened, according to Sauer, even "in a heathenish temple of idols," a Jewish school, or a Turkish mosque. Sauer's use of the colloquialism, "Jewish school" (*Juden Schule*), which can be applied either to a chaotic situation or a Jewish educational institution, may have been an intentional double meaning.[56] Meanwhile, Lutheran and Reformed pastors harshly criticized the Sauer Bible for including several apocryphal books that they

---

[54] Bonomi, *Under the Cope of Heaven*, 66, 162-7; William G. McLoughlin, *Isaac Backus and the American Pietist Tradition* (Boston, Mass.: Little, Brown and Company, 1967), 116-20; and Stephen A. Marini, *Radical Sects of Revolutionary New England* (Cambridge, Mass.: Harvard University Press, 1982), 23-4.

[55] Muhlenberg an J. B. Gabler, December 22, 1749, *Die Korrespondenz Muhlenbergs*, I, 356; and *Pensylvanische Berichte*, August 16, 1747.

[56] Ibid., August 16, 1747, and February, 16, 1748.

disliked. Muhlenberg also accused the Sauer newspaper of encouraging undesirable attitudes, including the "perverted notions" of people who did not value God's Word, and he maintained that the prolific Sauer press did more damage than ten preachers could repair. He frequently but always unsuccessfully requested European supporters to fund a printing establishment to compete with the Sauers.[57]

Neither the sectarians nor the more formal denominations accepted the few Catholics in Pennsylvania, who were often the lepers of the German Christian community. In 1757 colonial authorities, fearing Catholic fifth-column activities on behalf of the French, took a census that enumerated 849 German Catholics and apparently assigned them to Protestant citizens who would accept responsibility for their conduct. However, Catholics were scattered so widely that supervision of them could not have been very close. One citizen was responsible for Catholics in a five-county area, and another watched over those in four counties. Conversely, Schwenkfelder leader Christopher Schultz, of Berks County, noted that he lived between a Mennonite preacher and a large Catholic church but that they were "always at peace with each other." He boasted that the Jesuit priest "confides more in me than in those who come to him for confession." The priest held title for eight years to the land occupied by the Mennonite meetinghouse, and the Mennonites helped build the Catholic chapel.[58]

Thus, although Pennsylvania's diverse fellowships occassionally lapsed into quarreling, just as they did elsewhere, what made Pennsylvania different was the early appearance of tolerance. Cooperation was especially strong between Lutherans and the Reformed, and the collegial relations between Schlatter and Muhlenberg enhanced it. The two missionaries enjoyed many common aspects of objective, strategy, and background. At their first meeting Muhlenberg said he wished for

---

[57] Longenecker, *The Christopher Sauers*, 52-6; Muhlenberg, *Journals*, I, 143.; and Muhlenberg to G. A. Francke and F. M. Ziegenhagen, May 24, 1747, *Die Korrespondenz Muhlenbergs*, I, 292; Muhlenberg to Boltzius, January-March, 1750, ibid., I, 365; Muhlenberg to G. A. Francke and F. M. Ziegenhagen, May 15, 1751, ibid., I, 412; and Muhlenberg to Albinus, February 17, 1756, ibid., II, 288. See also Muhlenberg to G. A. Francke and F. M. Ziegenhagen, May 24, 1747, ibid., I, 288.

[58] Schultz is quoted in MacMaster, *Land, Piety, Peoplehood*, 138, 186. See also *PA*, William Henry Egle, ed. (Harrisburg: Commonwealth of Pennsylvania, 1853), Series I, Vol. 3, 144-5.

neighborliness and peace between Lutheran and Reformed communions and hoped that "such traces of harmony might also be found in Germany." Muhlenberg's esteem extended to other non-Lutheran clergy; he defended Otterbein from charges of sectarianism, contending that his relationship with the Reformed minister was rewarding, and he exchanged compliments with George Whitefield. Schlatter, who married a Lutheran in Pennsylvania, told a German acquaintance "with great satisfaction" that in Pennsylvania, at least, Lutherans and Reformed "lived together in pleasant neighborly harmony."[59] Perhaps inspired by the personal example of their spiritual leaders, German church people in Pennsylvania clung to an Old World tradition of cooperation that included "Simultan-Kirchen," or shared buildings. Between 1710 and 1800 the two denominations established over one hundred union congregations--over half the total number in each.[60]

Union schools were also commonplace in colonial Pennsylvania and greatly aided education. Of the 140 Lutheran and 138 Reformed schools found in eighteenth-century Pennsylvania, ninety were cooperative efforts. In six counties of southeastern Pennsylvania Lutheran parishes co-sponsored twenty-nine of the fifty-one schools that Reformed congregations supported. In Warwick Township trustees of both groups secured a land patent for a cemetery as well as a schoolhouse, and sometimes schools stipulated that Lutheran and Reformed students pay identical tuition or that the master be alternately Lutheran and Reformed.[61]

---

[59] Muhlenberg an G. A. Francke und F. M. Ziegenhagen, October 24, 1763, 100-1, November 10, 1763, 121, and November 12, 1764, 212; Muhlenberg an Boltzius, November 22 and 27, 1764, and Muhlenberg an Roemer, March 16, 1768, 591--all in *Die Korrespondenz Muhlenbergs*, III; Muhlenberg, *Journals*, I, 502-4; George W. Richards, "Henry Melchior Muhlenberg and Michael Schlatter," *LCQ* 15 (July 1942): 274-84; Schlatter, "Journal," 138-9, 344-5; and Abdel Ross Wentz, "Relations Between the Lutheran and Reformed Churches in the Eighteenth and Nineteenth Centuries," *LCQ* 6 (1933): 307.

[60] Howard K. Macauley, "A Social and Intellectual History of Elementary Education in Pennsylvania to 1850" (Ph.D. diss.: University of Pennsylvania), 1972, 316-22.

[61] I counted schools as union efforts if cooperation existed anytime in the eighteenth century; this survey, however, does not consider denominational schools with an interdenominational student body, which may have been commonplace. The six counties are Montgomery, Lancaster, Philadelphia, Berks, Lehigh, and Bucks. See Frederick

Bilingual worship further lowered denominational boundaries and on occasion also reduced ethnic barriers. Particular examples of it depended upon the preacher's language skills, of course, but whenever it became possible, Pietists welcomed it. Muhlenberg enthusiastically delivered sermons in German, English, and Dutch, especially at one of his permanent charges, Molatton, a multi-ethnic congregation with Irish, Swedish, English, and German members who were both Lutheran and Reformed. Several elderly Swedes and one whom Muhlenberg called an "awakened" Anglican had issued him his first invitation to preach at Molatton. He met it by mounting his horse immediately after Sunday morning service at New Hannover and riding as hard as possible for several hours during "the sun's greatest heat." His sermon was in English, but afterwards he exhorted both Lutherans and Reformed in German. They invited him back soon. This time Peter Brunnholtz delivered the German message. In a subsequent Molatton service Muhlenberg apparently blessed the congregation's multi-ethnicity by preaching about Cornelius, the Roman centurion whom Peter had baptized; his text was from Acts 10, which underlines the Holy Spirit's availability to all nations, including Romans and other gentiles as well as Jews.

Such bilingualism became commonplace. German and Swedish Lutheran clergy often met jointly, and participants at the first Lutheran synod, held at Brunnholtz's residence, heard prayers in both languages. In 1749 Muhlenberg agreed to preach for an English congregation that had no pastor. After his bilingual service, held in an Anglican church, many of the Germans, who were mostly servants, wept. Their singing in harmony, Muhlenberg recalled, "amazed" the English. Bilingual pastors sometimes preached in one language in the morning and in another later in the day. For example, in a barn near Neshaminy Muhlenberg delivered a morning sermon to Dutch Lutherans and an evening one to an English congregation, presumably Anglican. On another Sunday morning and afternoon, at barn services in Ancrum,

George Livingood, *Eighteenth Century Reformed Church Schools* (Norristown, Pa.: Pennsylvania German Society, 1927), 26-132. The figure of ninety union schools comes from Macauley, "Social and Intellectual History of Education in Pennsylvania," 322-6.

Muhlenberg led worship in German and English.[62] Joachim Zubly, a German itinerant from Charleston, South Carolina, attracted bilingual and interdenominational audiences in Philadelphia when in 1753 he visited the city to raise money for Whitefield's orphanage. Both English and German preachers endorsed him and offered their pulpits for his use, and Sauer compared the power of his preaching to Whitefield's.[63]

Pastors able to use both languages often ministered to individuals as well as groups. On visiting a deathly ill Dutchman, Muhlenberg knelt by the bed and prayed in Dutch alongside the man's distressed wife. When Brunnholtz became ill with dysentery, nearby English preachers visited him frequently. Muhlenberg translated a German catechism into English to assist a teenager who wanted communion but spoke no German, and he also baptized several English adults, closing one such ceremony with an English hymn.

Interethnic marriages produced several baptismal candidates, including the grown children of a Dutch women who regularly attended Muhlenberg's services and whose husband was English. He also baptized the daughter of a Swedish father and his Quaker wife, whom, Muhlenberg concluded, "allowed her to grow up in ignorance."[64]

If Muhlenberg was typical, bilingual Pietist preachers triggered among their multi-ethnic listeners the emotional response that they considered vital. He told of a young Englishwoman who tearfully testified that "in past years she had wandered about like a lost sheep in the wilderness." A "genteel" woman stated to Muhlenberg that at every one of his services at Molatton she "had been awakened; the Lord had opened her heart."[65]

At funerals, especially, Christians of various faiths gathered, mourning together but sometimes in different languages. Sauer I rejoiced when a Mennonite, the only available preacher, presided over a Reformed minister's funeral. When such occurrences were "regular,

---

[62] The Molatton congregation became St. Gabriel's Epicopalian of Douglassville; see Glatfelter, *Pastors and People*, 248. Also see Mittelberger, *Journey to Pennsylvania*, 46; and Muhlenberg, *Journals*, I, 115, 187-8, 196, 202, 223, 241, 246, 252, 367.

[63] *Pensylvanische Berichte*, April 1, 1753.

[64] Muhlenberg, *Journal*, I, 146, 196, 197, 202, 215, 234, 311.

[65] Ibid., 196, 208.

customary, and usual," then, he predicted, "all factional disputes and grudges will come to an end."[66] Muhlenberg gained a better appreciation for Mennonites at the funeral of Maria Salome Hallman, whose husband, a Lutheran elder at Providence, owned a family plot in the nearby Mennonite graveyard because he had helped build their meetinghouse. At her burial Muhlenberg intended to preach under a tree, but the elderly Mennonite minister invited him to use the large church building. The Lutheran leader at first declined, citing Pennsylvania's tolerance and his reluctance to "cause strife" by interfering with religious freedom there, but the Mennonite persuaded Muhlenberg not to "shun" his denomination. As they entered the building, however, the pastor requested Muhlenberg to avoid "strange ceremonies," but afterwards he apologized for the remark, explaining that he had not understood Lutheran practices. Muhlenberg recalled in his journal that the Mennonites

> were thankful with weeping eyes, that I, the Heavenly Messenger, (as they called me) had spoken in their edifice. Since then I have frequently been obliged to speak in the same place at the funerals of our neighbors. The ministers were always present and declared that their souls were revived and hallowed thereby and bespake for themselves good friendship and neighborliness.[67]

At another funeral in a "so-called" Mennonite cemetery Muhlenberg preached in English and German to a "large crowd of every nationality." At a February service in another Mennonite graveyard Muhlenberg tramped with mourners through drizzle and several miles of deep snow, sweating heavily, but all were "very attentive" to his sermon on repentance. Afterwards a Mennonite preacher approached him and, after a deep sigh, cited a Scriptural passage that began an "edifying conversation." (After this strenuous ceremony Muhlenberg was ill for four weeks and twice fainted in the pulpit; to restore his health he bled himself.) The Lutheran leader avoided doctrinal

---

[66] *Pensylvanische Berichte*, May 16, 1749.

[67] Quoted in John C. Wenger, *History of the Mennonites of the Franconia Conference* (Scottdale, Pa.: Mennonite Publishing House, 1938), 28.

differences at such multi-ethnic funerals, proclaiming instead "atonement, faith, and holiness--so we all without discrimination may be
complete in all things necessary."[68]

Muhlenberg dominates the record of interdenominational services
because his journals and correspondence--both bound in three thick vol-
umes--dwarf other sources, but other Germans also supported
interdenominationalism. A traveller reported, perhaps with some
exaggeration, that sometimes a single household contained members of
six denominations.[69] Sauer II's burial in 1784 was in the Methacton
Mennonite Cemetery because no Dunker meetinghouse was nearby;
Martin Urner, a Brethren, and Samuel Hopkins, a Philadelphia Quaker,
led the service.[70]

In fact, the Sauer press became an example of Pennsylvania's
mixture of tolerance and intolerance by balancing its opposition to other
sects with nondenominational news. Sauer I endorsed Boehm's publication of Reformed pastor Johann Jacob Hochreutiner's last sermon,
calling it "highly useful and valuable" and advising Christians "to preserve the teachings and to do the exercises."[71] A few years later Sauer
notified the public when Boehm and Benjamin Franklin printed Johann
Arndt's popular Pietist devotional, *Wahres Christentum* (True Christianity).[72] Eventually even Muhlenberg and Sauer II stopped complaining
about each other.[73]

Hymnals also transcended denominations, especially the Dunker's
hymnbook, *Der Kleine Davidische Psalter-Spiel* (The Little Davidic
Psalter), which became the most commonly used German hymnal in
Pennsylvania. Released in 1744, its anonymous editors emphasized
their "great effort" to make "quite an impartial hymn-book, indeed, a

---

[68] Muhlenberg, *Journals*, I, 215, 370. For other examples of Muhlenberg's participation in bilingual funerals, see *Journals*, I, 312, 318, 357.

[69] Mittelberger, *Journey to Pennsylvania*, 41.

[70] Durnbaugh, *Brethren in Colonial America*, 423.

[71] *Pensylvanische Berichte*, March 16, 1749.

[72] Ibid., May 1, 1753.

[73] Muhlenberg rarely mentions Sauer II in his later correspondence, a contrast to the
running complaints about the founder of the Sauer press. See *Die Korrespondenz
Muhlenbergs*, III, 710.

guileless flower-garden containing all manner of flowers or songs for all those who praise the Lord with hearts and lips." The Dunker's patterned their book, commonly called "*Little David's*" or the "*Little Psalter*," after a hymnal that the Inspired published and European Pietists used widely. The organization of the book demonstrated the Dunker world view by grouping hymns under categories such as holy baptism, "brotherly and universal love," and feetwashing, but the first nine sections of hymns followed the seasons in a fashion similar to the larger Inspirationist hymnal, and the portions on human misery, repentance, and true faith showed deep Pietist influences. Contemporary European Pietist books contained most of the *Little Psalter's* hymns. Eberhard Ludwig Gruber, an Inspirationist, placed four selections in it, including *Jesus ist Je-suss* (Jesus is ever sweet), a punning, mystical Jesus-hymn, as well as a more conventional one (*Wohlauf, zum rechter Weinstock her*) about Christ being the true vine. Among the other hymnists in the *Little Psalter* were Conrad Beissel, Lenaert Clock, a sixteenth-century German Mennonite, and Count von Zinzendorf.[74]

In addition to being interdenominational and bilingual, the spirit of Pietism occasionally became interracial. While the overnight guest of a Dutch family, Muhlenberg noted that in the evening he "catechized the children and Mr. van Horn's Negro slaves." Schlatter termed a former slave, whom he baptized, "an unblamable member" of the congregation at Germantown.[75]

Pennsylvania Germans, then, gradually softened the intensity of organizational rivalries and doctrinal disputes and accepted one another. Religious intolerance had existed for centuries among Christians; the emergence of tolerance was both new and significant. The German population slowly evolved towards Christopher Sauer I's vision of

---

[74] Hedwig T. Durnbaugh, *The German Hymnody of the Brethren, 1720-1903* (Philadelphia: Brethren Encyclopedia, 1986), 41-57; and MacMaster, *Land, Piety, Peoplehood*, 169-70. Hymnals of other denominations, as well, showed ecumenical inclinations. The Mennonite *Ausbund* had an ecumenical term--"unparteyische" (nondenominational)--on its title page. The Moravians also produced a hymnal intended for interdenominational use. See Hostetler, *American Mennonites and Protestant Movements*, 54.

[75] Muhlenberg, *Journals*, I, 367; and Schlatter, "Journal," 165. See also Mittelberger, *Journey to Pennsylvania*, 45.

"only one shepherd and one flock. "[76]

VI

Tolerance, denominationalism, and Pietism thus complemented one another, each expanding during the Pennsylvania German awakening. The limited growth of denominational organization early in the eighteenth century deprived anti-Pietists of leverage they had in most other colonies, and, therefore, organized opposition to Pietism in Pennsylvania was practically nil, enabling it to spread unchecked. When denominations rejuvenated, they often drew energy from revivalism, but the new structures rose from foundations laid by the laity, who crossed the Atlantic ahead of their pastors and acquired a stronger voice in church affairs. (Popular ministers, such as Schlatter and Muhlenberg, nevertheless retained the admiration of their parishioners.) Differences diminished between church Germans and Anabaptists, whose polity had emphasized lay authority from its beginning in Europe, and between clergy and laity.

As denominations strengthened and ethnicity persisted, religious disputes continued, but German Christians also learned to live with pluralism. Tolerance increased, encouraged by circumstances, but also endorsed by Pietistic beliefs that deemphasized doctrinal detail and rejoiced in nondenominational efforts. If God extends salvation to all who partake of the water of life, Pietists reasoned that denominational identity must be less consequential. Though not yet matured, ecumenical seeds had sprouted among the tares of narrow-mindedness, contributing much to tolerance in colonial Pennsylvania.

The 1752 Lutheran synod sang the hymn, *Wachet auf, ruft uns die Stimme* (Sleepers, Wake), following a sermon on Jesus' healing of a paralytic. Its words and music predated Pietism and incorporated imagery from the *Minnesänger* era, but the hymn conveyed a different meaning for these Pennsylvania Lutherans. All Pietists loved its call for rebirth and the Biblical metaphors that symbolized the indwelling of the Spirit of Christ. As the Lutheran pastors sang *Wachet auf*, they testified to Pietism's strength in Pennsylvania.

[76] *Pensylvanische Berichte*, May 16, 1749.

Wake, awake, for night is flying,
The watchmen on the heights are crying.
Awake, Jerusalem, at last!
Mid-night hears the welcome voices
And at the thrilling cry rejoices:
Come forth, ye virgins, night is past!
The Bridegroom comes, awake,
Your lamps with gladness take;
Alleluia!
And for his marriage feast prepare,
For ye must go to meet him there.

Following the singing, the Lutherans baptized a black man.[77]

---

[77] Handschuh's "diary" in *Lutheran Ministerium*, 37. The translation is from *Service Book and Hymnal of the Lutheran Church in America* (Minneapolis, Minn.: Augsburg Publishing House, *et al.*, 1958), 7-8. In 1731 Johann Sebastian Bach performed this hymn in Leipzig in his Cantata 140, *Wachet auf*. The lyrics of the recitatives and duets in this work are even more personal and intimate, and critics charged that Bach's church music was too theatrical and Pietistic; see Bach, *Wachet auf, ruft uns die Stimme*, *The Score of the New Bach Edition: Backgrounds, Analysis, Views, and Comments by Gerhard Herz* (New York: W. W. Norton, 1972), 55-7, 109-112; and Jaroslav Pelikan, *Bach Among the Theologians* (Philadelphia: Fortress Press, 1986), 56-71.

CHAPTER 5

"No deeptoned organ":
The Rise of the New Revivalists

*No loud-clanging bell called them together; no deeptoned
organ accompanied their hearty voices in song: no learned,
college-bred priest explained to them the difference between
ecclesiastical tweedledee and tweedledum, and yet they carried home with them in their simple hearts much peace and
charity.--Ezra Grumbine, United Brethren in Christ, Stumps-
town, Pennsylvania.[1]*

In the late eighteenth century a new tide of revivalism surged over
Pennsylvania, sweeping many Germans into the next century's revival
and camp meeting movement. Just as the earlier Pietism of the Dunkers, Mennonites, Lutherans, and German Reformed went hand in hand
with organizing congregations and building denominations, this
turn-of-the-century movement spawned four new denominations: the
United Brethren in Christ, the Evangelical Association, the River
Brethren, and the Reformed Mennonites. Although much of what these
new evangelists preached and practiced was consistent with earlier
Pietism, the new levels of emotion and the infusion of Wesleyanism
into Pennsylvania German religion broadened the traditional revivalism
and swelled Pennsylvania's pluralism. Sometimes this new revivalism
heightened denominational walls, but it also nurtured cooperation and
supported the near-universal doctrines of free will, universal grace, and
the new birth.

---

[1] Grumbine, who attended revivals as a young person in the 1840s, is quoted in Don
Yoder, *Pennsylvania Spirituals* (Lancaster, Pa.: Pennsylvania Folklife Society, 1961),
147-8.

I

The new revivalists were especially fond of dramatic moments of new birth. Like eighteenth-century Pietists, they believed that regeneration began when anguished sinners realized the depths of their guilt. They often depicted their pre-awakened life as spiritually dead, confused, and corrupted, and, according to Jacob Hershey, a River Brethren preacher and revival enthusiast, this awareness of sin made the penitent feel "soul sick and sin sick."[2] Sometimes transgressors sank into severe depression and, occasionally, into physical collapse just prior to experiencing unbounded joy at their conversion. A desperate struggle with sin had been integral to Pietism from its beginnings in Europe, but for Pennsylvania Germans the battle now rose to new heights.

Revivalists such as Philip William Otterbein occasionally denied that a moment of crisis was mandatory, but in practice they prized dramatic conversions.[3] Martin Boehm's experience, for example, closely followed the sequence of depression and jubilation. In 1756 Boehm's congregation of Lancaster County Mennonites chose him by lot to be their pastor. Despite his own doubts that he was truly converted, he reluctantly accepted the calling because he believed the selection process to be divinely inspired. At first, the young minister spoke little, only witnessing briefly and exhorting after the older men preached, as was customary. But when, after a year or so, other ministers granted him the privilege of preaching, Boehm found he could not articulate his Bible studies and memorizations. After mumbling only a few lines, he returned to the preachers' bench in shame. One day as Boehm plowed his fields, he became deeply depressed over what he thought was his unfitness for the ministry and knelt in prayer at the end of each furrow. Finally, overcome with grief, he slumped behind

[2] Jacob Hershey, *Confession of Jacob Hershey* (n.p., 1825), 22; and James D. Nelson, "Jacob Albright: Founder, Reformer, or Model Pietist" (unpublished paper, n. d.), 5.

[3] See Otterbein's unsigned, undated letter in Arthur C. Core, *Philip William Otterbein: Pastor, Ecumenist* (Dayton, Ohio: Board of Publication of the Evangelical United Brethren Church, 1968), 101; and George Miller's account of his conversion experience in his autobiography, "Life, Experience, and Ministerial Labors of George Miller, Evangelical Preacher," in Reuben Yeakel, *Jacob Albright and His Co-Laborer* (Cleveland: Publishing House of the Evangelical Association, 1883), 174-88. See also Martin Schrag, "Influences Contributing to an Early River Brethren Confession of Faith," *MQR* 38 (October 1964): 348-9.

the plow in mid-field, crying, "Lord, save, I am lost!" Immediately he sensed what he called a "voice or thought" assuring him that God would "save that which is lost," and he left the field in a "stream of joy." Suddenly eager to preach, Boehm soon recounted this experience to his congregation, who listened approvingly, some tearfully.[4]

Many other revivalists reported similar experiences of sudden resolution of inner conflict. Christian Newcomer, another Lancaster County Mennonite, underwent several spiritual crises in the 1760s. Newcomer said he had first become conscious of his need for salvation when a peach pit stuck in his throat. Facing "death and eternity," and fearing to come before the "awful tribunal of the great Jehovah," Newcomer saved his life by ramming his back against a nearby apple tree and dislodging the pit. But his spiritual turmoil now became intense. On another occasion he ran outside his house during a severe thunderstorm, knelt by the garden fence, and gave himself "wholly and without reserve" to Christ. Brilliant lightning and deafening thunder confirmed his experience of grace, and the "anguish of the soul" left him. His doubts, however, returned. Newcomer then submitted to Mennonite baptism, but the ceremony had little effect. Several years later he contracted measles and on death's doorstep again experienced what he believed was God's grace, this time permanently. He yearned to speak to his congregation but felt unequal to the lofty task of preaching, so he sold his farm and moved to Maryland, where he slowly began a wide-ranging ministry.[5]

[4] Kenneth E. Rowe, "Martin Boehm and the Methodists," *MH* 8 (July 1970): 52-3, contains the Martin and Henry Boehm conversation of April 12, 1811.

[5] Christian Newcomer, *The Life and Journal of Christian Newcomer, Late Bishop of the Church of the United Brethren in Christ*, ed. John Hildt (Hagerstown, Md.: F. G.W. Kapp, 1834), 3-5, 7. For other examples of dramatic moments of conversion, see John Herr, *Complete Works, Comprising the Way to Heaven, the Illustrating Mirror; [and] an Appendix Relating to John Herr's Life* (Buffalo, N.Y.: Peter Paul and Bro., 1890), 376-83; Samuel Huber, *Autobiography of the Rev. Samuel Huber, Elder in the Church of the United Brethren in Christ, Containing Sketches of His Life, and Religious Experience*, ed. John Denig (Chambersburg, Pa.: M. Kieffer and Company, 1858), 14-23; W. W. Orwig, *History of the Evangelical Association: From the Origin of the Association to the End of the Year 1845*, 2 vols. (Cleveland: Charles Hammer, 1858), I, 11; Samuel P. Spreng, *History of the Evangelical Association*, The American Church History Series, 12 (New York: The Christian Literature Company, 1894), 392-3; and Reuben Yeakel, *History of the Evangelical Association*, 2 vols. (Cleveland, Ohio: Mattill and Lamb, 1902), I, 39.

Hershey, Boehm, and Newcomer became denominational leaders, but rank and file members also experienced similar emotions at their conversion. On one occasion, Huber testified, a woman tried to run out of the meeting, but she fell down and "lay there in agony for some time, wrestling in prayer, until she was blest." A Virginian named Carper became so angry over Martin Boehm's preaching that he resolved to kill him for being a false prophet. While Boehm spoke, Carper waited to ambush him outside the door. But the preacher's words entered his heart, Carper recalled, "like arrows from a strong bow," and he ran home. The next day in the woods Carper saw, he said, a long-bearded man (Boehm?) approaching, whom he fled by jumping a fence. But on the other side another bearded man pulled him down. When, in his vision, both strangers pinned him to the ground, "the earth opened," Carper testified, and he "went down into hell." He lay unconscious in the fence corner all day, but awoke believing that he had been born again.[6]

As these guilt-stricken sinners experienced their moments of conversion, they ascended an emotional peak that mirrored the trough of their recent despair. Such passion, although usually less intense, had been common among earlier Pennsylvania German Pietists, but in the early republic it had declined among some of them, especially the Dunkers. Displays of unrestrained joy became characteristic in conversions obtained by the new revivalists.

Converts expressed their joy in a variety of ways. According to one revivalist, new-born Christians could "leap for joy," and some of them did. Repentant sinners often cried aloud. Newcomer reported that at a meeting with Reformed Mennonites several persons were "in distress and cried for mercy" while "others were rejoicing and praising God with shouting." John Seybert, a revivalist preacher, frequently spoke approvingly of the "jubilation" and shouting at the climax of gatherings in which some worshippers had fallen to the ground unconscious. Newcomer lost his voice in one lively meeting. George Miller, a leader in the Evangelical Association, recalled that after listening to three sermons, those attending a service in Union County witnessed such "a mighty outpouring of the Spirit" that "the cries of

---

[6] Huber, *Autobiography*, 44-7, quotes "B. Carper's" testimony. See also ibid., 54.

penitent souls" resounded throughout the house.[7] Meetings often lasted late into the night. At a quarterly meeting of the Evangelical Association, John Dreisbach celebrated Holy Communion at one o'clock in the morning.[8] Tears flowed frequently, just as they had among eighteenth-century Pietists. Newcomer observed that at one such gathering "all were melted into tears," and he approved of worshippers in Lancaster who tearfully approached the communion table.[9] Sometimes the power of the experience physically overwhelmed worshippers. When George Miller first heard Jacob Albright, founder of the Evangelical Association, preach, he said that the "powerful sermon" so overwhelmed him that he would have fallen to the floor had he not held on to a table. At one of the first United Brethren camp meetings Samuel Huber remembered that, like many other sinners, he fell down "as if dead" but soon "rose again shouting victory." He explained that he had received there a spiritual blessing that overpowered both his soul and body. At the conclusion of a camp meeting in the Shenandoah Valley, a Mrs. Snyder approached Huber, asking if he intended to leave her husband "lying in the altar." Huber went to look, and there lay Snyder, powerless to move. They loaded him in a wagon, but before Snyder arrived home he regained his strength and professed the new birth.[10]

---

[7] Miller is quoted in Yeakel, *Jacob Albright and His Co-Laborers*, 97-8. Seybert is quoted in Don Yoder, *Pennsylvania Spirituals* (Lancaster, Pa.: Pennsylvania Folklife Society, 1961), 56-7. See also Hershey, *Confession*, 21; Huber, *Autobiography*, 60; and Newcomer, *Life and Journal*, 20, 31, 135, 139, 321.

[8] John Dreisbach, *Diary, 1817-1818* (typewritten manuscript, Commission on Archives and History, The United Methodist Church), 2. See also Newcomer, *Life and Journal*, 135, 136, 139, 146, 147, 215; and Seybert, quoted in Yoder, *Pennsylvania Spirituals*, 57-8.

[9] Newcomer, *Life and Journal*, 21, 55. For other references to tears, see Newcomer, 19-20, 22, 25, 27, 31, 32, 33, 38; Dreisbach, *Diary*, 1, 3, 8; *Doctrine and Discipline of the United Brethren in Christ* (Hagerstown, Md.: Gruber and May, 1819), 40; Huber, *Autobiography*, 31; Miller, quoted in Yeakel, *Jacob Albright and His Co-Laborers*, 97-8; and Seybert, quoted in Yoder, *Pennsylvania Spirituals*, 57. Other examples of instantaneous conversions are in Henry G. Spayth, *History of the Church of the United Brethren in Christ* (Circleville, Ohio: Conference Office of the United Brethren in Christ, 1851), 89-93.

[10] Huber, *Autobiography*, 37-9, 70. For other examples of fainting and unconsciousness, see Huber, 33, 60, 69-70; and Miller, "Life, Experience, and Ministerial Labors," 185.

Christian perfectionism, or the doctrine of sanctification, further characterized the preaching of many revivalists. Perfectionism, with roots that extended deeply into German pietism, taught that following conversion believers could continue their spiritual development until, as one German hymnist wrote, an inward "fire of love" consumed the "monster of sin." Make the soul "pure and chaste" on earth, the writer urged, "completely freed from the power of sin."[11] Purity came from justification through Christ although Spener, like Charles Wesley, acknowledged that a perfected heart still committed sins out of ignorance or original sin. (Wesley said that sanctified souls committed sins of omission but not those of commission.) Most German Pietists suggested that although the sanctified conquered their sinful nature and old habits, they never became perfect in the sense that growth ended, and true purity came only after death when the soul became reconciled to God, unlike Wesleyan sanctification, which was possible in the earthly life.[12]

In Pennsylvania many Germans continued to discuss perfectionism, but some, including early-nineteenth-century revivalists, gave it less priority than other parts of the conversion process. Christian Newcomer's 330-page journal mentions sanctification only briefly while endlessly documenting dramatic and emotion-filled conversions, and Miller's exhortation to an early conference, urging other Evangelical leaders "to seek entire sanctification," suggests that not all Evangelical Association pastors professed the experience of perfect love.[13] The River Brethren confession of 1790 ignored Christian perfectionism although Jacob Hershey's 1825 *Confession* describes the "third part of the new birth" in which the believer with God's help "lays aside wrath,

---

[11] Hedwig T. Durnbaugh, *The German Hymnody of the Brethren, 1720-1903* (Philadelphia: Brethren Encyclopedia, 1986), 52.

[12] August Hermann Francke, "On Christian Perfection," ed. Peter C. Erb, *Pietists: Selected Writings* (New York: Paulist Press, 1983), 114-5; J. Steven O'Malley, *Pilgrimage of Faith: The Legacy of the Otterbeins* (Metuchen, N.J.: Scarecrow Press, 1973), 64-5, 72-4; Timothy L. Smith, *Wesley and Whitefield on the New Birth* (Grand Rapids, Mich.: Francis Asbury Press, 1986), 84-6; and K. James Stein, *Philipp Jakob Spener: Pietist Patriarch* (Chicago: Covenant Press, 1986), 165-6.

[13] Newcomer, *Life and Journal*, 171, 232; and Miller, "Life, Experience, and Ministerial Labors," 247. See also "Entire Sanctification," *Evangelical Messenger* 2 (September 8, 1849): 67.

anger, covetousness, unbelief and all uncleanness so that the heart is cleansed of all."[14] Reformed Mennonite documents also devoted little attention to sanctification. Their founder, Francis Herr's, deathbed description of the new birth as created "after the image of God in righteousness and true holiness," words the New Testament attributes to the Apostle Paul, uses language similar to that employed by advocates of perfect love. The confession of his son, John, declared that only the atonement made him "perfect in [Christ]."[15] Aside from these passing remarks, however, Reformed Mennonite writers concentrated on other matters.

Others, however, laid greater emphasis on perfectionism. In 1763 Otterbein, sounding very much like his brothers Johann and Georg, preachers who remained in Germany, maintained that anybody who disavowed the "possibility of living with sin," denied God, and at a United Brethren ministers' conference in 1801 he proclaimed that those who "become free from sin" had God to thank.[16] This was consistent with his Reformed Pietistic heritage that stressed sanctification leading to Christian perfection as a progressive order of salvation. In 1789 a gathering of evangelistic pastors, who later became the hub of the United Brethren movement, confessed that Christians must be sanctified through the Holy Spirit, "thereby being cleansed from all filthiness of the flesh and spirit." A draft of the first United Brethren confession, adopted in 1814, used similar language. The following year delegates to the denomination's ministers' conference affirmed that through God "we are enlightened, justified through faith, and we become holy (or

---

[14] In the late nineteenth century the holiness movement became popular with large numbers of River Brethren, then called Brethren in Christ, in Kansas. See Carton O. Wittlinger, *Quest for Piety and Obedience: The Story of the Brethren in Christ* (Nappanee, Ind.: Evangel Press, 1978), 227-53, and, for the confession, 551-4. See also Hershey, *Confession*, 23.

[15] John Herr, *Complete Works*, 381, 383.

[16] Johann Otterbein filled a Reformed pulpit in Wittgenstein-Berleburg, the Radical Pietist haven. See O'Malley, *Pilgrimage of Faith*, 64-5, 72-4, 97, 153-8; Philip Wilhelm Otterbein, unsigned and undated letter in Core, *Otterbein*, 101; "Minutes of the United Brotherhood in Christ Jesus," Core, 121; and Daryl M. Elliot, "Entire Sanctification and the Church of the United Brethren in Christ to 1860," *MH* (July 1987): 207.

sanctified)."[17]

The Evangelical Association's first statement of doctrine, Martin Boehm's German translation of the Methodist *Discipline*, and its first hymnal gave prominence to Christian perfection, and the doctrinal statement included essays on the subject by John Fletcher and John Wesley.[18] Albright's preaching assistant, John Walter, found Scriptural support for perfection in the Song of Solomon 6:10, "Who is this that looks forth like the dawn, fair as the moon, bright as the sun, terrible as an army with banners?" Walter explained that "dawn" represented receding darkness and sin, "fair as the moon" depicted new Christians who partially reflected Christ, and "bright as the sun" symbolized entire sanctification.[19]

The growing Wesleyan influence seemed especially evident as more revivalists taught that purity could be both spiritual and literal. Otterbein declared that it was "obvious error" to believe that people cannot in their "earthly life be freed from sin," although he acknowledged that this blessing would not come "in one week or in one's sleep," a rejection of Wesley's second moment of grace.   Jacob Albright, however, followed the Wesleyan pattern more closely when he helped George Miller achieve holiness after they rode together all day, with Miller spending much of the time in tears. That night Miller prayed for an hour until "a mighty storm of love" poured over him and brought him what he believed was heart purity. Dreisbach also showed traces of Wesleyanism by praying for "sanctifying power" and asserting that God's grace kept him from sinning "willfully." Christian Newcomer claimed to have discovered independently of Methodism that sin

[17] The 1789 statement is in D. Berger, *History of the Church of the United Brethren in Christ*, The American Church History Series, 12 (New York: The Christian Literature Company, 1894), 348. The 1815 statement is in J. Steven O'Malley, "A Distinctive German-American Credo: The United Brethren Confession of Faith," *ATJ* (1986): 3, 5.

[18] Dreisbach, *Diary*, 4-5; J. Bruce Behney and Paul H. Eller, *The History of the Evangelical United Brethren Church* (Nashville, Tenn.: Abingdon Press, 1979), 83-4. The Methodist Discipline's statement on sanctification, which Boehm translated and enlarged, and the Evangelical Association's 1832 English translation of Boehm are in Ralph Kendall Schwab, *The History of the Doctrine of Christian Perfectionism in the Evangelical Association* (Menasha, Wisc.: The Collegiate Press, 1922), 24, 114-29. The hymnal title was *Das Geistliche Saitenspiel*.

[19] Schwab, *The History of the Doctrine of Christian Perfectionism*, 14-5.

could be "totally subdued, destroyed, and wholly eradicated" from the Christian heart. Later in his ministry, however, he prayed in precisely Wesleyan fashion that a "deeper work of grace be wrought" in the hearts of believers, "even the perfect love of God and the sanctification of their souls."[20]

Thus the new revivalists occupied a distinctive point on the spectrum of Pennsylvania German theology. The belief that perfection could come prior to death differentiated some of them from other Protestants, and their emphasis on the moment of conversion and the consequent emotions in worship further set many apart from earlier Pietists.

II

Just as the new revivalists found novel ways to express jubilation in conversion, so they created fresh applications for the egalitarianism within Pietism, similar to trends among English-speaking revivalists.[21] Women, for example, realized new opportunities. According to Samuel Huber, the old dogma that "women should keep silent in churches" disappeared. He reported that females of all ages fully participated in revivalist activities, including exhorting, prophesying, and "talking about the Savior in public," though he never used the word "preaching" to describe them. The result, he added, was the "utter consternation of old dry Pharisees, who beheld this new way with horror and dismay."[22] Female education received an endorsement from an anonymous contributor to the *Evangelical Messenger*, the Evangelical Association's magazine, encouraging women to increase their literary activity, particularly by becomimg correspondents of religious publications.[23] In Dunker council meetings, in which congregations conducted

[20] Dreisbach, *Diary*, 4-5; Newcomer, *Life and Journal*, 7, 276; and Elliot, "Entire Sanctification," 208-11.

[21] Nathan O. Hatch, *The Democratization of American Christianity* (New Haven: Yale University Press, 1989).

[22] Huber, *Autobiography*, 34.

[23] Philomatheus, "Woman," *Evangelical Messenger* 5 (October 13, 1852): 167.

business, "the voice of the youngest brother or sister," according to one of their leaders, carried the same weight "as if the oldest brother or sister" had spoken. Few women, however, preached, although one female, Sarah Righter Major, the daughter of a Philadelphia minister, became a well-known non-ordained preacher in her denomination. She held frequent meetings in Maryland, and after marrying a Philadelphia minister in 1842, moved to Ohio, where she and her husband often exhorted together. Some opposed her activities, but when elders decided to silence her, the committee delegated to inform her was unable to perform its assignment. One committee member explained that he would not silence someone who could "outpreach" him. [24]

Revivalists revealed their populist directions more clearly when singing translated versions of the ballads, choruses, and spirituals that roused English-speaking evangelicals. During revivals, especially, worshippers appended hymns with choruses that were easily learned and had, as one worshipper reminisced, "lively and catchy music." These popular choruses, usually in the Pennsylvania German vernacular, often called "Pennsylvania Dutch," expressed unadorned theology, such as

Ei ei! vee iss des duch so seess,
Vos ich in Yaisoo shoon ganeess!

(Oh, my, how sweet is this,
what I already enjoy in Jesus!)[25]

Another favorite proclaimed,

[24] "Correspondence," *Gospel-Visiter* (February 1852): 177-8; and Roger E. Sappington, *The Brethren in the New Nation: A Source Book on the Development of the Church of the Brethren, 1785-1865* (Elgin, Ill.: Brethren Press, 1976), 232-5, contains documents relevant to Lightner as follows: Sophia Lightner, Pipe Creek, Maryland, February 22, 1840, to "Dear Uncle"; Sophia Lightner, Pipe Creek, Maryland, July 12, 1840, to "Very dear Uncle and Aunt and Cousins"; 1834 and 1859 Yearly Meeting Minutes; J. H. Warstler, "Sister Sarah Major," *Brethren's Family Almanac*, 1901; and an account by Henry R. Holsinger.

[25] Daniel Bertolet, "Der Heiland rufet mir und dir," in *Geistliche Viole*, 1835, No. 141, v. 5, quoted in Yoder, *Pennsylvania Spirituals*, 12. See also Yoder, 10-18.

Weid ivver dem Yordon
Schau das Landt, schau das Landt!
Weid ivver dem Yordon
Schau das Verheis'ne Landt!

(Far over the Jordan, view the land, view the land!
Far over the Jordan, view the Promised Land.)[26]

Die geistliche Schmiede-Kunst, or "Jesus the Blacksmith," invoked the familiar imagery of the village smith. It implored the "master" to file and polish "my black and cold iron"; "hit away," the repentant sang, "so I come to the end of my misery." Sinners promised to lay themselves upon the anvil, where "the master commences to strike" blow after blow at their "black and cold" hearts. Then, "the soft iron yields," allowing itself to be "turned, bent, worked."[27] No ecclesiastical tweedledee or tweedledum here!

Critics disliked the simplicity of revivalist music. They charged that at least half of the choruses had been written "by the less-informed classes,"[28] and one disapproving worshipper noted that participants who were not gifted vocalists still wanted to lead the singing. Some congregations sang lengthy hymns with ten or fifteen verses to their very end. Others memorized a few beloved hymns and then sang them with favorite choruses several times in the same service, regardless of the appropriateness of the words and circumstances; like singing "evening hymn in the morning," one antagonist contended, "and a morning hymn in the evening." Another charged that some congregations sang their favorites "from January to December, at home, and at church, by day and by night." Evidently for some evangelical musicians enthusiasm counted more heavily than proficiency.[29]

Whether singing or preaching, new revivalists often avoided educated forms in favor of popular customs. Services typically favored Pennsylvania Dutch over High German, and, according to one listener,

---

[26] Ibid., 155-6, 331.

[27] Ibid., 373-75.

[28] Yoder quotes the *Evangelical Messenger,* August 8, 1849, in ibid., 148.

[29] Yoder quotes Maria Alspach in *Geschäftige Martha,* October 14, 1851, in ibid., 147-8.

were "less pedantic and learned, and hence more easily understood" than in the "older churches," whose ministers generally were college graduates. When Brother Barber preached "with power and not like the University Educated and pharisaic hypocrites," Seybert believed that "the foundations of Hell trembled." Another itinerant bragged that a Reformed cleric who scheduled a preaching appointment that conflicted with his service spoke to the "Scribes and Pharisees" while the "Publicans and sinners" attended his service.[30]

Indeed, revivalists relished opportunities to distinguish themselves from the dignified mainstream, especially in matters of dress. Seybert, who preached in an unfashionably cut coat, remembered that during his first camp meeting sermon in Lebanon County in 1821, a young woman became so disgusted with her stylish apparel that she tore off portions of it and fell to her knees crying for mercy and salvation. Some tried to pull her away, but other worshippers stopped them and prayed with her in a tent until she could believe that her conversion was complete.[31] Samuel Huber also recalled the conversion of a well-dressed woman, "embellished in full regalia of worldly fashion." He described her as sitting conspicuously in the middle of the meeting with a hat so "decorated with artificials" that it "might have been taken for a flower-pot." She displayed obvious contempt for the proceedings and its participants until midway through the service, when she knelt down and began seeking God's mercy. This set off considerable commotion; some ran for the door, but others fell to their knees or on their backs.[32] One humorist poked fun at young men who tried to "palm themselves on the public as gentlemen." The writer ridiculed their "dandified coat, green glasses, shining boots, costly finger-rings, or large whiskers" and added that these swells "nod and hop around, as though they were made of gum elastic, and worked in wire springs." Artificial ways of speaking, such as, "Foin weathah this moining--a delightful atmosfear--yes-am," likewise received censure.[33]

Thus new revivalists, like the eighteenth-century Pietists, lessened

---

[30] Grumbine in ibid., 141. See also ibid., 79; and Seybert, *Journal*, 5.

[31] Spreng, *John Seybert*, 53-4; and Yoder, *Pennsylvania Spirituals*, 60.

[32] Huber, *Autobiography*, 55-8.

[33] U. Eberhart, "Hints to Young Men--or True Gentility," *Evangelical Messenger* 2 (September 22, 1849): 70.

distinctions of rank and status. Their criticism of fancy dress resembled Anabaptist simplicity, though by the mid-nineteenth century Dunkers had begun to specify distinctive garb and hairstyles. The straightforward sermons and music of the new revivalists paralleled worship in the Pietist awakenings of the previous century, but their treatment of women broke new ground.

III

Drawn together by their distinctive beliefs and practices, the new revivalists developed their informal organizations into new denominations. United Brethren historians date the beginning of their communion from an unplanned encounter in 1767 between Martin Boehm, the Mennonite preacher, and William Otterbein, the Reformed minister, at an interdenominational meeting. Boehm, following his conversion, had visited Mennonites and New Light Baptists in the Shenandoah Valley, seeking, he said, "to find the truth more fully." Then he returned to Lancaster much encouraged and began a revival ministry, preaching to large congregations on both the Sabbath and weekdays. Although some Mennonite meetinghouses now barred him, he found "many doors opened in different directions," including large, nondenominational gatherings in barns and other unusual settings. These "big meetings," forerunners of nineteenth-century camp meetings, lasted several days and consisted primarily of singing and preaching, but they often closed with a love feast, reflecting possible Dunker, Moravian, and Methodist influences. At a barn meeting near Lancaster Otterbein heard Boehm preach on the new birth and afterwards embraced him, exclaiming, "We are brothers!" and giving birth to a new denomination.[34]

Thereafter Otterbein laid a foundation for the United Brethren by organizing informal gatherings among German revivalists. In 1774 he began the semi-annual "Pipe Creek Conference" among chiefly Reformed pastors. The name "Pipe Creek" came from the first

---

[34] Rowe, "Martin Boehm and the Methodists," 52. The story of the first Boehm-Otterbein meeting appears in many places; for example, see O'Malley, *Pilgrimage of Faith*, 176-8.

gathering's location, but subsequent conferences met in various places, mostly in Maryland. The group soon referred to themselves as the "United Ministers," indicating a self-identity wider than that provided by the coetus, and they appointed class leaders, many of whom became ministers. As their number grew, they established a general conference, which met for the first time in 1789 in Otterbein's parsonage in Baltimore. Ten of the eighteen preachers present were Reformed, though only three were ordained; of the others, six, including Boehm, were Mennonites, one was Amish, and one was Moravian. This conference adopted a confession of faith and a discipline, which Otterbein's Baltimore congregation had probably used previously. Two years later Otterbein's followers held another conference near York, Pennsylvania, with nine ministers present, but thirteen members of the associated group were absent. In 1800 the group's third conference, near Frederick, Maryland, formally adopted the designation United Brethren in Christ, and chose Boehm and Otterbein to be superintendents, or bishops. Growth came so rapidly that the organization soon divided into four conferences: Pennsylvania, Maryland, Virginia, and Miami (Ohio). In 1815 representatives of these met in southwestern Pennsylvania, at Mt. Pleasant, just a few years after both Otterbein and Boehm died, for their first denominational General Conference. They elected Christian Newcomer bishop and Andrew Zeller to be his associate and re-affirmed the 1789 confession.[35]

From the time of their informal beginnings in Boehm's barn meetings and Otterbein's Pipe Creek Conferences, the United Brethren displayed little interest in denominational discipline, thus distinguishing themselves from other Wesleyans and revivalistic fellowships. Otterbein's Baltimore congregation admitted to communion all believers, regardless of their denomination, because according to their constitution, "the differences of people and denominations end in Christ."[36] The United Brethren, perhaps showing the influence of former Mennonites among them, abandoned the tightly organized Methodist classes in favor of optional, informal prayer groups without membership lists. Methodists, praising the usefulness of a Christian discipline in

[35] Berger, *United Brethren in Christ*, 340-54; and O'Malley, *Pilgrimage of Faith*, 182.

[36] This quotation from "The Constitution and Ordinances of the Evangelical Reformed Church of Baltimore, Maryland, 1785," is in Behney and Eller, *Evangelical United Brethren Church*, 48-9.

encouraging members to be obedient, "earnestly" urged the United Brethren to prepare one, but the conference that received this communication deferred the request. Their first *Book of Discipline*, adopted ten years after the Methodist inquiry, acknowledged that Christian societies should practice the "outward means" of grace, such as baptism and communion, but allowed individuals to determine the manner. Feetwashing as well, it said, "must remain free to the judgement of everyone"; their 1789 confession had recommended feetwashing only "when desired." The United Brethren further departed from earliest Methodist polity in America by electing delegates to their general conferences, by giving local preachers as well as itinerants a vote in the conference, and by electing bishops for four-year terms rather than for life.[37]

This relaxed attitude toward denominational discipline did not prevent the United Brethren from instructing their members to "lead a strict and godly life." Although Mennonite and Dunker critics complained that the revivalists' preoccupation with the moment of conversion left them little room to stress obedience, the denomination's rules, adopted in 1814, set high standards for members. The United Brethren required attendance at all worship services and class meetings. Members were expected to practice their faith in business dealings, to assist the poor, to use strong drink only for medicinal purposes, and "to practice love towards friend and foe." Sundays were for devotions and "singing spiritual songs," rather than "ordinary occupations, buying and selling." And the *Discipline* counseled United Brethren to obey the "laws of the land," noting that every Christian should live "a peaceable, quiet, and godly life."[38]

The Evangelical Association, organized under Jacob Albright's leadership in 1803, adopted the Methodist discipline much more quickly

---

[37] Berger, *United Brethren in Christ*, 349. See also Francis Asbury and William McKendree to the Conference of the United Brethren, and Martin Boehm, George Adam Geeting, and Christian Newcomer to Baltimore Conference of English Methodist Episcopal Church (May 10-12, 1809), in *Minutes of the Annual and General Conferences of the United Brethren in Christ, 1800-1818*, ed. and trans. A. W. Drury (Dayton, Ohio: United Brethren Historical Society, 1897), 46, 49; *Doctrine and Discipline of the United Brethren in Christ* (Hagerstown, Md.: Gruber and May, 1819), 21; and Donald K. Gorrell, "'Ride a Circuit or Let It Alone': Early Practices That Kept the United Brethren, Albright People and Methodists Apart," *MH* 25 (October 1986): 9, 11.

[38] Drury, *United Brethren in Christ*, 283-4.

than the United Brethren. Albright was determined that his community of believers be tightly organized so that the members might "edify each other in the bonds of Christian fellowship." He recalled having prayed recurrently "with hot tears" while still a layperson for God to provide ecclesiastical leadership for his fellow Germans, but soon he felt God calling him to perform this task. After much soul-searching, in 1796 he began to preach without credentials or the support of ministerial colleagues in eastern Pennsylvania, Maryland, and the Shenandoah Valley. Frequent, lengthy fasting became part of his new life of intense devotion, a regimen so strenuous, he said, that he often bathed "in cold water to cool off the fever that raged within." Albright felt strong bonds with the Methodists but apparently began his individual effort becuase Bishop Francis Asbury disliked preachers skilled only in German.[39]

True to his beliefs about a community of faith, Albright proceeded rapidly to make his band of followers a formal one. After four years of itinerating, he organized three widely scattered classes in eastern Pennsylvania. Two years later Albright and forty followers held their first "big meeting" at Colebrookdale in Berks County, and the development of denominational order progressed quickly. In 1803 the Association's first council, which consisted primarily of lay leaders, ordained Albright and two young preaching assistants, and four years later the first regular or annual conference attracted twenty-eight of Albright's approximately 200 followers. When Albright died in May 1808, his group adopted its founder's name and became known as "Albright People." In 1816 they renamed themselves the "Evangelical Association."[40]

The River Brethren differed from the Evangelical Association and the United Brethren by retaining a vigorous Anabaptist emphasis on

---

[39] Behney and Eller, *Evangelical United Brethren Church*, 70; Nelson, "Jacob Albright," 14, 18-20; and Yeakel, *Evangelical Association*, 42-4, 53. See also the quotation from Albright in Spreng, *Evangelical Association*, 393-6.

[40] The membership estimate is from S. C. Breyfogel, *Landmarks of the Evangelical Association, Containing All the Official Records of the Annual and General Conferences from the Days of Jacob Albright to the Year 1840* (Reading, Pa.: Eagle Book Printing, 1888), 12-6. See also Behney and Eller, *Evangelical United Brethren Church*, 94; Spreng, *Evangelical Association*, 397-408; Yeakel, *Evangelical Association*, 51-7, 102; and Albright's comments in Yeakel, *Jacob Albright and His Co-Laborers*, 78-9.

obedience and, as described earlier, by avoiding for a century or more Wesley's doctrine of perfect love, or sanctification by faith. According to tradition, the River Brethren emerged from a fellowship of persons, mostly Mennonites, who had been awakened under Martin Boehm's influence. The most prominent of their early founders was Jacob Engel, a Swiss Mennonite who immigrated to America as an infant. The name "River Brethren" comes from their location near the Susquehanna River in western Lancaster County.[41]

The River Brethren confession, written in 1780, fused the fervor of late eighteenth-century revivalism with the Anabaptist understanding of obedience and the ordinances of baptism and communion. Their confession agreed with the Wesleyans that conversion emerged from a fierce, inward struggle with guilt in which the sinner felt "inner soul-pains" that ended when God's grace brought repentance and the sense of victory over sinning. For River Brethren, however, the new birth was a "revival of the mind" as well as of the emotions, so that those born anew obeyed all the injunctions of the Bible. The first River Brethren, for example, were convinced of the Biblical correctness of trine immersion but, according to tradition, were unable to persuade a Dunker to administer it, so they baptized themselves, consciously following the example of the first eight Dunkers who had baptized themselves in Germany. Their confession prohibited members from bearing the sword on any occasion, whether "for revenge or defense." They refused militia service during the Revolution, avoided election or appointment to public office, and did not swear oaths to the Revolutionary governments. The confession called for a believing community, operating through "unity of the Spirit"; it directed members to marry only persons of their denomination and to consult with their congregation before moving or purchasing land. Their deacons regularly visited members. Perhaps in imitation of the Dunkers, River Brethren banned the unfaithful, elected leaders rather than cast lots, wore beards, held

---

[41] Details are murky regarding the founding of the River Brethren, but they probably organized themselves in approximately 1780, when their confession has been dated; see Wittlinger, *Quest for Piety and Obedience*, 15-8.

love feasts, and washed one another's feet at the Lord's Supper.[42]

Of the new groups, only the Reformed Mennonites viewed themselves as a remnant, trying to preserve or recover the righteousness of a previous generation. They developed from a dispute in Lancaster County between Francis Herr and his congregation around 1800. Herr, a layperson, then left his Mennonite fellowship and led his supporters in home services. Contemporaries advanced two explanations for the division: either Herr's congregation spurned his demands for reform, or else he refused to reimburse a neighbor whom he had victimized in horse-trading. After his death in 1810, John, his son, assumed leadership and organized the denomination. It declared itself an independent organization in the 1830s.[43]

Like the River Brethren, Reformed Mennonites combined revivalism with the Anabaptist emphasis on discipleship. In 1790 Francis Herr had called for "spiritual, regenerated men whose hearts were changed": "new creatures" who prayed daily for God "to light the fire" of God's love in their hearts. He argued that those who were regenerate humbled themselves "with a low and contrite heart" and strived "to crucify their flesh and to mortify and subdue their lusts." Later, the Herrs sharply criticized other Mennonites for deviating from the teachings of Menno Simons concerning obedience, particularly for neglecting to shun unfaithful members, serving on juries, participating in political campaigns, and bringing lawsuits. Opponents observed that Reformed Mennonites were "extremely rigid in the observance of all

---

[42] Ibid., 551-4. See also Wittlinger, "The Vision of the River Brethren" (Lancaster Mennonite Historical Society; unpublished, undated manuscript), 11-4; Richard K. MacMaster, *Land, Piety, Peoplehood: The Establishment of Mennonite Communities in America, 1683-1790* (Scottdale, Pa.: Herald Press, 1985), 223; Martin H. Schrag, "The Eighteenth-Century River Brethren Confession of Faith," an unpublished paper presented at a conference on the Mennonite Experience in America, October 25-27, 1979; and Schrag, "The Impact of Pietism upon the Mennonites in Early American Christianity," *Continental Pietism and Early American Christianity*, ed. F. Ernest Stoeffler (Grand Rapids, Mich.: William B. Eerdmans Publishing Company, 1976), 87-121.

[43] "Francis Herr," *The Mennonite Encyclopedia: A Comprehensive Reference Work on the Anabaptist-Mennonite Movement*, 4 vols. (Hillsboro, Kan.: Mennonite Brethren Publishing House, 1955-1959), III, 712.

outward forms and customs."[44] Thus Reformed Mennonites uniquely blended the idea of a moment of conversion with the theology of an old order movement.

By 1820, then, German revivalists had added four new denominations to Pennsylvania's "mixed multitude."[45] The Evangelical Association and United Brethren both combined revivalism with Wesleyanism, with the former adopting more fully the Methodist emphasis on discipline. The River Brethren mingled revivalism with Anabaptist obedience, and the Reformed Mennonites united revivalism with an old order, possibly reactionary, movement. But all preached essentially the same doctrine of dramatic conversion and new birth through grace.

IV

For Germans the rise of the new revivalists represented only a degree of theological and institutional change. The revivalists and older Pietists had much in common, including the belief in the importance of repentance, grace, the new birth, and discipleship. The Mennonites' excommunication of prominent Wesleyans, for example, stemmed from reasons other than revivalism, perfectionism, or the teaching of a moment of conversion. Revivalist methods become controversial for Mennonites near Harrisonburg, Virginia, when several objected to the attendance of one of their preachers, Frederick Rhodes, at revivals led by the United Brethren and, according to unconfirmed reports, he occasionally led the meetings in prayer. His opponents charged that he

[44] John E. Funk, *The Mennonite Church and Her Accusers: A Vindication of the Character of the Mennonite Church of America from Her First Organization in This Country to the Present Time* (Elkhart, Ind.: Mennonite Publishing Company, 1878), 5-6, 18-9, 28-9, 388; Francis Herr, "A Short Explication of the Written Word of God, Likewise of the Christian Baptism and the Peaceable Kingdom of Christ, to the People Called Quakers" (a typescript of this manuscript, dating purportedly from 1790, is available at the Lancaster Mennonite Historical Society), 27-34; and Theron F. Schlabach, "Mennonites and Pietism in America, 1740-1880: Some Thoughts on the Friedmann Thesis," *MQR* 57 (July 1983): 233-5.

[45] I have borrowed this term from the title of Sally Schwartz's book, *"A Mixed Multitude": The Struggle for Toleration in Colonial Pennsylvania* (New York: New York University Press, 1987).

preached loudly, similar to the United Brethren preachers. Offended Mennonites drafted a letter that challenged only Rhodes' style, not his doctrine, and acquired forty signatures. Rhodes' supporters and opponents had argued previously over the use of English and whether worship should be in meetinghouses or private homes, both of which, like revivalism, raised larger questions of assimilation. The Rhodes controversy festered for approximately five years until ministers from Pennsylvania restored peace; the mediators declared Rhodes' behavior acceptable because Mennonite and United Brethren ministers in Maryland and Pennsylvania commonly travelled and worshipped together. The offended party as consolation received recognition for several ordinations they had performed.[46]

Mennonites in Pennsylvania took sterner action against Martin Boehm. For several decades they had accepted his revivalism, and Boehm's emotional sermons on regeneration apparently did not prevent his promotion to bishop in 1761, but undiplomatic statements--"that we might burn the Scriptures," that Satan benefitted humanity, and that faith comes from unbelief, life from death, and "light out of darkness" --caused prominent criticism. Finally, the Mennonite leadership censured Boehm because he increasingly associated with Methodists, whom they accused of walking "in the broad way, practicing warfare, and the swearing of oaths." Boehm partially confirmed Mennonite motives by recalling years later that they excommunicated him "for keeping fellowship with people of other denominations and tongue"; he claimed that his children were among the first Methodists in his neighborhood. Central to the Mennonite action, therefore, were the concepts of church discipline and community. Informal fellowship with revivalists who belonged to other denominations was permissible, but when Boehm's primary spiritual home came to be located outside their own fellowship, Mennonites no longer tolerated him.[47]

The Reformed synod's dismissal by a narrow majority of George

---

[46] Harry Anthony Brunk, *History of Mennonites in Virginia*, 2 vols. (Harrisonburg, Va.: published by the author, 1959), I, 79-83. Brunk based his account on the memory of Bishop Peter Burkholder's daughter, Margaret Burkholder Blosser, who was a young woman during the schism.

[47] The untitled statement of the Lancaster County Mennonite ministers is in Funk, *The Mennonite Church and Her Accusers*, 41-56. See also Rowe, "Martin Boehm and the Methodists," 53; and MacMaster, *Land, Piety, Peoplehood*, 213, 220-2.

Geeting, an Otterbein convert, resembled the Mennonite ouster of Boehm. The synod did not mention Geeting's Pietism but instead cited his absences and disorderly conduct, the latter probably being a veiled reference to his unrestrained emotional worship.[48]

In fact, despite Geeting's ouster support among church Germans for revivalist practices was widespread. When Otterbein's successor at Frederick, Maryland, Charles Lange, heavily criticized his doctrine and methods, the coetus upheld both, including independent prayer and Bible study, and requested Lange to "confess his error." At one of William Hendel's Thursday afternoon prayer meetings in Tulpehocken, a neighboring preacher, according to a participant, "prayed so earnestly that there was not a dry eye to be seen in the house." In the early nineteenth century many German Reformed and Lutheran congregations reported local revivals. At one in Chester County penitents, who had been long-time members of the church, wept openly and asked the pastor to kneel with and pray for them. A Lutheran pastor described a "glorious and blessed" awakening during which a "grey-headed man came trembling and weeping to the feet" of his Savior. The Lutherans' denominational newspaper, the *Lutheran Observer*, published in Baltimore by Benjamin Kurtz, endorsed revivals as "in spirit and principle as old as Christianity," and a Reformed revivalist admitted that certain "extravagant measures" deserved condemnation but asked who were "more zealous in promoting genuine revivals of religion" than Michael Schlatter and other "fathers of our church."[49] Revivals were the church's "true life," Kurtz declared, influencing the secular world in addition to congregations and multiplying converts like "the drops of the morning dew."[50]

---

[48] James I. Good, *History of the Reformed Church in the United States in the Nineteenth Century* (New York: Board of Publication of the Reformed Church in America, 1911), 126-9.

[49] The coetus minutes are in Joseph Henry Dubbs, *The Reformed Church in Pennsylvania* (Lancaster, Pa.: The Pennsylvania German Society, 1902), 236-9. See also "Evangelist," *Reformed Messenger* 1 (November 25, 1835): 56; and Good, *History of the Reformed Church*, 125, 130-4, 137-140.

[50] "Revivals," *Lutheran Observer* (December 20, 1844): n.p.; R. Weiser, id. (December 27, 1844): n.p. See also G. Scherer, "Letter to the Editor," id.; and "What Is a Revival of Religion?" id. (January 11, 1850): 213.

Although the various denominations thus shared considerable common ground, differences remained. Disagreement grew especially sharp over the Wesleyan emphasis upon a critical moment of conversion, which many Dunkers and Mennonites thought neglected obedience. Peter Nead, a Dunker from Virginia and a confirmed anti-revivalist, believed that because Christ, "our exemplar," spent his life obeying God's will, his followers were "to walk in his footsteps" with a like commitment to discipleship.[51] Christian Burkholder's 1804 essay, which all Lancaster County Mennonite preachers probably endorsed, rejected the idea that subjective experience confirmed the new birth. Instead, he wrote, obedience was "the only sign whereby the children of God can be known." Abraham Godschalk, writing in 1838, similarly declared that new creatures are those who keep Christ's commandments. Godschalk asserted that regeneration was not "fanaticism, but a most sober and rational thing." "When to the will is added the deed," he believed, "we have regeneration in a good degree."[52] Dunkers and Mennonites, therefore, assumed that those truly reborn followed Christ's commandments, and the Wesleyans' perceived failure to assert this disappointed them.

Many Anabaptists additionally claimed that personal testimonies to conversion, which the revivalists cherished, violated humility, a pillar of Christian discipleship. Peter Nead told his Brethren not to "make a public song" of their conversion by boasting that they were "the salt of the earth, the children of God"; conduct rather than words, he said, identified the saints. Christians were to "answer in meekness" when persons inquired about personal faith. Christian Burkholder told Mennonites, "My experience can help you nothing; nor can your experience help me anything," and he added that crowing about their conversion was "the work of the 'old man.'" Burkholder further warned that persons who talked freely about their conversion but had not changed their lifestyle were hypocrites and "a laughing stock before

---

[51] Peter Nead, *Theological Writings on Various Subjects: Or a Vindication of Primitive Christianity as Recorded in the Word of God* (new ed., Dayton, Ohio: 1866), in Sappington, *Brethren in the New Nation*, 128-9, 131.

[52] Harold S. Bender, ed. and trans., "A Few Words about the Mennonites in America in 1841: A Contemporary Document by Jacob Krehbiel," *MQR* 6 (January 1932): 51-3; Burkholder, "Third Address," *Useful and Edifying Address*, 198, 236; Godschalk, *The New Creature*, 30, 32-4, 51-9; and Schlabach, "Mennonites and Pietism," 229-30.

the world."[53]

Dunkers and some Mennonites also worried that the emphasis upon a moment of conversion diminished the role of the congregation in admitting new Christians to the faith community. Nead pointed out that the Apostle Peter sought approval from the church before baptizing Cornelius. From this he inferred that the congregation "has a right to be heard" on the reception of new members; applicants should "be instructed, and examined, and the church counseled." Christian Burkholder also described briefly the instruction congregations should give baptismal candidates.[54]

Many also dissented from the doctrine of sanctification, usually by suggesting that perfection came in another time, or in "the heavens themselves." August Spangenburg's *An Exposition of Christian Doctrine*, published in 1796 for the Moravians, asserted that those who believed that they could not "offend in a single word" and no longer needed to pray "forgive us our trespasses" did not understand the Bible. Abraham Godschalk acknowledged that the "perfect man" should be the "constant aim" of Christians and pointed out that Stephen kept "one of the hardest commandments of Christ, to love your enemy." But he explained that David, although "a man after God's heart," committed "great sins" and that Peter denied Christ. Critics stressed the continuing struggle against sin, and Godschalk interpreted the phrase "those who are born of God cannot sin" to mean that Christians could not sin as freely as others because of their conscience. God does not, said Spangenburg, "change any one so suddenly, nor in such a manner, as to make him incapable of sinning," and he rejected the Wesleyan distinction between sins of omission and commission.[55]

Camp meeting practices, as well, drew criticism, especially from professors at the German Reformed seminary in Mercersburg, Pennsylvania, and from the Dunkers. Peter Nead complained that

[53] Burkholder, "Third Address," *Useful and Edifying Address*, 221-2; and Nead, "Primitive Christianity," in Sappington, *Brethren in the New Nation*, 129.

[54] Burkholder, "Third Address," *Useful and Edifying Address*, 239-43; and Nead, "Primitive Christianity," in Sappington, *Brethren in the New Nation*, 142.

[55] Abraham Godschalk, *A Description of the New Creature* (Doylestown, Pa.: William M. Large, 1838), 49-50, 59-60, 63; and August Gottlieb Spangenburg, *An Exposition of Christian Doctrine as Taught in the Protestant Church of the United Brethren, or, Unitas Fratrum*, preface Benjamin La Trobe (Bath: S. Hazard, 1796), 255, 269-70, 276, 286-7.

camp meeting revivalists "believe in anything, and everything," and at last in nothing. They had "no established principles" except "to become numerous." The Dunker Yearly Meeting of 1842 advised its people "at all times to keep good order" and decided against "innovations, like the mourner's bench," or anxious bench, a special pew on which the unconverted sat, enabling evangelists to preach directly to those most troubled by their sins. Dunker leaders found the Scriptures silent on "protracted meetings" and warned that attendance at camp meetings or protracted meetings would "not be profitable" although refusing to limit "the frequency of the saints meeting together." The Brethren censured benedictions with "uplifted hands" as unbiblical and cautioned that meetings should be "held in the order of the house of God." Four times between 1838 and 1851 Yearly Meetings ruled against giving ministers from other denominations the liberty to preach.[56]

Even more severe criticism of camp meetings came from the Mercersburg Movement, led by Philip Schaff and John Nevin, German Reformed professors who promoted the liturgy and the catechism. For these "confessionalists," Christians grew as they learned doctrine through the ministry of the church, especially the catechism and the sacraments, a gradual process that Nevin and Schaff considered antithetical to the new birth. Nevin's book, *The Anxious Bench*, first published in 1844, repudiated the new measures of early-nineteenth-century revivals, including expressions of emotion, protracted meetings, prayer rooms, and the anxious bench, which Nevin used as a metaphor for all the new measures. Evangelists, he wrote, created "a false issue for the conscience"; their noise and commotion disturbed those who were "truly serious." He suspected that the "modest, the humble, the broken-hearted" usually remained seated while others moved to the anxious bench to be seen. As a result, Nevin charged, the revivalists produced "precarious and insecure" conversions that left the impression that outward form brings a spiritual blessing. Agreeing with the Anabaptists, he feared that excitement rather than "instruction or reflection" predominated. Nevin advocated instead the catechism,

---

[56] *Classified Minutes of Annual Conference of the Brethren: A History of the General Councils of the Church from 1778 to 1885* (Mt. Morris, Ill.: The Brethren Publishing Company, 1886), 139-41, 143; Nead, *Primitive Christianity*, in Sappington, *Brethren in the New Nation*, 141; and Sappington, 246.

which through knowledge of truth built sinners into symmetrical growth toward "everlasting life."[57] After a circuit rider visited the Reformed Theological Seminary in Mercersburg, he remarked that he had "seen the Beast!"[58] Evidently portions of the general public also opposed the revivalists. One critic asserted that the revivalists' main objective was to "make a good deal of noise, screw and twist from one side to the other, stamp with the feet, and change the face into different shapes."[59] Epithets, such as "*strabbler*" (struggler, or foot-stamper) and "*Knierutscher*" (knee-slider), mocked revivalists. According to one resident of south central Pennsylvania, many feared itinerants as "false prophets, deceivers, and bewitchers" and often denied them overnight hospitality. Apparently popular interest in the occult, which was strong in the colonial period, continued into the next century because some even feared that shaking hands with an evangelist would make them spellbound.[60]

Albright and his followers especially provoked reaction. When Albright, Newcomer, and Geeting dedicated a Reformed church in Schaefferstown, Albright began preaching from a pile of lumber, but several onlookers attacked him, and a sturdy friend carried him to safety. In another incident in Schaefferstown, Albright suffered a beating so severe that he could barely ride two miles to a friend's farm, and he spent two weeks there recuperating. In Berks County Albright preached from atop a worn-out millstone with words so powerful that he broke up a "frolic" at a nearby hotel, but the proprietor tried to chase him away with a whip.[61]

Albright occasionally returned the fire. In one sermon he faulted Lutherans, Reformed, Dunkers, and Mennonites. Lutherans thought

[57] John B. Frantz, "Revivalism in the German Reformed Church in the United States to 1850, With Emphasis on the Eastern Synod" (Ph.D. diss.: University of Pennsylvania, 1961), 94, 154-6, 161; and John Nevin, *The Anxious Bench: A Tract for the Times*, intro. John S. Stahr (third ed.; Reading, Pa.: Daniel Miller, 1892; originally published in 1844), 63-78, 109, 120-1.

[58] Yoder, *Pennsylvania Spirituals*, 79.

[59] The quote is from the *Evangelical Messenger* (November 9, 1853), in ibid., 149.

[60] Ibid., 96; and Huber, *Autobiography*, 12-4.

[61] The witness was Joseph Zoll, whose testimony is in Yeakel, *Jacob Albright and His Co-Laborers*, 80-1.

they had Luther, he said, but lived sinful lives that contradicted "God's Word and Luther's teaching." Reformed Germans, Albright continued, had "turned from God and towards the world" but to be "reformed" meant "to be converted from sin and the world." Dunkers and Mennonites comforted themselves with "peculiar dress and outward plainness," but notwithstanding their large farms and wealth, they would be "lost without the new birth."[62]

Like the colonial period, early nineteenth-century Pennsylvania often endured religious disputes. Non-Wesleyans distanced themselves from the individualism of instantaneous conversion, and Anabaptists repeatedly stressed that the new birth's fruits were obedience. But all Pietists agreed on the importance of regeneration, making this experience vital to most Germans in the early republic.

V

If German Protestants disagreed on the validity of the emotional conversion, they found quick agreement on the menace posed by two evils: Roman Catholicism and rum. Pietistic tolerance simply did not include Catholics, and periodicals published by the German denominations often depicted the decadence in Catholic countries and reported on Protestant missions to save them. The *Messenger*, for example, ran a story about immoral priests in Chile and endorsed an anti-Catholic periodical, the *Protestant Banner*. "Things in Europe," in the Evangelical Association's magazine, described French life as corrupt and immoral, exemplified by a high rate of illegitimate births, and denounced French worship services as "cold, dark, ceremonial superstition." "Even the Italian mind," professed one zealot, though "almost extinguished" by the "evil influences" of Rome, questioned the validity of Catholicism. The Dunker's *Gospel-Visiter* recounted the Irish priest who snatched a Bible out of a boy's hands and tossed it into the fire; the boy, so the *Gospel-Visiter* said, merely smiled back at the priest

---

[62] Quoted in Cecil P. E. Pottieger, "The History and Influence of the Evangelical Church in Monroe County; the Third Class Founded by Jacob Albright (Phillips Class): A Treatise of the Existing and Defunct Evangelical Churches in that County" (Master's Thesis: Lutheran Theological Seminary, Philadelphia, Pa., 1953), 10.

because he could not "burn those ten chapters" he had memorized. Opponents of the Mercersburg movement branded it with the mark of Catholicism by attacking the confessionalists' emphasis on good works, i.e., sacraments and catechisms, and similar "Roman abominations." If the Reformed followed John Nevin, asserted one of his antagonists, "the dark abysses of Popery" would follow. Charles Porterfield Krauth, a Lutheran preacher from Winchester, Virginia, considered "silly jokes about Pope Joanna" or "hotblooded" pamphlets and insults to be useless but nonetheless felt determined to suppress error by "teaching truth" to the children of America. Catholicism, he concluded, was the "leading power of darkness." According to Protestants, at stake was nothing less than the public schools, which if Catholic-controlled would brainwash students; religious freedom, especially menaced by crafty Jesuits; and the frontier, imperiled by vast numbers of degraded Catholic immigrants.[63]

The same denominational magazines that defended the cross by attacking Catholics took aim at alcohol. Periodicals warned of the corrupting might of drink and looked forward to the "blessed" time when the nation would expel its "abominable, and destructive enemy." "A Drunkard on Fire," in the *Evangelical Messenger*, recounted the tragic tale of an alcoholic who burst into flames when he strolled into the blacksmith's shop, and another story reported the testimony of a soldier in Napoleon's defeated army in Egypt, who survived the ordeal because he never drank. A German-language publication of the Evangelical Association, *Der Christliche Botschafter*, cautioned against the myth that hard drink enhances strength, noting instead that persons who

---

[63] Charles Porterfield Krauth, "Address to the teachers of the Lombard Street Sabbath-school" (February 1843), in Adolf Spaeth, *Charles Porterfield Krauth* (New York: Arno Press and The New York Times, 1969), 68-9; "Protestant Banner," *Messenger* 7 (June 22, 1842): 1397; "Pius IX and the Clergy of Chile," id., 12 (April 21, 1847): 2415; "Kirwan's Reply to Bishop Hughes," id., 13 (August 16, 1848): 2681; A Member of the Church, "The Winter Is Past," id., 17 (April 7, 1852): 3651; D. E. F., "The Crisis in the German Reformed Church," id., 17 (April 21, 1852): 3658; "Conversation Between Two Ministers," *Evangelical Messenger* 1 (October 9, 1848): 73; "Urgency of the Present Crisis in the West," id., 2 (October 8, 1849): 76; "Things in Europe," id., 5 (October 13, 1852): 167; "Something the Priest Couldn't Burn," *Gospel-Visiter* 5 (November 1855): 271; "Romanism Outspoken," *Lutheran Observer* (January 2, 1852): 622 [a reprint from the *Western Christian Advocate* appearing under a heading, "Romanism"]; and "Are the Jesuits to Be Incorporated?" id. (October 29, 1852): 815 [reprinted from the *Montreal Witness*].

bragged about the strengthening effects of rum were actually "weak in body and soul." The Dunkers' magazine explained away Jesus' miraculous transformation of water into wine by pointing out that wine is not hard liquor, that the amount consumed was minimal rather than excessive, and that the wine was for a "select and holy company."[64] The Reformed *Messenger* and the *Evangelical Messenger* regularly featured columns, "Temperance Department," that reported on the latest developments in the movement.[65]

Temperance-minded Germans enthusiastically supported the Maine Law, enacted in 1852 to ban the sale of alcoholic beverages in that state. The *Lutheran Observer* approved the switch from moral suasion to prohibition, arguing that unless the "fountains" were "dried up," their "waters [would] continue to flow," and the *Evangelical Messenger* followed the Maine Law's progress in Minnesota and New York. In 1853 the Lutheran periodical blessed victorious Maine Law politicians in Maryland, including an aspirant for sheriff, elected by "a most gratifying majority"; whether the candidate was a Whig or Democratic was irrelevant, pronounced the editor. The Lutheran Synod of Maryland endorsed a Maine Law for its state, Virginia's Lutheran clergy urged the Old Dominion to enact a comparable statute, and the Reformed magazine advocated similar legislation in Pennsylvania.[66]

---

[64] "Put It Down in Ink," *Messenger* 1 (November 25, 1835): 56; "Hitzige Getränke und deren Wirkungen," *Der Christliche Botschafter* 5 (November 16, 1840): 169-70; "Bertus," letter to the editor, *Evangelical Messenger* 1 (April 22, 1848): 30; "A Drunkard on Fire," id. (October 23, 1848): 80; "A Temperance Man," id., 3 (November 8, 1850): 84; and "About Temperance," *Gospel-Visiter* 4 (August 1855): 193-4.

[65] For examples, see "Temperance Dept.," *Messenger* 1 (February 17, 1836): 104; 1 (March 2, 1836): 110; 1 (March 9, 1836): 116; 7 (July 13, 1842): 1420; 8 (September 6, 1843): 1662; "Temperance Department," *Evangelical Messenger* 1 (January 24, 1848): 8; (February 15, 1848): 15; and (April 8, 1848): 25.

[66] "The Evangelical Lutheran Synod of Virginia," *Lutheran Observer* (November 5, 1852): 816; "Evangelical Lutheran Synod of Maryland," id. (November 4, 1853): 100; "The Election in Maryland," id. (November 11, 1853): 100; "Thoughts on the Liquor Question," id. (July 21, 1854): 117 [This letter was the first in a series on temperance]; see id. (July 29, 1854): 122-3; (August 4, 1854): 126; and (August 11, 1854): 130; "The Maine Law," *Messenger* 18 (September 22, 1852): 3747; "The Maine Law in Minnesota," *Evangelical Messenger* 5 (May 26, 1852): 88; and "New York for the Maine Law," ibid. (August 18, 1852): 135. See also "The Maine Liquor Law," *Lutheran Observer*

VI

The wars against papists and drunkards, however, lacked sufficient power to enable Germans in the young nation to overcome their denominational loyalties. Rather, the common emphasis on experiential religion inspired German Christians to raise higher the banner of religious toleration when they gathered in interdenominational settings. Germans who tended towards Pietism seem to have believed more deeply than others that the experience of the new birth transcended denominations and language differences. They chastised denominational advocates for obscuring Christ and urged them instead to apply their zeal to religious experience.[67]

Thus Samuel Huber, a United Brethren evangelist, declared that upon conversion he received God's love, which enabled him "to unite with all His true followers." Huber held revivals at which River Brethren, Dunkers, Methodists, Presbyterians, Lutherans, and Mennonites as well as his United Brethren colleagues spoke; in them he proclaimed "love to all mankind, and hatred to none."[68] Christian Newcomer also enthusiastically encouraged interdenominational worship. He recorded that Lutheran, Dunker, Mennonite, and Moravian pastors appeared at his meetings, and he worshipped at Mennonite, Reformed, River Brethren, Albright, and Dunker services, though he complained that the latter refused him communion. "When will bigotry be banished from the world?" he asked. Newcomer also held services in a Methodist meetinghouse in York, a German Reformed church in Lancaster County, and many Mennonite houses of worship. In 1795 he stayed at the Virginia home of his uncle, a Mennonite preacher, and spoke at a house meeting "with considerable liberty" on Psalms 34:15. He once attended a Quaker meeting but did not speak, fearing that he might break the rules. Sometimes preachers of other persuasions sitting in the congregation affirmed his words, as did a Mennonite pastor near Lancaster and a Moravian in nearby Elizabethtown. Henry Boehm re-

(April 9, 1852): 689; and "The Maine Law and Christian Law," id. (November 5, 1852): 818.

[67] "Creeds and Formulas," ibid. (March 12, 1852): 672.

[68] Huber, *Autobiography*, 11, 37, 61.

marked that a Mennonite offered "a powerful exhortation" when in 1800 he toured the Shenandoah Valley with Newcomer, Asbury, and his own father.[69]

Other revivalist preachers matched Newcomer's commitment to interdenominational worship. Non-Mennonites flocked to Boehm's early meetings. He explained that after his conversion experience he no longer confined his labors "to Jew only--but also to Greek." George Geeting, of the United Brethren, preached in German Reformed churches in Harrisburg, Lebanon, and York. Newcomer once spoke to a small but attentive Amish congregation near Lancaster, and he often shared pulpits with preachers from other denominations. In 1796 at the laying of a cornerstone for a union church, Geeting, Newcomer, Hautz, and a Lutheran named Herbst jointly led the service, and the following day Geeting preached to the nearby German Reformed congregation. Between 1791 and 1801 George Pfrimmer, a United Brethren preacher, spoke in both Reformed and United Brethren congregations, and in 1806 Jacob Albright delivered a sermon at a United Brethren quarterly meeting. Lutherans sponsored a nondenominational revival in Schaefferstown, and Newcomer noted that as "Lutherans, Presbyterians, Mennonites, Baptists, and Methodists drew near the Lord's table" in a barn in Rockingham County, Virginia, sectarian differences became "lost in Christian love" as they shouted and praised God's "unbounded mercy and goodness."[70]

Relations between the German revivalists and English-speaking Methodists were always close, reinforcing a bilingual tradition that began with the birth of Methodism. John and Charles Wesley first fellowshipped with Germans in 1736 when they encountered Moravians aboard their ship en route to Georgia. Two years later, Peter Boehler, a Moravian visiting London, was instrumental in the Wesleys' spiritual

---

[69] MacMaster, Land, Piety, Peoplehood, 211; and Newcomer, Life and Journal, passim.

[70] Raymond Martin Bell, "John George Pfrimmer, 1762-1825: Early United Brethren Minister" (unpublished paper; Washington, Pa.: 1983), 1; Henry Boehm, The Patriarch of One Hundred Years: Being Reminiscences, Historical and Biographical, of Rev. Henry Boehm, ed. Joseph B. Wakely (Lancaster, Pa.: Nelson and Phillips, 1866), 22-3; Newcomer, Life and Journal, 41, 55, 63, 99, 145, 149, 165, 182, 315; Rowe, "Martin Boehm and the Methodists," 52; and S. M. B---r, "Revival," Lutheran Observer (April 9, 1852): 688.

transformation. Methodists, including their first gathering in Fetter Lane, London, adopted the Moravians' love feasts and choirs or classes. John Wesley translated thirty-six German hymns, largely Moravian, although the tradition that Boehler's remark--"Had I a thousand tongues, I would praise Him with them all"--led to the Wesleys' great hymn is probably inaccurate because other variations of it were widespread.[71]

Cooperation between Germans and Methodists continued in the New World. They often shared preaching duties, and when Methodists ordained Asbury as superintendent and bishop, Otterbein joined in the ceremony of the laying on of hands. In 1805 Newcomer rode circuit for a few weeks with Lorenzo "Crazy" Dow, an American Methodist nicknamed by English Anglicans who disapproved of him. Dow, with shoulder-length hair, harsh voice, and ill-fitting clothes, mocked the powerful and delighted worshippers with his quick wit, theatrical style of preaching, and earthy doggerel and anecdotes. Newcomer listened to Dow in Williamsport, Maryland, and then travelled with him across the Mason-Dixon Line to Greencastle, Chambersburg, Shippensburg, and Carlisle in Pennsylvania's Cumberland Valley. At Carlisle Dow gave an afternoon talk in the markethouse and an evening one in the Methodist building. In 1823 Dow, back from his long tour of Britain, preached to Hagerstown's German Reformed congregation in the afternoon and to Newcomer's United Brethren in the evening. Later that year Newcomer rode with and exhorted for another Methodist, John Chambers, who preached with such "liberty and power" at Shippensburg as to astonish him. At a York service Bishop Richard Whatcoat preached in the morning, and Newcomer spoke in the evening by candlelight.[72]

Evangelical Association and United Brethren itinerants also cooperated closely. Preachers from both denominations provided lodgings for one another, occasionally found hospitality from the same families, and held meetings in the same homes. Philip Bishop, for

[71] A German hymn, *O dass ich tausend Zungen hatte*, was published in 1704, and George Whitefield used the phrase a month before Charles Wesley wrote his memorable lines. See Clifford W. Towlson, *Moravian and Methodist: Relationships and Influences in the Eighteenth Century* (London: The Epworth Press, 1957), 35-67, 184-215.

[72] Hatch, *Democratization of American Christianity*, 36-40, 130-33; and Newcomer, *Life and Journal*, 131, 132, 135-6.

example, who resided near Hanover, Pennsylvania, welcomed itinerants from both denominations, and Jacob Kleinfelter's large farm in York County hosted several interdenominational services. Kleinfelter was one of Albright's people, but he testified to Otterbein's influence upon his conversion. John Dreisbach (Evangelical Association) once led worship at John Meyer's, near Carlisle, where, he recalled, "some reacted as though they were drunk and praised God, others sank on their knees and asked God for a greater measure of grace," i.e., sanctification; Newcomer, of the United Brethren, also appeared there frequently. In all of these cases, journals do not identify particular persons with either denomination.[73]

Besides sharing pulpits and preaching platforms, German revivalists contemplated closer institutional cooperation. On a journey down the Susquehanna River in 1810, John Dreisbach, an Albright preacher, conversed amiably with Asbury and Henry Boehm about merging their denominations. Although Asbury dismissed as "inexpedient" Dreisbach's request for German circuits, districts, and conferences, the discussion remained friendly, and on departing Asbury presented Dreisbach with John Fletcher's perfectionist volume, *The Character of St. Paul.*[74]

The United Brethren and Methodists took several steps towards union, including an agreement to issue certificates so that each could include the other's preachers and laypersons in services, including communion. The United Brethren honored a Methodist request to refuse any ministers and laypersons whom the Methodists had expelled and asked for reciprocal exclusion. Methodists typically initiated the suggestions for cooperation, but the United Brethren welcomed them, expressing in 1811 the hope that the "mutual friendship and love" between their denominations would "be increased yet more and more" and that the exchange of letters and messengers between them could become annual. Merger, however, failed because the Methodists, especially Asbury, judged the United Brethren discipline to be unacceptable, especially its provisions that made itinerating optional for preachers and classes voluntary for local societies. The United

[73] Ibid., 23, 59, 64, 70, 75, 89, 101, 106, 121, 131, 133, 134, 137, 139, 142, 143, 145, 163, 184, 226, 233, 240, 252, 289, 298, 304; and Dreisbach, *Diary,* 1, 7, 9.

[74] Spreng, *Evangelical Association,* 408-9.

Brethren custom of accepting non-itinerating preachers as full members of annual conferences also blocked union between themselves and the Evangelical Association. Disagreements further arose over the name of the proposed denomination, and a misunderstanding over the voting authority of conference delegates angered the Evangelical representatives.[75]

Ethnic barriers for nineteenth-century revivalists were just as easily crossed as denominational boundaries. Newcomer, for example, frequently exhorted or preached in English. At one service a Methodist named Hinkel spoke in English, then Geeting preached and Newcomer exhorted, presumably in German. At a predominantly English funeral at Pipe Creek, Maryland, Newcomer preached to the mourners in their native tongue. He spoke to Methodists at Chambersburg in English, but on another occasion in York, he used German, after which Methodist Bishop William McKendree followed in English. Martin Boehm often hosted English-speaking Methodist preachers, including Robert Strawbridge and Benjamin Abbott, for services at his home. When Sylvester Hutchinson preached there, Henry Boehm remembered that "a glorious revival followed." At a New Year's Day communion service, Dreisbach shared preaching duties with an English preacher named Dinkel, who assisted in distributing the bread and wine after Dreisbach's German prayer.[76]

Dunkers practiced bilingual worship just as enthusiastically as the revivalists. The 1841 Yearly Meeting declared "that it is our right, and our duty, to preach the Gospel to every nation" and encouraged a bilingual service even if the majority of worshippers were German. In 1845 it reaffirmed the "commission of our Savior to preach the Gospel

---

[75] "An Address from the United Brethren in Christ to the Methodist Episcopal Conference," May 25, 1811, in Drury, *Minutes of the Annual and General Conferences of the Church of the United Brethren in Christ, 1800-1815*, 54-5; Francis Asbury and William McKendree, "To the Conference of the United Brethren," id., 45-7; the exchange of letters in id., 45-63; and Gorrell, "'Ride a Circuit or Let It Alone," 12, 14-5. Finally in 1946 the two German Wesleyan fellowships formed the Evangelical United Brethren, which merged with the Methodists in 1968.

[76] See examples of German/English services in Newcomer, *Life and Journal*, passim. See also Henry Boehm, *Patriarch of One Hundred Years*, 19-25; and Dreisbach, *Diary*, 9. Dreisbach mentions other bilingual services on 2, 3, 8, 9.

to all nations, and in every tongue."[77]   An anecdote about a young
Dunker demonstrates the comfort of nineteenth-century members of that
denomination with bilingualism.   The preachers' bench was full one
Sunday morning and included a young visiting preacher.   After an
opening hymn and prayer the elder turned to the preachers and said,
"Now Brethren, take up the subject."   Because it was customary to
allow a guest minister to speak first, each preacher extended "the
liberty" down the bench until it rested with the visitor.   Being last on
the bench, there was no one to whom he could pass the liberty, so he
looked to the elder for consent to speak.   The elder, despite the
courtesy of allowing guests to begin the preaching, was annoyed that
one so young would speak first, so he asked the young man if he could
deliver a sermon in German, expecting a negative reply.   But the
visitor answered, "O yaw," to which the elder could only say, "All
recht."   The guest preacher then delivered a stirring message in the
finest German heard there in many years.[78]

Further demonstrating the growth of interdenominational and
bilingual fellowship was the interchange of hymns among denominations and language groups.   In 1791 Peter Leibert, a Germantown
minister, published the Dunkers' first English hymnal, called *The
Christian's Duty*.   Its 352 songs included Isaac Watts' "Am I a Soldier
of the Cross," Robert Robinson's "Come, Thou Fount of Every
Blessing," and three by Charles Wesley, "O!   For a Thousand
Tongues," "Christ the Lord Is Risen Today," and "Jesus, Lover of My
Soul."   Another Dunker hymn book, *Die kleine Lieder Sammlung*,
published in 1826, contained among the hymns of invitation three
borrowed from the earliest United Brethren hymnal, including a song
popular among young people whose author was a Dunker, William
Knepper.   Numerous selections from the Dunkers' *Kleine Davidische
Psalterspiel* edition of 1795 and a supplement to it compiled by two
United Brethren found their way into the first River Brethren hymnal,
issued in 1874.   John Kline, an influential Dunker from Linville,
Virginia, quoted one of Charles Wesley's hymns in a sermon, and
another time he spoke severely about a Methodist service he visited in

---

[77] *Classified Minutes of Annual Conference*, 137-8.

[78] This event occurred after 1850, but its moral is relevant for this paper.   See James
H. Lehman, *The Old Brethren* (Elgin, Ill.:   Brethren Press, 1976), 118-9.

Washington, D.C., except that the hymn was "familiar" and "very enjoyable." The many editions of the popular Evangelical Association hymn book, *Geistliche Viole*, included German translations of popular English-language hymns, such as Wesley's "A Charge to Keep I Have" (*Ein Werk ist mir vertraut*) and "Jesus, Lover of My Soul." Another hymnal also included "A Charge to Keep I Have" but used a different translation (*Ein' Pflicht zu thun ich hab'*).[79]

Despite the debates, then, over music, protracted meetings, mourners' benches, personal testimonies, and other revivalist methods, the evangelists nevertheless promoted both tolerance and bilingualism. Revival meetings attracted participants from all German communions. Ministers of different denominations shared the speakers' platform, attended each other's services, and supported one another so much that sometimes denominational affiliation became obscured, particularly among revivalists. Pennsylvania Germans had created a religious society in which denominational labels and ethnic identification often meant less than one's spiritual life. As Jacob Albright put it, "Christ operates spiritually upon every heart that yields itself to Him."[80]

Although Pennsylvania Germans worshipped in many ways, they often agreed on large issues. They lacked unanimity on Christian perfection, instantaneous conversion, and methods of procedure and disagreed over the usefulness of camp meetings and unrestrained emotional behavior, but they maintained a consensus on the new birth. Nothing so exemplified the growing tolerance and variety surrounding this consensus than when Mennonites used Charles Wesley's Christmas hymn, "Hark, the Herald Angels Sing," with its powerful declaration of spiritual awakening:

---

[79] *The Christian's Duty*, 8, 37, 48, 122, 196; Durnbaugh, *The German Hymnody of the Brethren*, 68-70; Benjamin Funk, *Life and Labors of Elder John Kline, the Martyr Missionary* (Elgin, Ill.: Brethren Publishing House, 1900), 97, 346; Donald R. Hinks, *Brethren Hymn Books and Hymnals, 1720-1884* (Gettysburg, Pa.: Brethren Heritage Books, 1986), 39-40; Herbert Royce Saltzman, "A Historical Study of the Function of Music Among the Brethren in Christ" (Ph.D. diss.: University of Southern California, 1964), 94-110; and Yoder, *Pennsylvania Spirituals*, 357-8, 363.

[80] Yeakel, *Evangelical Association*, 54-5.

Born to raise the sons of earth,
Born to give them second birth.[81]

---

[81] By a Committee of Mennonites, *A Selection of Psalms, Hymns, and Spiritual Songs, from the Most Approved Authors Suited to the Various Occasions of Public Worship and Private Devotion, of the Church of Christ* (Harrisonburg, Va.: J. H. Wartman and Bros., 1847), 61. George Whitefield also contributed to the text.

CHAPTER 6

Proclaiming Liberty to the Captives

In 1811 Christian Newcomer, the United Brethren itinerant, preached in Baltimore to an enthusiastic congregation of over one thousand African Americans. "Before I had spoken many minutes," he recalled, "the noise and uproar became so great that my voice was entirely drowned, and could be heard no longer."

Newcomer, who clearly relished preaching to blacks, embodied the crosscurrents that slavery sent swirling through the German community. In 1797 he had purchased a twelve-year-old African American servant girl, named "Patience," under terms that she be freed at age thirty. (Patience probably died of an unidentified disease at twenty-one.)[1]

If salvation is available to everyone, regardless of rank and birth, as Newcomer believed, how could Pietists hold slaves? And how could they debate the most controversial issue in American history without destroying the Christian unity that they so prized?

I

Among Germans before the Revolution the most easily identifiable slaveholders were Moravians. Moravians kept slaves but treated those admitted to their congregations as spiritual brothers and sisters.

---

[1] Christian Newcomer, *The Life and Journal of Christian Newcomer, Late Bishop of the Church of the United Brethren in Christ*, ed. John Hildt (Hagerstown, Md.: F. G.W. Kapp, 1834), 195; and J. Bruce Behney and Paul H. Eller, *The History of the Evangelical United Brethren Church* (Nashville, Tenn.: Abingdon Press, 1979), 65.

Although they believed that slavery was part of God's plan, they assumed that conversion would greatly lighten the burden of being born a heathen, and Zinzendorf's entourage included an African convert from the Virgin Islands who came to Pennsylvania to evangelize blacks. In 1746 Moravians baptized another African American, Andrew the Moor, at Bethlehem; he later married a black woman from Philadelphia, and the pair lived at Bethlehem until their deaths in 1779. African American Moravians like Andrew met all the obligations of membership, including the preparation of an autobiography, and their material life, including food, clothing, and work, matched that of their white co-religionists. But black members also remained slaves, and Andrew, at least, lacked the dignity of a surname.[2]

Most Germans, however, disdained bondage from the moment of their arrival in colonial Pennsylvania. The supply of German indentured servants was adequate, and the large initial investment plus a hefty tax assessment made slaves less profitable. Pennsylvania farmers often considered slaves to be inefficient in the types of agricultural work they required. Slaves, therefore, usually became objects of conspicuous consumption, conferring status rather than productivity on their owners. The newly emerging elite not only adorned themselves with watches and shoe buckles and rode expensive riding horses; they also kept black slaves.[3]

Practical considerations, therefore, undoubtedly discouraged Germans from purchasing slaves. According to tradition Samuel Pennypacker, a Mennonite from Skippack, owned a black named "Schwartz Piet" (Black Pete), and a Mennonite slaveholder appears on

---

[2] Kenneth G. Hamilton, ed. and trans., *The Bethlehem Diary: Volume I, 1742-1747* (Bethlehem, Pa.: Archives of the Moravian Church, 1971), 121; Joseph Mortimer Levering, *A History of Bethlehem, Pennsylvania, 1741-1892: With Some Account of Its Founders and Their Early Activity in America* (Bethlehem, Pa.: Times Publishing Company, 1903), 122-3; and Daniel B. Tharp, "Chattel with a Soul: The Autobiography of a Moravian Slave," *PMHB* (July 1988): 433-46.

[3] Gary B. Nash, "Slaves and Slaveowners in Colonial Philadelphia," *WMQ* 30 (April 1973): 230-4; Alan Tully, "Patterns of Slaveholding in Colonial Pennsylvania: Chester and Lancaster Counties 1729-1758," *JSH* 6 (Spring 1973): 287-92; and Jerome H. Wood, Jr., "The Negro in Early Pennsylvania: The Lancaster Experience, 1730-1790," ed. Elinor Miller and Eugene D. Genovese, *Plantation, Town, and County: Essays on the Local History of American Slave Society* (Urbana: University of Illinois Press, 1974), 446-78.

the 1779 and 1780 Berks County tax lists. But tax lists reveal no Dunkers who owned slaves, and only a rare Mennonite who did.[4]

Several Germans, however, were not content with a silent witness of non-participation but publicly opposed the peculiar institution of slavery. Extant comments center on the inhumanity of owning servants, although it seems logical that the Anabaptist interpretation of simplicity and humility would have encouraged objection to these pricey status symbols. Mennonites claim a role in the first written antislavery protest in North America, a 1688 statement by a group of Dutch Quakers in Germantown. (The basis of the claim is that several of the signers had formerly been Mennonites and at least one later rejoined the communion.) Tradition also maintains that a York County Mennonite spent a night in an open field rather than accept the hospitality of a slaveholder.[5]

The Christopher Sauers were especially outspoken critics of slaveholding. In 1754 the elder Sauer speculated that the prayers of Jamaican slaveholders for rain might go unanswered because they "mercilessly" whipped their slaves, "treating them worse than cattle." This attacked the ill-treatment of slaves, not the institution, but Sauer's son assaulted slavery itself. In 1761 the latter's front-page editorial called the "inhumane business" of the slave trade "an evil and a sin," and he published a lengthy report detailing the corruptness of trading in slaves.[6] Several months later Sauer printed an advertisement for a runaway slave in which the master described the runaway as wearing tattered clothing. To this Sauer appended a comment that

> One has to wonder why the Negro was so senseless and ran away barefoot and wearing old clothes; he should have put on new ones! If masters often did to their employees what is just and equal and remembered that they also have a Lord in heaven (Col. 4:1), many would not run away. But money is the root of all evil.[7]

---

[4] Richard K. MacMaster, *Land, Piety, Peoplehood: The Establishment of Mennonite Communities in America, 1683-1790* (Scottdale, Pa.: Herald Press, 1985), 100-1, 297n47.

[5] Ibid., 43-4, 101.

[6] *Pensylvanische Berichte*, February 2, 1761; and July 16, 1754.

[7] Ibid., July 31, 1761.

Sauer's words must have fallen on receptive ears. Most Germans in colonial Pennsylvania avoided slavery, and the German Anabaptists, among the earliest American opponents of slavery, more consistently resisted bondage than colonial-era Quakers, many of whom were slave-holders.[8]

II

In the next century slavery became more than just a consumer choice or moral question but an all-consuming political quagmire. Moreover, the fiery exchange in this argument threatened to split denominations as well as the union. Some German Christians, fearing the capacity of the debate over slavery to split their fellowships, attempted to censor themselves, pledging never to allow this topic, so often poisoned with controversy, to pass their lips.

Slavery's threat to denominational unity especially concerned many Lutherans and Reformed, the two largest German denominations, so their official bodies spoke very little about the institution. During the Civil War, Pennsylvania's Eastern Synod of the Reformed Church met several times in the shadow of bloody battlefields and marching armies but took little notice. In 1862 they gathered at Chambersburg only five days after Confederate cavalryman J. E. B. Stuart's raid; rebel troops still occupied nearby Hagerstown, Maryland, and reports circulated that Stonewall Jackson's army had crossed the Potomac. But the Synod busied itself for eight days discussing the Liturgy and educational institutions. The following year they met in Carlisle several months after the Battle of Gettysburg without officially mentioning the war or related topics. The Lutheran synods of Central and Eastern Pennsylvania were equally silent.[9]

---

[8] In Chester County between 1729 and 1758, seventy percent of the slaveholders were Quakers. See Tully, "Patterns of Slaveholding in Colonial Pennsylvania," 294.

[9] Robert Fortenbaugh, "American Lutheran Synods and Slavery, 1830-60," *JR* 13 (January 1933): 88; and H. M. J. Klein, *The History of the Eastern Synod of the Reformed Church in the United States* (Lancaster, Pa.: Eastern Synod of the Reformed Church in the United States, 1943), 243-5.

Likewise, Lutheran and Reformed newspapers only gingerly approached slavery. As early as 1837, Benjamin Kurtz, editor of the *Lutheran Observer*, pledged never again to mention the subject and told potential letter writers to avoid it. After angry abolitionists canceled subscriptions, Kurtz reiterated that his journal would not discuss divisive and trivial issues. The *Messenger*, the Reformed journal, pursued a similar hands-off policy, and a southern reader caught the spirit of its editorial policy by boasting that "ultraism, disunion, and abolitionism" were nonexistent among Reformed Germans and that sectional loyalties, so damaging to other denominations, found no place in his communion. Kurtz agreed that the Reformed were "truly one" with "no such dividing lines as North and South." Despite Kurtz's attempted neutrality, northerners accused him of proslavery sentiment while southerners charged that his heart lay in the abolitionist camp. Kurtz feared that "between the two" he might be squeezed to death.[10]

Although many Lutheran and Reformed leaders strived to avoid debating slavery, they rarely missed an opportunity to praise colonization, a popular scheme to rid America of slavery by resettling blacks in Africa. The *Messenger* blessed the American Colonization Society as "praiseworthy and benevolent," and the *Lutheran Observer* thought it deserved the "support of the whole Christian world." Glowing accounts of the Liberian Republic, the fledgling democracy planted in Africa by former slaves, compared it to early American colonies in Plymouth and Jamestown. A missionary confessed her preference for the new African nation over Mississippi, and in 1852 the editor of the *Messenger* defined Liberia's success as "beyond dispute." Peter Schaeffer, a Lutheran pastor in Frederick, Maryland, was certain that colonization enjoyed "the smiles of the Almighty."[11]

Many border-state Lutheran clergy became leaders in the colonization movement. Benjamin Kurtz belonged to the Board of

---

[10] *Lutheran Observer* 4 (July 28, 1837): 194; id., 4 (August 3, 1837), n.p.; and id., 12 (December 20, 1844), n.p.; "J. L.," "The Church of the South--Her Claims Upon the North," *Messenger* 16 (March 26, 1851): 3234; and the editorial comments on p. 3235.

[11] *Lutheran Observer* 18 (November 8, 1850): 383; id., 12 (November 29, 1844): n.p.; "Local," *Messenger* 17 (February 25, 1852): 4035; id., 16 (January 1, 1851): 3188; "Mr. Webster on the Colony of Liberia," id., 17 (March 10, 1852): 3444; and Douglas C. Stange, "Lutheran Involvement in the American Colonization Society," *Mid-America* 49 (April 1967): 142-4.

Managers of the Maryland chapter of the Society, and Charles Henkel served in a similar capacity in Ohio. Charles Porterfield Krauth was Secretary of the Shepherdstown, Virginia, chapter, and Peter Schaeffer was Vice-President for Frederick County, Maryland; in 1842 the Maryland Lutheran synod unanimously approved Schaeffer's resolution encouraging colonization. Lewis Eichelberger, pastor in Winchester, Virginia, published a sermon preached in 1830 and donated the profits to the American Colonization Society. (His text, Deuteronomy 8:18-20, was that God gives humans the "power to get wealth.") He praised the Society for opposing immediate abolition, which, he wrote, would make conditions for slaves much worse and ruin the country, whereas colonization, he predicted, would make blacks "independent and happy."[12]

Occasionally, support for colonization surfaced in smaller and newer denominations usually opposed it. The *Evangelical Messenger*, published by the Evangelical Association, printed an open letter to clergy from the president of the Pennsylvania Society,[13] and a Dunker Yearly Meeting permitted members to promote "the liberty of the African race" by contributing financially to the Society but did not sanction membership. A letter from a southern reader published in the *Gospel-Visiter*, the Dunker's periodical, argued that although free blacks in Virginia lived as poorly as slaves and blacks in free states fared little better, in Africa one hundred and fifty million people dwelled "in total heathenism, barbarism, ignorance, and wickedness, under the influence of the most superstitious idolatry." Thus bondage, the southern Dunker concluded, served God's purpose because freed slaves would be "pioneers," preparing Africa for civilization.[14]

Colonization, however, was more than an antidote for the

[12] Stange, "Lutheran Involvement in the American Colonization Society," 140-2, 146-8.

[13] Joseph R. Ingersoll, "To the Clergy of All Denominations in the State of Pennsylvania, in Behalf of the Pennsylvania Colonization Society," *Evangelical Messenger* 4 (June 9, 1851): 14. The *Messenger* also ran a reprint from the *Western New Yorker*, "African Colonization," 7 (February 1, 1854): 17-8.

[14] "A Voice from the South," *Gospel-Visiter*: 322-4; *Classified Minutes of Annual Conference of the Brethren: A History of the General Councils of the Church from 1778 to 1885* (Mt. Morris, Ill.: The Brethren Publishing Company, 1886), 378; and "Colonization," *Religious Telescope* 1 (May 20, 1835): 44.

barbarism of African jungles and, therefore, drew considerable praise as offering an alternative to abolitionist fanaticism. Lewis Eichelberger, although conceding that slavery was disgraceful, charged that abolition "by its moral guilt and sin" was so impractical as to be unthinkable. Pro-colonization Germans compared the antislavery campaign to radical movements, including socialism, women's rights, and bloomerism, which, one editor said, were "at bottom essentially infidel." He gleefully described the rebuke that free blacks in Massachusetts gave to Harriet Beecher Stowe for reneging on her promise to contribute financially to black education, running the story under the sarcastic headline, "Mrs. Stowe and Her Colored Friends." The *Messenger* also reported the denunciation that abolitionists Theodore Parker and Wendell Phillips received for "inflammatory speeches," allegedly resulting in the murder of a U.S. Army officer during the attempted rescue of Anthony Burns, a jailed runaway. Kurtz, the Lutheran, agreed that abolitionists scattered "firebrands throughout the community."[15]

While rebuking abolitionists, such moderates found kind words for slaveholders. The *Messenger* wrote that Anthony Burns was anxious to return home to his kindly master. Although Kurtz affirmed that his paper was no friend of slavery, he refused to chastise "a Christian brother" who merely happened to own black persons. Kurtz pointed out that many masters struggled to teach their slaves to read and write and to bring religion to them, partly by distributing Bibles. Such men, he wrote, often had "more of the graces and virtues of the Christian life" than their critics. He believed that those who frequently documented cruelty towards slaves often ignored the "religious and other advantages" bondsmen and -women enjoyed, including a death rate disproportionately lower than that of free blacks.[16]

Giving slaveholders the benefit of the doubt, Lutheran and Reformed leaders naturally discouraged support for antislavery legisla-

[15] "Radicalism and Infidelity," *Messenger* 18 (March 3, 1852): 3437; "Mrs. Stowe and Her Colored Friends," id., 19 (May 10, 1954): 4087; "Boston Riot," id., 19 (June 8, 1854): 5003; *Lutheran Observer* 4 (July 28, 1837): 194; and Stange, "Lutheran Involvement in the American Colonization Society," 147.

[16] *Lutheran Observer* 2 (February 1, 1833): 104; id., 18 (August 23, 1850): 339; "Remarks," *Messenger* 17 (March 10, 1852): 3445; and "News of the Week," id., 19 (June 15, 1854): 4107.

tion. The *Observer* chose silence during the national debate on the
Compromise of 1850, except to vigorously endorse the higher-law
concept that antislavery spokesperson William Seward articulated on the
Senate floor. Kurtz supported the return of fugitive slaves although he
used a German proverb to suggest that the law was overly stringent:
Zu scharf schneid't nicht, und zu spitzig sticht nicht (Too sharp doesn't
cut, and too pointy doesn't stick). The Lutheran editor decided,
"without a moment's hesitation," that resistance to such a law, even if
unconstitutional, was unthinkable. The Reformed publication regretted
that the Kansas-Nebraska bill "was agitated at all" and denounced the
Anti-Nebraska Remonstrance of three thousand New England clergy as
inappropriate behavior for preachers.[17]

Slavery's best friend among prominent Pennsylvania Germans was
probably Philip Schaff, the Reformed theologian at Mercersburg.
Schaff affirmed the "graces and virtues" of American bondage, which,
he said, was more ethical than servitude in ancient Rome; American
slavery was confined to the South and one-eighth of the population,
whereas Roman bondage covered the whole empire and one-half of its
inhabitants.   Furthermore, Schaff said, Romans enslaved people
regardless of race or color, but Americans based their system "on the
inferiority of the African race," banned foreign slave trade, and
encouraged religion among black persons. Schaff acknowledged abuses
in American slavery and considered selling human beings "repugnant
to the spirit of the Gospel," but he nevertheless joined the chorus that
applauded slavery for replacing heathenism with Christian civilization,
"an immense blessing" to the Africans. The New Testament, he said,
both "tolerates and ameliorates" slavery by injecting it with morality.
He was convinced that abolitionists secularized "the holy philanthropy
of the Gospel" and that benevolent masters could train "inferior races"
to govern themselves.   Neither did the Bible require emancipation,
define holding slaves as a sin, nor make church membership conditional
upon the renunciation of owning them. Schaff confessed that he could
not explain why innocent and guilty blacks alike felt the "special
severity" of the institution, but he still thought that northerners should

[17] "The Nebraska Bill," *Messenger* 19 (April 5, 1854): 4066; and *Lutheran Observer* 18 (December 13, 1850): 402.

refrain from meddling with it.[18]

Although theologians like Schaff and the border-state Lutherans found little Scriptural support to encourage freedom for enslaved blacks, the salvation of Africans concerned them greatly, as it did all Germans. A lengthy story about "Black Jerry" published in the *Lutheran Observer* and the *Evangelical Messenger*, the latter staunchly abolitionist, exemplified this. Jerry, a Maryland slave, became a fervent Christian when a minister requested worshippers to give the slave a seat and then preached directly to him "with all the simplicity he could muster." Tearfully, Jerry accepted the preacher's hand of fellowship and went home born again. But his master, Colonel Greenway, suspecting that this new life would make his bondsman disobedient and proud, forbad Jerry to pray. Jerry counterargued that every person ought to pray; then, perhaps confirming his master's fears of rebelliousness, admonished him, "Don't say dat, massa; sartinly prayin' wont make a nigga no wos." Jerry's prayers brought him a whipping, but his owner softened when he overheard Jerry appeal for the master's crops and children. He made Jerry chaplain of the house, and eventually the black man's witness at Sunday services brought about Colonel Greenway's conversion. Jerry and his master, so the story goes, were finally buried side by side, as brothers in Christ.[19]

Other moderates agreed that redeemed African Americans would go to heaven and labored to bring God's word to them. Black Lutheran congregations, founded by J. Jones, a black clergyman, appeared in Gettysburg, Chambersburg, and Philadelphia. Peter Schaeffer catechized a slave girl, but his congregation opposed her confirmation and requested that she come to communion last. When Charles Porterfield Krauth preached for two hours in a packed church building near Staunton, Virginia, he described listeners as "aided, abetted, and

---

[18] Schaff referred to Ephesians 6:5-9, Colossians 3:22-25 and 4:1, I Timothy 6:1-2, Titus 2:9-10, and I Peter 2:18-20. See Philip Schaff, *Slavery and the Bible: A Tract for the Times* (Chambersburg, Pa.: M. Kieffer, 1861), 1-32.

[19] *Lutheran Observer* 18 (August 16, 1850): 337; id., 18 (August 23, 1850): 341; "Black Jerry, the Praying Negro: A Story That Is No Fiction," *Evangelical Messenger* 3 (September 9, 1850): 68; and id., 3 (September 23, 1850): 72.

aggravatingly backed by a choir of black babies in the gallery. "[20]

German moderates, then, quietly acknowledged the abuses of slavery but refused to condemn the institution itself. They spurned abolitionists but demonstrated their compassion for slaves by occasionally nurturing black Christians and by promoting colonization, finding the latter both an act of benevolence and a balm for inflamed passions.

III

A few Germans rejected both colonization and abolitionism, denouncing each as impractical. Samuel S. Schmucker, for example, was a prominent Lutheran opponent of bondage, but his passion for denominational unity overshadowed his antislavery feelings. A Virginian who taught at the seminary in Gettysburg, Pennsylvania, Schmucker became a slaveholder through marriage and freed two of his slaves, but the third declined manumission.

Schmucker insisted that American slavery had no Biblical basis. He claimed that Old Testament servants, unlike American slaves, had religious rights equal to their masters, endured only a temporary bondage, bore arms, and ate at the master's table. They enjoyed marriages with legal recognition and sometimes married into the master's family. According to Schmucker, every human being belonged to the "same family" because God had created all nations from "one blood" (Acts 17:26). It was just as sinful to enslave other nations as to enslave one's brothers and sisters; skin color and cultural variation were inconsequential. Colonization he condemned because its sluggish pace doomed at least an entire generation of blacks to their "present grievous privations," and he believed that the New Testament, especially the Golden Rule, demanded that Christians explicitly ban slavery.

---

[20] James I. Good, *History of the Reformed Church in the U.S. in the Nineteenth Century* (New York: Board of Publication of the Reformed Church in America, 1911), 199; Charles Porterfield Krauth to his wife, May 11, 1852, *Charles Porterfield Krauth*, Adolf Spaeth, ed. (New York: Arno Press and The New York Times), 283-4; and Stange, "Lutheran Involvement in the American Colonization Society," 141.

Yet Schmucker held back from strongly criticizing slaveholders. He favored gradual emancipation despite his repudiation of colonization, writing in early editions of his book, *Elements of Popular Theology*, that advocates of "entire immediate abolition do not understand the subject." He prepared an antislavery resolution for the West Pennsylvania Synod, but it died when illness prevented him from attending. He then made the resolution the basis of a seminary lecture. Though Schmucker's home was reportedly a station on the underground railroad, he refused to join the antislavery society because he opposed its confrontational methods. If early Christians had criticized bondage, he asserted, Roman power would have snuffed out the very faith that would eventually destroy slavery. Antislavery agitation also damaged the ecumenism that he and other Pietists cherished. At an ecumenical gathering in London that created the Evangelical Alliance, Schmucker resisted a English suggestion to bar slaveholders from the organization because he believed that the membership test was divisive and irrelevant, that it would generate other political tests, and that the test inappropriately questioned the morality of conference participants.

Even though the Gettysburg professor tempered his criticism of slavery, he nonetheless suffered for his opinion. His opponents observed the silence on slavery, but they bitterly criticized his other positions, especially his encouragement of revivalism and opposition to confessionalism. Other Lutherans who rejected confessionalism escaped such scathing attacks, and fellow anti-confessionalists from the South allowed Schmucker to brave the storm alone because they considered him an abolitionist. During the Battle of Gettysburg he fled the seminary amidst reports that General Lee's men had singled him out for arrest; Confederate troops vandalized his home and scattered personal papers on the floor, tossed them out the windows, and trampled them in the mud. In contrast, a nearby colleague lost only a silver set, which he recovered after complaining to the Confederate Army.[21]

---

[21] Paul Phillip Kuenning, "American Lutheran Pietism, Activist and Abolitionist" (Ph.D. diss.: Marquette University, 1985), 208, 229-55, 268-73; Samuel S. Schmucker, *Elements of Popular Theology; with Occasional Reference to the Doctrines of the Reformation, as Avowed before the Diet at Augsburg, in MDXXX, Designed Chiefly for Private Christians and Theological Students* (Philadelphia: E. W. Miller, 1848), 332-6; and Abdel Ross Wentz, *Pioneer in Christian Unity: Samuel Simon Schmucker* (Philadelphia: Fortress Press, 1967), 269-76, 316, 322, 324, 326-30.

Like Schmucker, John Winebrenner, founder of the Church of God, condemned slavery but counseled moderation, especially later in his life. Winebrenner had been pastor of a German Reformed congregation in Harrisburg but left after quarrelling with his vestry over the new measures. After losing a vote in the synod, Winebrenner left the congregation to become an independent minister and conduct camp meetings and revivals in the Harrisburg area. About 1825 he led his followers into a new denomination, calling it the Church of God. They adopted baptism by immersion and feetwashing, partly because of Winebrenner's experience at a United Brethren camp meeting.[22]

Initially inclined towards colonization, Winebrenner became briefly an outspoken abolitionist. He was one of three managers of the local affiliate of the American Antislavery Society and edited a periodical, the *Publisher*, that printed news of the petition campaigns in Congress, various fugitive slave cases, the murder of abolitionist printer Elijah Lovejoy in Alton, Illinois, and the campaign to admit Texas into the Union as a slave state. Abolitionism, Winebrenner proclaimed, "aims at the destruction of a corrupt tree."

But soon he rejected the exclusion of slaveholders from church membership. He agreed with C. U. Harn that in northern Maryland many faithful ministers had washed the feet of slaveholders. (Conversely, some of Harn's Maryland neighbors branded him an abolitionist.) Winebrenner affirmed that those who loved others as Christ loved them would never cast members out of the church "for opinion's sake."

In the 1850s Winebrenner began calling himself a "liberal conservative." His journal, the *Advocate*, reported fugitive slave cases and Congressional debates, denounced kidnappings of free blacks, and defended such books as *Uncle Tom's Cabin* and Frederick Douglass's *My Bondage and My Freedom*. It reprinted a petition that 151 clergymen had signed against what Winebrenner called the "Nebraska iniquity." After listening to Stephen Douglas speak for ninety minutes, he decided that the "little giant" was "a good democrat, but a bad Christian." On the other hand, he published several articles favoring colonization and one that described the improving lifestyle of slaves in

[22] C. H. Forney, *History of the Churches of God in the United States of North America* (Harrisburg, Pa.: Publishing House of the Churches of God, 1914), 13-21, 41-3; and Richard Kern, *John Winebrenner: Nineteenth Century Reformer* (Harrisburg, Pa.: Central Publishing House, 1974), 23-48.

Virginia. He declared that critics of the Compromise of 1850 had "too much feeling and fire," and he counseled that "wrong legislation should never be set aside by resistance." In 1860 Winebrenner endorsed for president Simon Cameron, who lived in Harrisburg and allowed the Church of God to use his land for camp meetings. Winebrenner said he liked Cameron, a recent convert to free soil, because he opposed slavery's extension but pledged non-interference where it currently existed.

By 1858 many in the Church of God thought Winebrenner's position had become contradictory. He relinquished the editorship of the *Advocate* to his son-in-law, then openly feuded with him in a pamphlet, *Letter on Slavery*, proclaiming that the "real question [was] ultra and fanatical views." He admitted that slavery's abuses were immoral but insisted that the "ultra-abolition fraternity" could not justify its views, and he listed well-known religious leaders such as George Whitefield, William Ellery Channing, and Alexander Campbell, who believed that slavery enjoyed Biblical sanction. He still professed, however, that a faithful application of the gospel would kill the institution. His position by then had moved from abolition to moderation, though always without altering his fundamental conviction that slavery's abuses were sinful.[23]

Winebrenner and Schmucker, then, occupied a middle position between the colonizers and the antislavery Germans. They agreed with abolitionists that slavery occasioned sins for which colonization was unrealistic repentance, but they feared that attempts to purge bondage from the community of faith would only injure it.

IV

Other German Christians, particularly Anabaptists and the Wesleyan denominations, refused to compromise with slavery. If the church was to consist of those truly born anew, it could not, they believed, admit slaveholders to membership.

Statements and disciplines rejecting the institution became

---

[23] Forney, *Churches of God*, 81, 102-3; and Kern, *Winebrenner*, 93-139.

increasingly explicit after the American Revolution. As early as 1782 the Dunkers' Yearly Meeting banned slaveholders and participants in the slave trade from membership. They instructed "Brother John Van L.," who had purchased an African American woman many years previously (perhaps before he had become a member), that he must free her or, if she chose to stay with him, pay her wages. The meeting also required him to provide care and education for her four children until age twenty-one, then liberate them. Five years later the Yearly Meeting unanimously reconfirmed the decision to exclude slaveholders but allowed baptismal candidates to hold slaves long enough to recover the purchase price, after which slaves were to receive their freedom and a new suit of clothes, "as is given to a white servant." In 1812 the Brethren declared that both slavery and the slave trade "should be abolished as soon as possible," and the following year denounced, again unanimously, "making merchandise of souls" as among the "iniquities of Babylon." Yearly Meeting urged members to restrain, if possible, their children who were not yet members from buying slaves and directed members to liberate inherited slaves as soon as the congregation considered it "right and proper." In 1845 Dunkers decided that hiring slaves was "little better than purchasing" them. In 1853 another Yearly Meeting approved "after a lengthy discussion" the recommendation of a committee, which included southerners, that in states that outlawed free blacks, Brethren should help emancipated slaves purchase transportation to free territory. Other Dunker meetings affirmed these antislavery positions, citing the Scripture in Luke 6:31, "as you wish that men would do to you, do so to them."[24] Dunkers in Virginia sustained the denominational position although John Kline complained that the abolitionists within the denomination were impractical. A southern member, who supported colonization, acknowledged that the Brethren sometimes differed on tactics but affirmed that Dunkers on both sides of the Mason-Dixon Line opposed the institution; for the church, he said, "there is no north, no south."[25]

[24] Yearly Meeting considered slavery in 1782, 1797, 1812, 1813, 1837, 1845, 1846, 1853, 1854, 1857, 1862, 1863, and 1865. See *Classified Minutes*, 372-8.

[25] "A Voice from the South," *Gospel-Visiter* 6 (December 1856): 322; John Kline to George Shaver (February 1853), Roger E. Sappington, ed., *The Brethren in Virginia: The History of the Church of the Brethren in Virginia* (Harrisonburg, Va.: Committee for the Church of the Brethren History in Virginia, 1973), 62; and ibid., 63.

The Wesleyan denominations, like the Dunkers, explicitly disallowed slaveholding within the fellowship. Disciplines, published in 1809, 1817, 1821, and 1839, proscribed "under any pretence or condition whatsoever" slaveholding and "traffic in human beings."[26] The United Brethren required members to liberate any slaves they owned but allowed owners to recover the purchase price by hiring them out prior to manumission. A bishop acknowledged that several United Brethren in Virginia owned slaves in "peculiar circumstances" but claimed that even before the denomination banned slavery, congregations in Maryland and Virginia generally did not admit slaveholders to membership. The United Brethren suspected that their antislavery stance impeded mission work in slave states, and the Virginia conference may have feared that the postal service would confiscate the strongly abolitionist *Religious Telescope*. (One postmaster in northwestern Virginia had impounded it.) By a vote of 18-4 the conference established its own newspaper although it never implemented this decision.[27]

Winebrenner's Church of God also disfellowshipped slaveholders. Its first General Eldership met at Pittsburgh in 1846 and approved Winebrenner's draft condemning slavery as a "flagrant violation of the natural rights of man" and inconsistent with Christianity. A congregation in Greene County, Pennsylvania, excommunicated allegedly proslavery members who in the 1848 Presidential election voted for Lewis Cass (Democrat) or Zachary Taylor (Whig) instead of Free Soiler Martin Van Buren; Elder J. Hickernell restored the congregation to order only after several members withdrew. Winebrenner, as we have seen, had second thoughts about expelling slaveholders, but he could not persuade the East Pennsylvania Eldership to reverse its decision. Also contrary to Winebrenner's wishes, the Eldership eliminated

---

[26] Behney and Eller, *Evangelical United Brethren Church*, 146; and Eller, *These Evangelical United Brethren* (Dayton, Ohio: Otterbein Press, 1950), 72-3.

[27] A. W. Drury, *History of the Church of the United Brethren in Christ* (Dayton, Ohio: United Brethren Publishing House, 1931), 337-8; Paul R. Fetters, ed., *Trials and Triumphs: A History of the Church of the United Brethren in Christ* (Huntingdon, Ind.: Church of the United Brethren in Christ, 1894), 137; J. J. Glossbrenner, "Slavery in the United Brethren Church," *Religious Telescope* 7 (April 5, 1848): 283; and Patricia P. Hickin, "Antislavery in Virginia: 1831-1861" (Ph.D. diss.: University of Virginia, 1968), 439-40.

funds for Texas missionaries who threatened to baptize slaveholders.[28]

Journals became vigorous mouthpieces for the antislavery denominations, stressing the humanity of African Americans and the sinfulness of bondage. "Living up to the Divine rule," wrote a reader of the *Religious Telescope*, was never dangerous, and Henry Kurtz, editor of the *Gospel-Visiter*, observed that slavery was "no question at all" among the Dunkers because they agreed on its sinfulness. Even in slave states, he wrote, "hundreds, and perhaps thousands" of the Brethren agreed that slavery "was a great wrong." Others concluded that slavery was obnoxious to the God who made all nations "one blood," and that slavery was a sin and that sin was of the devil, whose works "Christ came to destroy." For antislavery Germans the Bible demanded that every bond "be rent, every shackle fall." Jesus, according to Luke 4:18, proclaimed "liberty to the captives."[29]

Secular arguments, particularly the doctrine of free labor, further persuaded many antislavery Germans, and they demanded that blacks receive the rights they deserved as "rational beings." Free labor, which came to dominate popular thought in the north, held that all persons have the opportunity to succeed or fail according to their ability to work, a basic right denied to bondsmen and -women. Thus African American hearts palpitated "with manly energy for the heaven-born privileges of Equal Rights," making slavery's greatest evil "its degradation of a man to a chattel, its robbery of manhood." The *Religious Telescope* denounced Virginia's slavery as resting on "the legal recognition of man as chattel," finding evidence in a Richmond newspaper's observations that slavery was "the only reliable means of liquidating debts." Free labor taught German abolitionists that slavery was inefficient as well as sinful; free workers in the middle states and even in thin-soiled New England outproduced the "sunny South," de-

---

[28] Forney, *Churches of God*, 68, 326-7, 330; and Kern, *Winebrenner*, 110-1, 121, 128, 135.

[29] "An Essay on Slavery" and "Remarks of the Editor," *Gospel-Visiter* 1 (January 1852): 158-9; "The Bible against Slavery," *Evangelical Messenger* 9 (July 23, 1856): 114-5; Andrew Funkhouser, "Is Slaveholding a Sin?" *Religious Telescope* 7 (December 24, 1847): 174; and W. R. Rhinehart, "Human Rights--Their Inviolability," id., 7 (August 19, 1857).

spite that region's valuable staples of cotton and tobacco.[30]

German publications often scorned southern life. To defend *Uncle Tom's Cabin* from the charge that slaveholders only whipped criminals or malingerers, not pious persons like Uncle Tom, the *Religious Telescope* printed an eyewitness account of the murder of a black preacher by two drunken Kentuckians; one of the sots allegedly had wagered that in thirty minutes he could "whip the religion out of any 'nigger' in the state." Another article, headlined "A Negro Hunt--Rare Southern Sport," recounted the chase of a fugitive slave and exemplified the Dixie-baiting that southerners detested.[31]

Strong antislavery sentiments also surfaced among Lutherans, Reformed, and Mennonites, although none of these communions took denominational action opposing the institution. In 1836 abolitionist Lutheran ministers in New York formed their own synod, named "Franckean" after August Hermann Francke. Members of that synod were also promoters of revival measures, and they eventually seceded from their parent denomination,[32] soon peppering the editor of the *Lutheran Observer* with letters supporting abolition. The Pittsburgh Lutheran synod became a second center of Lutheran antislavery sentiment, resolving in 1846 that slavery was "a moral and national evil" that deserved condemnation. In 1851 William A. Passavant, a pastor from that synod, led the Pittsburgh district in a boycott of the General Synod because of the presence of slaveholding delegates, and when the Lutherans from Pittsburgh returned to the General Synod,

---

[30] Andrew Funkhouser, "From Virginia," *Religious Telescope* 3 (February 7, 1838): 10-11; "Slavery in Virginia," id., new series 6 (June 9, 1847): 361; "Beauties of Slavery," id. (March 5, 1851): 108; "A Few Thoughts on Slavery," id., new series 1 (May 7, 1851); "Slavery and Its Appendages," *Evangelical Messenger* 1 (January 24, 1848): 8; "Free and Slave Labor," id. (March 22, 1848): 22; "Another Slave Case," id., 5 (June 23, 1852): 104; L. Kelly, "Slavery," id., 8 (April 4, 1855): 51; and Eric Foner, *Free Soil, Free Labor, Free Men: The Ideology of the Republican Party Before the Civil War* (New York: Oxford University Press, 1970).

[31] "A Negro Hunt--Rare Southern Sport," *Evangelical Messenger* 6 (October 12, 1853): 166-7; and "Uncle Tom," id. (December 8, 1852): 198.

[32] Other new abolitionist communions included the Wesleyan Methodist Connection, the American Baptist Free Mission Society, the Free Presbyterian Church, and the Progressive Friends.

they announced that their position on slavery remained unchanged.[33]

While Lutheran abolitionists tended to be revivalists, the most outspoken German Reformed opponent of slavery was an antirevivalist, John Nevin, Schaff's confessionalist colleague at the Mercersburg Seminary. Nevin was the only member of a German denomination to became an officer of a national abolition society. Born a Presbyterian, his antislavery views cost him the editorship of the *Friend*, a journal for young Presbyterians in Pittsburgh. His farewell editorial in 1835 denounced bondage as a sin involving the entire nation that "ought to be abolished." Colonization, Nevin charged, diverted attention from "the true question" and fostered "a most foolish and wicked prejudice" against blacks. Because of his outspokenness, a "prominent physician" accosted him in the street and condemned him as the most dangerous man in Pittsburgh.

Another antislavery German Reformed was Dr. George William Welker. A native of Pennsylvania and a graduate of the seminary at Mercersburg, Welker accepted a parish in North Carolina in 1841. Throughout the Civil War he remained a loyal Unionist, supported by most of his parishioners, though a dissenting faction charged that many of them were, like the pastor, "rank abolitionists."[34] And Jacob Eisenhower, a River Brethren of strong antislavery sentiment, named his son Abraham Lincoln Eisenhower; Abraham named his son, a future President, Dwight David.[35]

Because Mennonites employed a decentralized polity, official statements on the subject were few, but their leaders made clear their objections to slavery. In 1837 Peter Burkholder, then residing in Winchester, Virginia, wrote in his widely used confession that because "all are free in Christ," believers should not be slaveholders or

---

[33] William Herman Gehrke, "Negro Slavery among the Germans in North Carolina," *The North Carolina Historical Review* 14 (October 1937): 313-5; Robert Fortenbaugh, "American Lutheran Synods and Slavery, 1830-60," *JR* 13 (January 1933): 76-9, 85-6; *Lutheran Observer* 4 (August 3, 1837): n.p.; John R. McKivigan, *The War against Proslavery Religion: Abolitionism and the Northern Churches, 1830-1865* (Ithaca, N.Y.: Cornell University Press, 1984), 93; and E. Clifford Nelson, ed., *The Lutherans in North America* (Philadelphia: Fortress Press, 1975), 141-3, 239.

[34] Gehrke, "Negro Slavery among the Germans in North Carolina," 324.

[35] Carlton O. Wittlinger, *Quest for Piety and Obedience: The Story of the Brethren in Christ* (Nappanee, Ind.: Evangel Press, 1978), 532-3.

participate in the slave trade. In 1841 Joseph Funk of Singer's Glen, Virginia, lamented the "unhappy Negro traffick" and advised Mennonites "never to meddle with slavery." On July 4, 1856, John Funk, a Pennsylvania Mennonite, wrote in his diary of "the glorious event" that established "our great national independence." But slaves, he noted, still suffered "beneath the very folds" of the star-spangled banner. He urged freemen to "rise and draw the sword" on behalf of "our Brothers smarting beneath the cruel bond of oppression"--aggressive words for a Mennonite! During the Civil War, Mennonites living amidst military campaigns in the Shenandoah Valley courageously reaffirmed their "creed and discipline" prohibiting slavery. They refused to hire slaves unless the servant received the wages but accepted exchanges of labor with slave-owning neighbors.[36]

None of the antislavery German publications liked colonization. *The Religious Telescope* published a large chart to reveal the Colonization Society as a facade, or "shield," for slavery; it quoted colonization supporters who called free blacks "a nuisance," who condemned them to "remain forever a degraded caste," and who promised that colonization would "augment the value of property left behind."[37] Quinter in the *Gospel-Visiter* pointed out that during a nineteen-year period the Colonization Society had only transported 809 liberated slaves to Africa, equal to just over five days' increase of the slave population in America. He denounced those advocates of colonization who feared that free blacks would exert a subversive influence on slaves.[38]

But like the colonizers, antislavery Germans fondly recounted tales

---

[36] John Funk is quoted in James O. Lehman, "Mennonites in the North Face the Crisis of Civil War" (unpublished manuscript; Lancaster Mennonite Historical Society, 1982), 9. Joseph Funk (no relation) (March 22 and 26, 1841), is quoted in Willard M. Swartley, *Slavery, Sabbath, War, and Women: Case Studies in Biblical Interpretation* (Scottdale, Pa.: Herald Press, 1983), 287-8n151. See also Peter Burkholder, "Confession, Faith and Practice," *The Confession of Faith, of the Christians Known by the Name of Mennonites, in Thirty-Three Articles; With a ·Short Extract from Their Catechism*, trans. Joseph Funk (Winchester, Va.: Robinson and Hollis, 1837), 419; *Minutes of the Virginia Mennonite Conference*, 2 vols. (n.p.: Virginia Mennonite Conference, 1939; second ed., 1950), I, 6; and Swartley, *Slavery, Sabbath, War, and Women*, 55.

[37] "Colonization," *Religious Telescope* 1 (May 20, 1835): 44; and "The Shield of American Slavery," id., 3 (January 1, 1838): 4.

[38] James Quinter, "Remarks," *Gospel-Visiter* 6 (July 1856): 171.

of pious blacks. The *Evangelical Messenger* recorded the testimony of a elderly black woman at the grave of George Washington and told the story of a "respectable" white who sought instruction from a black preacher, "Uncle Jack," but received admonishment while the slave hoed corn on a warm summer day.[39]

Occasionally the antislavery denominations admitted African Americans to membership. The Evangelical Association received blacks as members by 1823. When locked out of a schoolhouse in Orwigsburg, Pennsylvania, John Seybert moved the meeting to a black man's home, which denominational historians celebrate as the birthplace of a major revival. Albright's people also met in a black residence in Allentown. Mennonites acquired black members more slowly; the Franconia conference in Eastern Pennsylvania did not have any until the 1930s.[40]

Dunkers believed that Jesus' command to preach the gospel "to all nations and races" meant that blacks should enjoy full membership in their communion. Yearly Meeting reminded congregations that a warning in the book of James against showing deference when seating wealthy worshippers also applied to race. They regretted that some of their white members (who were probably Virginians) felt "a repugnance" to greeting blacks with the holy kiss but counselled "colored members" to withhold it until these weak brothers and sisters became stronger and made the offer first. Moreover, the 1849 Yearly Meeting advised congregations not to deny members places at the Lord's table, which included feetwashing and the holy kiss, "on account of their color," but it nevertheless permitted local fellowships to make this decision.[41]

The most noteworthy nineteenth-century black Dunker was Sammy Weir, a Virginia slave freed when his master joined the Dunkers and rejected an offer of fifteen hundred dollars for his bonds-

---

[39] "An Old Negro's Religion," *Evangelical Messenger* 3 (May 8, 1850): 35; and "The Negro Preacher," id., 8 (July 25, 1855): 119.

[40] Albright, *A History of the Evangelical Association*, 231; and John L. Ruth, *Maintaining the Right Fellowship: A Narrative Account of Life in the Oldest Mennonite Community in North America* (Scottdale, Pa.: Herald Press, 1984), 220.

[41] James is quoted from the Revised Standard Version. See also *Classified Minutes of Annual Conference*, 162-3.

man. Out of gratitude for the communion responsible for his freedom, Weir applied for membership soon after his manumission, and in 1843 Peter Nead baptized him. Members received Weir with the right hand of fellowship but not a holy kiss. Because free blacks could not legally reside in Virginia, Weir left for Ohio, accompanied for protection by another Dunker, with a suit, horse, saddle, bridle, and cash given by his former master. The two arrived at the home of Thomas and Sarah Major, preachers in Scioto County, Ohio. The Paint Creek congregation welcomed Weir into its fellowship, and one of the families took him home because free blacks evidently had difficulty finding a place to live. In 1849, after a trial sermon before an all-white congregation, the Dunkers ordained Weir to preach among his own race.[42]

The political activity of antislavery Germans brought the same mixed results as their efforts to add African Americans to their membership rolls. Occasionally Germans participated in the abolitionist campaigns to petition Congress. A mid-1830s petition from Upper and Lower Providence Townships in Montgomery County included the signatures of Jacob Pennypacker and Jacob Hunsicker, both Mennonites, and James Quinter, the Dunker. The religious affiliation of several other Pennypackers on the document, perhaps related to Jacob, is unknown. John Winebrenner signed an 1838 petition, and Jacob Weidner, a German Reformed resident of Adams County, added his name to an Anti-Nebraska protest. In 1854 the East Pennsylvania Eldership of the Church of God advocated petitioning Congress for the repeal of both the Fugitive Slave Law and the Nebraska bill.[43] Several petitions from Potter County, near the New York border, and from Brady's Bend, a Scotch-Irish region east of Pittsburgh, contained names

---

[42] "The Life of Elder Samuel Weir: A Colored Brother," in Roger Sappington, ed. *The Brethren in the New Nation: A Source Book on the Development of the Church of the Brethren, 1785-1865* (Elgin, Ill.: Brethren Press, 1976), 265-72.

[43] "Memorial to the Senate and House of Representatives of the United States, in Congress Assembled," *Petitions and Memorials to the Congress of the United States*, Box 15, Legislative Records, Civil Archives Division, National Archives, Washington, D.C.; "Petition of James Wright and thirty of citizens of Dauphin County for the abolition of slavery in the District of Columbia," January 3, 1838, Box 22, id., "Remonstrance of Citizens of Adams Co., Penna., against the Nebraska Kansas Bill," April 7, 1854, Box 44, id.; Forney, *Churches of God*, 330; *History of Adams County, Pennsylvania* (Chicago: Warner, Beers and Co., 1886, reprinted 1980), 386; and Ruth, *Maintaining the Right Fellowship*, 238, 240.

of apparently recent German immigrants.[44]   Identifiable religious
leaders who signed an 1854 petition from Montgomery County against
the Kansas-Nebraska Act were Abraham Harley Cassell, a Dunker
bibliophile, Abraham Rosenberger, a Mennonite schoolteacher, John G.
Stauffer, who founded a Mennonite newspaper after the Civil War, and
John Hunsicker, deacon of an independent group of "Johnson Mennonites." Many others using Mennonite and Dunker surnames--including
Detweiler, Gratz, Hunsicker, Shearer, Markley, Krause, and Gerber--
placed their names on this petition although they are otherwise unidenti-
fiable.[45]

As a rule, however, Germans did not enlist in the great petition
campaigns. Almost all of the petitions from southeastern Pennsylvania,
with its large German populace, were Quaker. The only petitions from
Lancaster County--one from the city and the other from Quakers near
the Maryland border--contained only a few recognizably German names
and none of their religious leaders.[46]

Another political weapon that antislavery Germans sometimes used
was the ballot box, but evidence of activity is thin. John Funk, the
Mennonite, attended a rally for the Republican candidate, John C.
Fremont, and recommended that Mennonites vote for him, striking a

[44] The signatures are in *schrift* and liberally use umlauts, indicating that little
anglicization had occurred. See "Remonstrance signed by about 500 citizens of
Armstrong County, Pa., against the passage of the Nebraska-Kansas Bill," April 7, 1854,
Petitions and Memorials, Box 44; "A petition of Citizens of Abbott Township,
Pennsylvania, for the abolition of slavery in the Territories," March 3, 1854, id.,
"Remonstrance of H. Nixon and 77 other citizens of Pennsylvania against the Repeal of
the Missouri Compromise," id.; and an untitled, undated petition from Armstrong
County, ibid.

[45] "The petition of Citizens of Penn-a against the repeal of the Mo. Compromise,"
February 28, 1854, id. Other Mennonites were Abraham Meyer and Isaac Kratz. Three
Jacob Moyers were alive when one of them signed a petition: a bishop who died in 1859,
a trustee of the Towamencin congregation, and a Funkite Mennonite with a meetinghouse
on his property. See Ruth, *Maintaining the Right Fellowship*, 153, 284, 304, 350; J. C.
Wenger, *History of the Mennonites of the Franconia Conference* (Telford, Pa.: Franconia Mennonite Historical Society, 1937), 135, 326, 358, 360; and Theodore W. Bean,
ed., *History of Montgomery County, Pennsylvania* (Philadelphia: Everts and Park, 1884),
1069.

[46] "Against the Repeal of the Missouri Compromise," April 18, 1854, *Petitions and
Memorials*, Box 44. Also see other petitions in Boxes 15 and 37.

"blow for our freedom, and our Fremont." He repeated an attack made at the Republican rally on "the Democracy, Buchananites, nigger worshippers, and all others opposed to Freedom, Free Kansas, Free Speech, and Fremont." In 1848 the *Evangelical Messenger* elevated minor antislavery factions to the status of national political parties by including the Barnburners, Abolitionists, and Liberty Party in a list of national tickets, and in the next decade it printed the entire platform of the Know Somethings, an antislavery contingent that walked out on the nativist Know Nothing party. Voting patterns are difficult to discern, but Mennonite townships in Montgomery County cast ballots for Republicans during the Civil War despite threats of violence, and Mennonites in Lancaster County apparently contributed to large majorities for Congressman Thaddeus Stevens. In 1863 a meeting in Manheim, Lancaster County, complained of Dunkers and Mennonites who voted for abolitionists.[47]

Germans also made minor contributions to the underground railroad. Authorities arrested Daniel Kauffman for sheltering thirteen slaves in his barn in Boiling Springs, Pennsylvania, and transported them north. Kauffman's co-conspirators were Philip Brechbill, his brother-in-law, who was probably a Lutheran, and Stephen Weakley, an Irish abolitionist. The dragnet that followed the Christiana, Pennsylvania, riot in 1851 caught Samuel Kendig, who was for forty-four years a Mennonite deacon in southern Lancaster County. Two other Mennonites, Christian Frantz and Augustus W. Cain, were conductors on the underground railroad near Christiana.[48]

---

[47] Funk is quoted in Lehman, *Mennonites in the North*, 3-4. See also *Evangelical Messenger* (July 8, 1848): 51; "National Platform of the Know Somethings," id., 8 (July 11, 1855): 112; Lehman, *Mennonites in the North*, 9, 26B, 245-51, 253-4; and Andrew Robertson, "The Idealist as Opportunist: An Analysis of Thaddeus Stevens' Support in Lancaster County, 1843-1866," *Lancaster County Historical Society Journal* 84 (Spring 1980): 84-5, 98.

[48] For a Germanless survey of prominent antislavery people, see McKivigan, *The War against Proslavery Religion*, 623-780. See also Charles L. Blockson, *The Underground Railroad in Pennsylvania* (Jacksonville, N.C.: Flame International, 1981), 14-5, 55-6, 79, 97; William H. Siebert, *The Underground Railroad from Slavery to Freedom* (Gloucester, Mass.: Peter Smith, 1898; reprinted 1968), 102, 120-3; William Still, *The Underground Railroad: A Record of Facts, Authentic Narratives, Letters, etc.* (Philadelphia: Porter and Coates, 1872), 355; Conway P. Wing, *History of Cumberland County, Pennsylvania, With Illustrations* (Philadelphia: James D. Scott, 1879), 218-9;

Those who hid runaways or washed the feet of African Americans marched counter to the rabid racism prevalent in popular American thought. Northern states denied jury duty and the ballot box to blacks and assigned them to segregated schools and railroad cars. Most northerners often assumed that if slaves gained freedom, the only possible outcome, other than racial warfare, was miscegenation, or "amalgamation," as the white supremacists put it. Even some abolitionists considered blacks to be inferior. William Lloyd Garrison's newspaper, *Liberator*, the best-known and most radical antislavery journal, remarked that nature had branded blacks "with a perpetual mark of disgrace." Not surprisingly, then, attempts to assist African Americans often met resistance. When abolitionists in New Haven, Connecticut, proposed the establishment of a black college, citizens overwhelmingly denounced it. Prudence Crandall's intention to open a boarding school for black girls in Canterbury, Connecticut, triggered the outrage of the locals, who imprisoned her and vandalized her building.

Racism was equally strong in American politics. During the 1850s Democrats frequently smeared Republicans as abolitionists who belonged to a "Nigger party." In Indiana young women marched in a Democratic parade with a banner that read, "Fathers, save us from nigger husbands," and Democrats spread the rumor that Hannibal Hamlin, Lincoln's running mate in 1860, was a mulatto, expecting the accusation to be politically potent. Republicans typically responded to race-baiting by ignoring the issue as irrelevant or by claiming to despise blacks as much as anyone. Free soilers in both parties suggested that keeping the territories free of slaves would prevent amalgamation and that their purpose was to aid whites, not blacks. David Wilmot, the Pennsylvania Congressman who introduced free soil legislation to ban slavery from territory acquired from Mexico, called his proposal the "White Man's Proviso," and New York Barnburners seemed more opposed to "black slaves" than to the institution of

and n. a., *1886 History of Cumberland County, Pennsylvania: Originally Published as History of Cumberland and Adams Counties, With Complete Index* (Chicago: Warner, Beers and Co., 1886; reprinted 1977), 549-50.

slavery.[49]

Even in Philadelphia, the hub of Quaker antislavery activism, racist feelings rose steadily after the War of 1812. Intellectuals reasoned that blacks were innately inferior, outside the social contract described in the Declaration of Independence and, therefore, not entitled to citizenship. When blacks organized an African Fire Association, white companies forced it to disband. White Philadelphians stereotyped blacks as dirty, ignorant, and degraded, and satirized and occasionally assaulted free blacks who exhibited middle-class behavior and dress. Whites decorated their walls with popular lithograph caricatures that lampooned the social pretensions of blacks. These typically featured ape-like persons, wildly overdressed and uttering malaprops. In one, a black man, with top hat, walking stick, and gold chains, asks Miss Chloe, "How do you find youself dis hot weader?" Miss Chloe, adorned in an enormous hoop skirt, balloon sleeves as large as watermelons, and an umbrella-sized hat, replied, "Pretty well i tank you Mr. Cesar only I aspire too much!"[50]

Although many religious organizations avoided such vulgar racism, they provided minimal assistance for slaves. The Presbyterians and the Disciples of Christ refused to condemn slavery or individual participants as sinful. Many of the Disciples of Christ, Congregationalists, and Unitarians favored colonization. The Universalists opposed slavery but only appealed to the conscience of slaveholders. While antislavery Germans excommunicated slaveholders, white Baptists and Disciples of Christ purged abolitionists from influential positions in missionary and publication societies. Catholics and Episcopalians practiced a liturgical faith that seemed to exclude slavery as a religious issue. Catholics forbad discriminatory practices, but Catholic and Episcopal bishops prohibited their clergy from participating in abolition organizations. Although Methodists suffered schism over slavery, the northern denomination did not become more outspoken after their southern co-religionists departed. Parker Pillsbury, an antislavery

---

[49] Foner, *Free Soil, Free Labor, Free Men*, 260-7; and Leonard L. Richards, *"Gentlemen of Property and Standing": Anti-Abolition Mobs in Jacksonian America* (New York: Oxford University Press, 1970), 30-46.

[50] Gary B. Nash, *Forging Freedom: The Formation of Philadelphia's Black Community, 1720-1840* (Cambridge, Mass.: Harvard University Press, 1988), 223-7, 254-9.

Congregationalist, lost his license to preach, and Stephen S. Foster, also a preacher in that denomination, was expelled by his congregation in Hanover, New Hampshire. Only Quakers, who dominated abolition societies, and Freewill Baptists, who ordained blacks and banned slaveholders, took a vigorous antislavery position, although several denominations adopted stronger statements after 1845.[51]

In contrast to most northern Protestants, antislavery Germans concluded that slavery was a sin that believers could not tolerate. Although their political witness was usually restrained, their otherwise persistent efforts to rid American society of slavery were by contemporary standards conspicuous.

V

Several factors influenced the German interaction with slavery. Many antislavery Germans were revivalists, including the United Brethren, Evangelical Association, Winebrennarian Church of God, and Franckean Lutherans; some Mennonites also found revivalism attractive, and nineteenth-century Dunkers endorsed the new birth though denouncing camp meeting practices. The great opponent of revivalism, Philip Schaff, by contrast, favored colonization. Running counter to the correlation between evangelicalism and antislavery, however, were John Nevin, who was a confessionalist and an abolitionist, and the *Lutheran Observer*, which endorsed both revivals and colonization.

The notion of separation from "the world" further contributed to an antislavery position. It must have been easier for Dunkers and Mennonites to take a nonconformist antislavery position than for more socially mainstream groups, for in their own way they were come-outers long before the term became associated with slavery. Anti-elitist Wesleyans similarly considered themselves outsiders and thus found it easier to attack traditional race relations. Pietism and Anabaptism, moreover, stressed ethics and compassion as integral to a new-born Christian's daily life.

On the other hand, geographical distribution of membership had

---

[51] McKivigan, *The War against Proslavery Religion*, 25-32, 50-3, 67, 86-91, 163-4.

little influence on denominational positions on slavery. Lutherans and Reformed worried about sectionalism dividing their fellowship, but Mennonites, United Brethren, and Dunkers managed a degree of unified opposition to slavery despite having southern congregations. Perhaps smaller denominations found harmony easier.

Thus Pietism's egalitarian salvation process influenced the reponse of most Pennsylvania Germans to bondage. All agreed that the doctrine of freewill conversion applied equally to blacks and whites, a conclusion that elevated the spiritual, but not always temporal, status of African Americans. Even Germans who favored colonization usually exemplified the more benign wing of that movement, stressing its charitable impact on African Americans, which in the context of northern negrophobia was progressive. Other German Pietists joined the tiny minority of northerners who demanded on moral grounds the immediate end to slavery, demonstrating that Pietism's ability to remove distinctions between persons remained powerful.

CONCLUSION

Kummt tsoo Yaisoos

Although intolerance, particularly directed towards non-Protestants, has persisted throughout American history, a parallel tradition of tolerance and variety has become increasingly popular. As diversity rose to new levels of complexity in the early nineteenth-century Ohio Valley, for example, tensions often failed to expand correspondingly, and in the South camp meetings transcended denominations in the same way that "big meetings" did for Pennsylvania Germans. Later in the century liberal and conservative Protestants alike practiced interdenominational cooperation though usually not with each other. Social Gospel enthusiasts cut across denominational lines to apply the Bible to contemporary problems, mission workers collaborated to Christianize the world, and conservative evangelists, such as D. L. Moody and Billy Sunday, persuaded congregations of differing denominations to unite in supporting their efforts. By the late twentieth century the ability to see commonality across denominational, ethnic, racial, and class lines became routine among Protestants and Catholics, as ideology, perhaps the last bastion of intolerance, became the greatest determinant of religious loyalty. In modern fellowships with Pennsylvania German roots, progressive Anabaptists, for example, move comfortably among fellow liberals in the mainline while bitter feuds between conservative and liberal co-religionists threaten to split denominations and conferences.[1]

---

[1] Dickson C. Bruce, Jr., *And They All Sang Hallelujah: Plain-Folk Camp-Meeting Religion, 1800-1845* (Knoxville: University of Tennessee Press, 1974), 51-3; Robert T. Handy, *A Christian America: Protestant Hopes and Historical Realities* (New York: Oxford University Press, 1984, second ed.), 111-20, 147-51; William G. McLoughlin, Jr., *Modern Revivalism: Charles Grandison Finney to Billy Graham* (New York: The Ronald Press, 1959), 37-8, 54, 60,136, 150, 221, 422-5; Timothy L. Smith, "The Ohio Valley: Testing Ground for America's Experiment in Religious Pluralism," *Church*

Thus, despite the trend towards tolerance, consensus remains illusive, and modern religion still resembles a quilt or rainbow rather than a melting pot, much like the patchwork pattern among the eighteenth and early nineteenth-century Pennsylvania Germans. In fact, the denominational loyalty of German Christians increased, and Pennsylvania's abundant denominations and ethnic groups have reminded some historians of a Babel of religions.[2] Noah's ark, however, is the more appropriate Old Testament metaphor because in Pennsylvania, unlike at the ancient tower, a pluralistic population--from hermits who opposed all church structure to traditionalists seeking to recreate Europe's ecclesiology--co-existed despite disagreements. Among such a diverse population differences were almost inevitable, and German Christians often argued over the new measures and their emotional consequences or other controversies, such as Zinzendorf's scheme, paid clergy, or adult baptism. Not all Pietists embraced tolerance; those who were Anabaptists struggled with the impact of cooperation on the fellowship of believers as a separate community. Nevertheless, in Pennsylvania all fellowships, even the Radical Pietists and Anabaptists with their determined disdain for the mainstream, enjoyed tolerance.

Of course, tolerance was often unintentional, arising from conditions in early Pennsylvania. Sometimes institutional weaknesses made cooperation a logical choice; a dearth of ministers encouraged the sharing of preachers and the lack of meetinghouses facilitated union churches and schools. Furthermore, in the young colony the older, traditional denominations were too weak to effectively frustrate the new order. While Pietism became popular on both sides of the Atlantic in the eighteenth century, it spread almost unchecked in Pennsylvania because of Quaker attitudes towards dissenters--Penn, in fact, recruited them--and because the opponents of Pietism lacked the institutional

History 60 (December 1991): 461-79; Ronald C. White, Jr., and C. Howard Hopkins, *The Social Gospel: Religion and Reform in Changing America* (Philadelphia: Temple University Press, 1976), 202-13; and Robert Wuthnow, *The Restructuring of American Religion: Society and Faith since World War II* (Princeton, N. J.: Princeton University Press, 1988), 218-22.

[2] Dietmar Rothermund, *The Layman's Progress: Religious and Political Experience in Colonial Pennsylvania, 1740-1770* (Philadelphia: University of Pennsylvania Press, 1961), 12.

strength they enjoyed elsewhere. Organizers, who remained attached to European-style polity and who opposed Pietism, like Johann Philip Boehm, complained about the abundance of dissenters but realistically could do little about them.

In addition to happenstance, religion influenced the behavior of Pennsylvania Germans. The doctrine of the new birth permeated popular thought in Pennsylvania, inspiring believers as disparate as separatists by the Wissahickon, Henry M. Muhlenberg's multi-ethnic Lutheran congregations, and nineteenth-century camp meeting enthusiasts. This widely accepted conversion process frequently deemphasized social and racial distinctions among believers. Nineteenth-century revivalists sang and preached in a popular, vernacular style and expressed pride in the simplicity of their apparel and theology. Some Pietists enlarged their egalitarianism to include members of another race; the Dunker's Yearly Meeting even criticized members who refused to greet black Brethren with the holy kiss.

Most importantly, the belief that God democratically offered salvation to every man and woman who chose to accept it eroded intolerance. Most Pietists, despite their committment to denomination building, subordinated dogma and denominational loyalty to the state of the soul and became forces for tolerance. Nondenominational and bilingual worship flourished among them. Hymns, devotional literature, and schools enjoyed interdenominational and ethnic exchanges. Itinerants, ignoring denominational labels, shared lodgings and preaching platforms. Pennsylvania Germans created a religious landscape remarkably similar to modern America: characterized by division, sometimes severe, yet a maintaining a level of tolerance that promoted understanding among denominations, especially those inclined towards Pietism. Many Pennsylvania Christians lived together and often collaborated with one another despite their differences.

A favorite chorus of nineteenth-century revivalists expressed simply and directly the tolerant theology responsible for their society. Sung to the tune of "O My Darling, Clementine," or the parody, "Found a Peanut," it repeated the simple call of August Hermann Francke, the seventeenth-century German theologian, for all to come to Jesus, but now in the Pennsylvania Dutch vernacular.

Kummt tsoo Yaisoos, kummt tsoo Yaisoos,
Kummt tsoo Yaisoos grawd nou!

Grawd nou kummt tsoo Yaisoos,
Kummt tsoo Yaisoos grawd nou!

(Come to Jesus, come to Jesus,
Come to Jesus right now!
Right now come to Jesus,
Come to Jesus right now!)[3]

[3] Don Yoder, *Pennsylvania Spirituals* (Lancaster, Pa.: Pennsylvania Folklife Society, 1961), 16, 256.

Bibliography

Manuscripts

Egle, William Henry. *Pennsylvania Archives*. Harrisburg: Commonwealth of Pennsylvania, 1897.

National Archives. Petitions and Memorials to Congress. Legislative Records, Civil Archives Division.

Confessions, Diaries, Journals, etc.

Bender, Harold S., ed. "Palatine Mennonite Census Lists, 1664-1774." *Mennonite Quarterly Review* 14 (January 1940): 5-40.

Boehm, Henry. *The Patriarch of One Hundred Years: Being Reminiscences, Historical and Biographical of Rev. Henry Boehm.* Joseph B. Wakely, ed. Lancaster, Pa.: Nelson and Phillips, 1866.

Bowman, Peter. *A Testimony of Baptism, as Practiced by the Primitive Christians, from the Time of the Apostles.* Baltimore, Md.: Benjamin Edes, 1831.

Braun, Johannes. *Circular-Schreiben an die Deutschen Einwohner von Rockingham und Augusta, und den benachbarten Counties.* Harrisonburg, Va.: Laurentz Wartman, 1818.

Burkholder, Christian. *Useful and Edifying Address to the Young on True Repentence, Saving Faith in Christ Jesus, Pure Love, etc.* Lancaster, Pa.: 1857.

Burkholder, Peter. *The Confession of Faith, of the Christians Known by the Name of Mennonites, in Thirty-Three Articles; With a Short Extract from Their Catechism.* Winchester, Va.: Robinson and Hollis, 1837.

—————. *Christian Spiritual Conversation on Saving Faith, for the Young in Questions and Answers, and A Confession of Faith, of the Mennonites.* Trans. Joseph Funk. Lancaster, Pa.: John Baer and Sons, 1857.

Dreisbach, John. *Diary, 1817-1818.* Typewritten manuscript, Commission on Archives and History, The United Methodist Church.

Funk, John E. *The Mennonite Church and Her Accusers: A Vindication of the Character of the Mennonite Church of America from Her First Organization in This Country to the Present Time.* Elkhart, Ind.: Mennonite Publishing Company, 1878.

Godschalk, Abraham. *A Description of the New Creature.* Doylestown, Pa.: William M. Large, 1838.

Hamilton, Kenneth G., trans. and ed. *The Bethlehem Diary: Volume I, 1742-1744.* Bethlehem, Pa.: Archives of the Moravian Church, 1971.

Herr, Francis. "A Short History of the Written Word of God, Likewise of the Christian Baptism and the Peaceable Kingdom of Christ, to the People Called Quakers." Typewritten manuscript, Lancaster Mennonite Historical Society, 1790.

Herr, John. *Complete Works, Comrising the Way to Heaven, the Illustrating Mirror.* Buffalo, N.Y.: Peter Paul and Bro., 1890.

Hershey, Jacob. *Confession of Jacob Hershey.* N.p., 1825.

Huber, Samuel. *Autobiography of the Rev. Samuel Huber, Elder in the Church of the United Brethren in Christ, Containing Sketches of His Life, and Religious Experiences.* Chambersburg, Pa.: M. Kieffer and Company, 1858.

Hughes, Thomas. *A Journal by Thos. Hughes: For his Amusement, and Designed only for his Perusal by the time he attains the Age of 50 if he lives so long (1778-1789).* Port Washington, N.Y.: Kennikat Press, 1947, reissued 1970.

Kelpius, Johannes. *The Diarium of Magister Johannes Kelpius.* Julius Friedrich Sachse, ed. Lancaster, Pa.: The Pennsylvania German Society, 1917.

————. *A Method of Prayer.* E. Gordon Alderfer, intro. and ed. New York: Harper and Brothers, 1951.

Lamech and Agrippa. *Chronicon Ephratense: A History of the Community of Seventh Day Baptists at Ephrata, Lancaster County, Pennsylvania.* Lancaster, Pa.: S. H. Zahn, 1889.

Longenecker, Christian. "On True Conversion and New Birth." Vernard Eller, ed. and trans. *Brethren Life and Thought* 7 (Spring 1962): 23-34.

Mittelberger, Gottlieb. *Journey to Pennsylvania.* Cambridge, Mass.: Harvard University Press, 1960.

Muhlenburg, Henry Melchior. *The Journals of Henry Melchior Muhlenburg.* Theodore G. Tappert, ed. Philadelphia: Muhlenberg Press, 1942-1958.

Nead, Peter. *Theological Writings on Various Subjects: Or a Vindication of Primitive Christianity as Recorded in the Word of God.* Dayton, Ohio: 1866.

Nevin, John. *The Anxious Bench: A Tract for the Times.* Reading, Pa.: Daniel Miller, 1892.

Newcomer, Christian, *The Life and Journal of Christian Newcomer, Late Bishop of the Church of the United Brethren in Christ.* John Hildt, ed. Hagerstown, Md.: F. G. W. Kapp, 1834.

Newman, George Fredrick, and Clyde Lester Groff. *Letters from Our Palatine Ancestors, 1644-1689.* Hershey, Pa.: Gary T. Hawbaker, 1984.

Sauer, Christopher. *Von Georg Weitfields Predigten.* Germantown, Pa.: 1740.

Sangmeister, Ezechiel. "Life and Conduct of the Late Brother Ezechiel Sangmeister." Trans. Barbara M. Schindler. Ephrata, Pa.: Historical Society of the Cocalico Valley, 1986.

Schaff, Philip. *Slavery and the Bible: A Tract for the Times.* Chambersburg, Pa.: M. Kieffer, 1861.

Schmucker, S. Samuel. *Elements of Popular Theology; with Occasional Reference to the Doctrines of the Reformation, as Avowed before the Diet at Augsburg, in MDXXX, Designed Chiefly for Private Christians and Theological Students.* Philadelphia: E. W. Miller, 1848.

Simons, Menno. *The Complete Writings of Menno Simons, c. 1496-1561.* Scottdale, Pa.: Herald Press, 1956.

Spangenburg, August Gottlieb. *An Exposition of Christian Doctrine as Taught in the Protestant Church of the Untied Brethren, or, Unitas Fratrum.* Benjamin La Trobe, preface. Bath: S. Hazard, 1796.

Spener, Philipp Jacob. *Pia Desideria.* Philadelphia: Fortress Press, 1964.

Weiss, George Michael. *Der in der americanischen Wildnusz unter Menschen von verschiedenenen Nationen und Religionen hin und wieder herum Wandelte und verschiedentlich angesochtene Prediger.* Philadelphia: Andrew Bradford, 1729.

Whitefield, George. *George Whitefield's Journals (1737-1741): To*

Which Is Prefixed His "Short Account" (1746) and "Further Account" (1747). Intro. William V. Davis. Gainesville, Fla.: Scholars' Facsimiles and Reprints, 1969.

Disciplines and Minutes

Breyfogel, S.C. *Landmarks of the Evangelical Association, Containing All the Official Records of the Annual and General Conferences from the Days of Jacob Albright to the Year 1840.* Reading, Pa.: Eagle Book Printing, 1888.

Church Book: Zion Evangelical Lutheran Church, Manheim, Lancaster County, Pennyslvania. Photocopy at the Lancaster County Mennonite Historical Society.

Classified Minutes of Annual Conference of the Brethren: A History of the General Councils of the Church from 1778 to 1885. Mt. Morris, Ill.: The Brethren Publishing Company, 1886.

Doctrine and Discipline of the United Brethren in Christ. Hagerstown, Md.: Gruber and May, 1819.

Minutes and Letters of the Coetus of the German Reformed Congregations in Pennsylvania, 1747-1792. Philadelphia: Reformed Church Board, 1903.

Minutes of the Annual and General Conferences of the United Brethren in Christ, 1800-1818. Dayton, Ohio: United Brethren Historical Society, 1897.

Minutes of the Virginia Mennonite Conference, Including Some Historical Data, A Brief Biographical Sketch of Its Founders and Organizers, and Her Official Statement of Christian Funamentals, Constitution, and Rules and Discipline. 2 vols. N.p.: Virginia Mennonite Conference, 1939; 2nd ed., 1950.

Spaeth, A., H. E. Jacobs, and G. F. Spieker, eds. *Documentary History of the Evangelical Lutheran Ministerium of Pennsylvania and Adjacent States: Proceedings of the Annual Conventions from 1748 to 1821.* Philadelphia, Pa.: Evangelical Lutheran Church, 1898.

Newspapers and Periodicals

Der Christliche Botschafter
Evangelical Messenger
Gospel-Visiter
Messenger
Lutheran Observer
Pensylvanische Berichte
Reformed Messenger
Religious Telescope

Encyclopedias

The Brethren Encyclopedia. Donald F. Durnbaugh, ed.   3 vols. Philadelphia: Brethren Encyclopedia, Inc., 1984.
The Mennonite Encyclopedia: A Comprehensive Reference Work on the Anabaptist-Mennonite Movement.   4 vols.   Hillsboro, Kan.: Mennonite Brethren Publishing House, 1955-1959.

Dissertations and Theses

Bowman, Carl Frederick.   "Beyond Plainness: Cultural Transformation in the Church of the Brethren from 1850 to the Present." Ph.D. diss.: University of Virginia, 1989.
Frantz, John B. "Revivalism in the German Reformed Church in the United States to 1850, With Emphasis on the Eastern Synod." Ph.D. diss.: University of Pennsylvania, 1961.
Hickin, Patricia P. "Antislavery in Virginia: 1831-1861." Ph.D. diss.: University of Virginia, 1968.
Kuenning, Paul Phillip. "American Lutheran Pietism, Activist and Abolitionist." Ph.D. diss.: Marquette University, 1985.
Longenecker, Stephen L. "Democracy's Pulpit: Egalitarianism and Pietism among Early Pennsylvania Germans."   Ph.D. diss.: Johns Hopkins University, 1989.
Macauley, Howard K.   "A Social and Intellectual History of Elementary Education in Pennsylvania to 1850." Ph.D. diss.: University of Pennsylvania, 1972.

Pletcher, Nuba M. "Some Chapters from the History of the Rhine Country." Ph.D. diss.: Columbia University Press, 1907.

Pottieger, Cecil P. E. "The History and Influence of the Evangelical Church in Monroe County; the Third Class Founded by Jacob Albright (Phillips Class): A Treatise of the Existing and Defunct Evangelical Churches in the County." Master's Thesis: Lutheran Theological Seminary, Philadelphia, 1953.

Pritzker-Ehrlich, Marthi. "Michael Schlatter von St. Gallen (1716-1790), Eine Biographische Untersuchung zur Schweizerischen Amerika-Auswanderung des 18. Jahrhunderts." Ph.D. diss.: Universität Zürich, 1981.

Saltzman, Herbert Royce. "A Historical Study of the Function of Music Among the Brethren in Christ." Ph.D. diss.: University of Southern California, 1964.

Wokeck, Marianne. "A Tide of Alien Tongues: The Flow and Ebb of German Immigration to Pennsylvania, 1683-1776." Ph.D. diss.: Temple University, 1982.

Selected Books

This list omits many works cited only once in the book, particularly those which do not study Pennsylvania Germans but which have been used for comparative purposes. The notes contain full bibliographic information for each source upon first citation in each chapter.

Alderfer, E.G. *The Ephrata Commune: An Early American Counterculture.* Pittsburgh: University of Pittsburgh Press, 1985.

Appel, Theodore. *The Life and Work of John Williamson Nevin.* Philadelphia: Reformed Church Publication House, 1889.

Barker, Verlyn L. *John W. Nevin: His Place in American Intellectual Thought.* Saint Louis University, 1970.

Barthel, Diane L. *Amana: From Pietist Sect to American Community.* Lincoln, Neb.: University of Nebraska Press, 1984.

Bean, Theodore W., ed. *History of Montgomery County, Pennsylvania.* Philadelphia: Everts and Park, 1884.

Behney, J. Bruce, and Paul H. Eller. *The History of the Evangelical United Brethren Church.* Nashville, Tenn.: Abingdon Press,

1979.

Bender, Harold S. *Mennonite Origins in Europe.* Akron, Pa.: Mennonite Central Committee, 1957.

Berger, D. *History of the Church of the United Brethren in Christ.* New York: The Christian Literature Company, 1894.

Bonomi, Patricia U. *Under the Cope of Heaven: Religion, Society, and Politics in Colonial America.* New York: Oxford University Press, 1986.

Braudel, Fernand. *Capitalism and Material Life, 1400-1800.* New York: Harper and Row, 1973.

Brown, Dale W. *Understanding Pietism.* Grand Rapids, Mich.: William B. Eerdmans Publishing Company, 1975.

Brumbaugh, Martin Grove. *A History of the German Baptist Brethren in Europe and America.* Mount Morris, Ill.: Brethren Publishing House, 1899.

Brunk, Harry Anthony. *History of Mennonites in Virginia.* 2 vols. Harrisonburg, Va.: Published by the author, 1959.

Butler, Jon. *Power, Authority, and the Origins of American Denominational Order: The English Churches in the Delaware Valley, 1680-1730.* Philadelphia: Transactions and Proceedings of the American Philosophical Society, February, 1978.

Carpenter, Delburn. *The Radical Pietists: Celibate Communal Societies Established in the United States Before 1820.* New York: AMS Press, 1975.

Clasen, Claus-Peter. *Anabaptism, A Social History 1525-1618: Switzerland, Austria, Moravia, South and Central Germany.* Ithaca, N.Y.: Cornell University Press, 1972.

Core, Arthur C. *Philip William Otterbein: Pastor, Ecumenist.* Dayton, Ohio: Board of Publication of the Evangelical United Brethren Church, 1968.

Correll, Ernst H. *Das schweizerische Taufermennonitentum: Ein sozialogischer Bericht.* Tübingen: Verlag von J.C.B. Mohr, 1925.

Drumm, Ernst. *Zur Geschichte der Mennoniten in Herzogtum Pfalz-Zweibrucken.* Zweibrucken: Veroffentlichungen der Stadtverwaltung, 1962.

Drury, A. W. *History of the Church of the United Brethren in Christ.* Dayton, Ohio: United Brethren Publishing House, 1931.

—————. *The Life of Philip William Otterbein: Founder of the*

Church of the United Brethren in Christ. Dayton, Ohio: United Brethren Publishing House, 1890.

Dubbs, Joseph Henry. *The Reformed Church in Pennsylvania.* Lancaster, Pa.: The Pennsylvania German Society, 1902.

Durnbaugh, Donald F. *The Brethren in Colonial America: A Source Book on the Transportation and Development of the Church of the Brethren in the Eighteenth Century.* Elgin, Ill.: The Brethren Press, 1967.

——————. *European Origins of the Brethren: A Source Book on the Beginnings of the Church of the Brethren in the Early Eighteenth Century.* Elgin, Ill.: Brethren Press, 1958.

Durnbaugh, Hedwig T. *The German Hymnody of the Brethren, 1720-1903.* Philadelphia, Pa.: Brethren Encyclopedia, Inc., 1986.

Edwards, Morgan. *Materials towards a History of the American Baptists.* Philadelphia: Joseph Crukshank and Isaac Collins, 1770.

Eller, Paul. *These Evangelical United Brethren.* Dayton, Ohio: Otterbein Press, 1950.

Erb, Peter. *Pietists: Selected Writings.* New York: Paulist Press, 1983.

Ernst, James E. *Ephrata: A History.* Allentown, Pa.: Pennsylvania German Folklore Society, 1963.

Estep, William R. *The Anabaptist Story.* Grand Rapids, Mich.: William B. Eerdmans Publishing Company, 1975.

Fetters, Paul R., ed. *Trials and Triumphs: A History of the Church of the United Brethren in Christ.* Huntingdon, Ind.: Church of the United Brethren in Christ, 1894.

Forney, C. H. *History of the Churches of God in the United States of North America.* Harrisburg, Pa.: Publishing House of the Churches of God, 1914.

Franz, Gunter. *Der Dreissigjahrige Krieg und das deutsche Volk: Untersuchung zur Bevolkerungs und Agrargeschicte.* Stuttgart: Gustav Fischer Verlag, 1961.

Friedmann, Robert. *Mennonite Piety Through the Centuries: Its Genius and Its Literature.* Goshen, Ind.: Mennonite Historical Society, 1949.

Funk, Benjamin. *Life and Labors of Elder John Kline, the Martyr Missionary.* Elgin, Ill.: Brethren Publishing House, 1900.

Gewehr, Wesley M. *The Great Awakening in Virginia, 1740-1790.* Durham, N.C.: Duke University Press, 1930.

Glatfelter, Charles H. *Pastors and People: German Lutheran and Reformed Churches in the Pennsylvania Field, 1717-1793.* Breinigsville, Pa.: The Pennsylvania German Society, 1980.

Gollin, Gillian Lindt. *Moravians in Two Worlds: A Study of Changing Communities.* New York: Columbia University Press, 1967.

Good, James I. *History of the Reformed Church in the United States in the Nineteenth Century.* New York: Board of Publication of the Reformed Church in America, 1911.

Guth, Hermann. *The Amish-Mennonites of Waldeck and Wittgenstein.* Elverson, Pa.: Mennonite Family History, 1986.

Harbaugh, Henry. *The LIfe of Rev. Michael Schlatter: With a Full Account of His Travels and Labors among the Germans--1716-1749.* Philadelphia: S.R. Fisher, 1857.

Hinke, William J., ed. *Life and Letters of the Rev. John Philip Boehm, Founder of the Reformed Church in Pennsylvania, 1683-1749.* New York: Arno Press, 1972.

Hinks, Donald R. *Brethren Hymn Books and Hymnals, 1720-1884.* Gettysburg, Pa.: Brethren Heritage Books, 1986.

Hocker, Edward W. *The Founding of the Sower Press.* Philadelphia, Pa.: Germantown Historical Society, n.d.

Horsch, John. *Mennonites in Europe.* Scottdale, Pa.: Mennonite Publishing House, 1950.

Hostetler, Beulah Stauffer. *American Mennonites and Protestant Movements: A Community Paradigm.* Scottdale, Pa.: Herald Press, 1987.

Hostetler, John A., ed. *Amish Roots: A Treasury of History, Wisdom, and Lore.* Baltimore: The Johns Hopkins University Press, 1989.

Isaac, Rhys. *The Transformation of Virginia, 1740-1790.* Chapel Hill, N.C.: University of North Carolina Press, 1982.

Kern, Richard. *John Winebrenner: Nineteenth Century Reformer.* Harrisburg, Pa.: Central Publishing House, 1974.

Kisch, Herbert. *Prussian Mercantilism and the Rise of the Krefeld Silk Industry: Variations upon an Eighteenth-Century Theme.* Philadelphia: Transactions and Proceedings of the American Philosophical Society, November 1968.

Klein, H. M. J. *The History of the Eastern Synod of the Reformed*

Church in the United States. Lancaster, Pa.: Eastern Synod of the Reformed Church in the United States, 1943.

Lehman, James H. *The Old Brethren.* Elgin, Ill.: Brethren Press, 1976.

Lehmen, James O. "Mennonites in the North Face the Crisis of the Civil War." Unpublished manuscript: Lancaster Mennonite Historical Society, 1982.

Levering, Joseph Mortimer. *A History of Bethlehem, Pennsylvania, 1741-1892: With Some Account of its Founders and their Early Activity in America.* Bethlehem, Pa.: Times Publishing Company, 1903.

Littell, Franklin Hamlin. *The Anabaptist View of the Church: A Story in the Origins of Sectarian Protestantism.* Boston, Starr King Press, 1958.

Livingood, Fredrick George. *Eighteenth Century Reformed Church Schools.* Norristown, Pa.: Pennsylvania German Society, 1927.

Longenecker, Stephen L. *The Christopher Sauers.* Elgin, Ill.: The Brethren Press, 1981.

Lovejoy, David S. *Religious Enthusiasm in the New World: Heresy to Revolution.* Cambridge, Mass.: Harvard University Press, 1985.

MacMaster, Richard K., Samuel L. Horst, and Robert F. Ulle. *Conscience in Crisis: Mennonites and Other Peace Churches in America, 1739-1789, Interpretations and Documents.* Scottdale, Pa.: Herald Press, 1979.

——————. *Land, Piety, Peoplehood: The Establishment of Mennonite Communities in America, 1683-1790.* Scottdale, Pa.: Herald Press, 1985.

McKivigan, John R. *The War against Proslavery Religion: Abolitionism and the Northern Churches, 1830-1865.* Ithaca, N.Y.: Cornell University Press, 1984.

Nelson, E. Clifford, ed. *The Lutherans in North America.* Philadelphia: Fortress Press, 1975.

Nieper, Friedrich. *Die ersten deutschen Auswanderer von feld nach Pennsylvanien: Ein Bild aus der religiosen Ideen geschichte des 17. and 18. Jahrhunderts.* Neukirchen, Kreis Moers: Buchhandlung des Erziehung Vereins, 1940.

O'Malley, J. Steven. *Pilgrimage of Faith: The Legacy of the Otterbeins.* Metuchen, N.J.: Scarecrow Press, 1973.

Orwig, W.W. *History of the Evangelical Association: From the Origin of the Association to the End of the Year 1845.* Cleveland: Charles Hammer, 1858.

Pennypacker, Samuel Whitaker. *The Settlement of Germantown Pennsylvania and the Beginning of German Immigration to North America.* Lancaster, Pa.: The Pennsylvania German Society, 1899.

Renkewitz, Heinz. *Hochmann von Hochenau (1670-1721): Quellenstudien zur Geschichte des Pietismus.* Luther-Verlag Witten, 1969.

Riforgiato, Leonhard R. *Missionary of Moderation: Henry Melchior Muhlenberg and the Lutheran Church in English America.* Lewisburg, Pa.: Bucknell University Press, 1980.

Rothermund, Dietmar. *The Layman's Progress: Religious and Political Experience in Colonial Pennsylvania, 1740-1770.* Philadelphia: University of Pennsylvania Press, 1961.

Ruth, John L. *Maintaining the Right Fellowship: A Narrative Account of Life in the Oldest Mennonite Community in North America.* Scottdale, Pa.: Herald Press, 1984.

Sachse, Julius Friedrich. *The German Pietists of Provincial Pennsylvania.* Philadelphia: Published by the author, 1895.

Sagarra, Eda. *A Social History of Germany, 1648-1914.* New York: Holmes and Meier, 1977.

Sappington, Roger, ed. *The Brethren in the New Nation: A Source Book on the Development of the Church of the Brethren, 1785-1865.* Elgin, Ill.: The Brethren Press, 1976.

―――――. *The Brethren in Virginia: The History of the Church of the Brethren in Virgina.* Harrisonburg, Va.: Committee for the Church of the Brethren History in Virginia, 1973.

Schwab, Ralph Kendall. *The History of the Doctrine of Christian Perfectionism in the Evangelical Association.* Menasha, Wisc.: The Collegiate Press, 1922.

Schwartz, Sally. *"A Mixed Multitude": The Struggle for Toleration in Colonial Pennsylvania.* New York: New York University Press, 1987.

Sellin, Volker. *Die Finanzpolitik Karl Ludwigs von der Pfalz: Staatswirtschaft in Wiederaufbau nach dem Dreissigjahrigen Krieg.* Stuttgart: Klett-Cotta, 1978.

Sessler, John Jacob. *Communal Pietism Among Early American*

Moravians. New York: Henry Holt and Company, 1933.

Shambaugh, Bertha M.H. *Amana That Was and Amana That Is.* Iowa City, Iowa: State Historical Society of Iowa, 1932.

Smaby, Beverly Prior. *The Transformation of Moravian Bethlehem: From Communal Mission to Family Economy.* Philadelphia: Univeristy of Pennsylvania Press, 1988.

Smith, C. Henry. *The Mennonite Immigration to Pennsylvania.* Norristown, Pa.: Pennsylvania German Society, 1929.

Smith, Timothy L. *Revivalism and Social Reform: American Protestantism on the Eve of the Civil War.* Baltimore: The Johns Hopkins University Press, 1957, reprinted 1980.

Spaeth, Adolf. *Charles Porterfield Krath.* New York: Arno Press and The New York Times, 1969.

Spayth, Henry G. *History of the Church of the United Brethren in Christ.* Circleville, Ohio: Conference Office of the United Brethren in Christ, 1851.

Spreng, Samuel P. *History of the Evangelical Association.* New York: The Christian Literature Company, 1894.

——————. *The Life and Labors of John Seybert: First Bishop of the Evangelical Association.* Cleveland, Ohio: Laver and Mattill, 1888.

Stoeffler, F. Ernest, ed. *Continental Pietism and Early American Christianity.* Grand Rapids, Mich.: William B. Eerdmans Publishing Company, 1976.

——————. *German Pietism During the Eighteenth Century.* Leiden: E. J. Brill, 1973.

Stoffer, Dale R. *Background and Development of Brethren Doctrines, 1650-1987.* Philadelphia: Brethren Encyclopedia, Inc., 1989.

Studer, Gerald C. *Christopher Dock: Colonial Schoolmaster.* Scottdale, Pa.: Herald Press, 1967.

Swartley, Willard M. *Slavery, Sabbath, War, and Women: Case Studies in Biblical Interpretation.* Scottdale, Pa.: Herald Press, 1983.

Towlson, Clifford W. *Moravian and Methodist: Relationships and Influences in the Eighteenth Century.* London: The Epworth Press, 1957.

Tully, Alan. *William Penn's Legacy: Politics and Social Structure in Provincial Pennsylvania, 1726-1755.* Baltimore: The Johns Hopkins University Press, 1977.

Walker, Mack. *German Home Towns: Community, State and General Estate, 1648-1871.* Ithaca: Cornell University Press, 1971.

Weinlick, John R. *Count Zinzendorf.* New York and Nashville, Tenn.: Abingdon Press, 1956.

Wenger, John C. *History of the Mennonites of the Franconian Conference.* Telford, Pa.: Franconia Mennonite Historical Society, 1937.

Wentz, Abdel Ross. *A Basic History of Lutheranism in America.* Philadelphia: Muhlenberg Press, 1955.

──────. *Pioneer in Christian Unity: Samuel Simon Schmucker.* Philadelphia: Fortress Press, 1967.

Willoughby, William G. *Counting the Cost: The Life Of Alexander Mack, 1679-1735.* Elgin, Ill.: The Brethren Press, 1979.

Wittlinger, Carlton O. *Quest for Piety and Obedience: The Story of the Brethren in Christ.* Nappanee, Ind.: Evangel Press, 1978.

Yeakel, Rubin. *History of the Evangelical Association.* Cleveland, Ohio: Mattill and Lamb, 1902.

──────. *Jacob Albright and His Co-Laborers.* Cleveland: Publishing House of the Evangelical Association, 1883.

Yoder, Don. *Pennsylvania Spirituals.* Lancaster, Pa.: Pennsylvania Folklore Society, 1961.

Articles

Bell, Raymond Martin. "John George Pfrimmer, 1762-1825: Early United Brethren Minister." Unpublished paper, General Commission on Archives and History, United Methodist Church, 1983.

Bender, Harold S. "A Few Words about the Mennonites in America in 1841: A Contemporary Document by Jacob Krehbiel." *Mennonite Quarterly Review* 6 (January 1932): 43-57.

──────. "Palatine Mennonite Census Lists, 1664-1774." *Mennonite Quarterly Review* 14 (January 1940): 26-31.

Boecken, Charlotte. "Early Brethren in Krefeld--Lists and Documents: Some Supplements to Previous Research, Part I." *Brethren Life and Thought* 35 (Spring 1990): 122-39.

Butler, Jon. "Magic, Astrology, and the Early American Religious Heritage, 1600-1760." *American Historical Review* 84 (April

1979): 317-46.

Calvert, Karen. "The Functions of Fashion in Eighteenth-Century America," Paper presented at the Capitol Historical Society Symposium, Washington, D.C., 1986.

Coalter, Milton J., Jr. "The Radical Pietism of Count Nicholas Zinzendorf as a Conservative Influence on the Awakener, Gilbert Tennant." *Church History* 49 (March 1980): 35-46.

Durnbaugh, Donald F. "Johann Adam Gruber: Pennsylvania German Prophet and Poet." *Pennsylvania Magazine of History and Biography* 83 (October 1959): 382-408.

——————. "Relationships of the Brethren with the Mennonites and Quakers, 1708-1865." *Church History* 35 (March 1966): 35-59.

——————. "Religion and Revolution: Options in 1776." *Pennsylvania Mennonite Heritage* 1 (July 1978): 2-9.

——————. "Was Christopher Sauer a Dunker?" *Pennsylvania Magazine of History and Biography* 83 (July 1969): 383-91.

Elliot, Daryl M. "Entire Sanctification and the Church of United Brethren in Christ in 1860." *Methodist History* 25 (July 1987): 203-21.

Fisher, Elizabeth W. "'Prophecies and Revelations': German Cabbalists in Early Pennsylvania." *Pennsylvania Magazine of History and Biography* 109 (July 1985): 299-333.

Fortenbaugh, Robert. "American Lutheran Synods and Slavery, 1830-60." *Journal of Religion* 13 (January 1933): 72-92.

Frantz, John B. "The Awakening of Religion among the German Settlers in the Middle Colonies." *William and Mary Quarterly* 33 (April 1976): 266-88.

Gehrke, William Herman. "Negro Slavery among the Germans in North Carolina." *The North Carolina Historical Review* 14 (October 1937): 307-24.

Gorrell, Donald K. "'Ride a Circuit or Let It Alone': Early Practices That Kept the United Brethren, Albright People and Methodists Apart." *Methodist History* 25 (October 1986).

Kadelbach, Ada. "Hymns Written by American Mennonites." *Mennonite Quarterly Review* 44 (July 1974): 343-70.

Lodge, Martin E. "The Crisis of the Churches in the Middle Colonies, 1720-1750." *Pennsylvania Magazine of History and Biography* 95 (April 1974): 192-210.

Nash, Gary B. "Slaves and Slaveowners in Colonial Philadelphia."

William and Mary Quarterly 30 (April 1973): 223-56.

Nelson, James D. "Jacob Albright: Founder, Reformer, or Model Pietist?" Unpublished paper, n.d.

O'Malley, J. Steven. "A Distinctive German-American Credo: The United Brethren Confession of Faith." *American Theological Journal* (1986): 1-12.

Pritzker-Ehrlich, Marthi. "Michael Schlatter: A Man in Between." *Swiss American Historical Society Newsletter* 19 (1983).

Richards, George W. "Henry Melchior Muhlenberg and Michael Schlatter." *Lutheran Church Quarterly* 15 (July 1942): 274-84.

Robertson, Andrew. "The Idealist as Opportunist: An Analysis of Thaddeus Stevens' Support in Lancaster County, 1843-1866." *Lancaster County Historical Society Journal* 84 (Spring 1980): 49-107.

Rowe, Kenneth E. "Martin Boehm and the Methodists." *Methodist History* 8 (July 1970): 49-53.

Schlabach, Theron F. "Mennonites and Pietism in America, 1740-1880: Some Thoughts on the Friedmann Thesis." *Mennonite Quarterly Review* 57 (July 1983): 222-40.

Schrag, Martin H. "The Eighteenth Century River Brethren Confession of Faith." Unpublished paper, presented at a conference on the Mennonite experience in America, October 25-27, 1979.

——————. "The Impact of Pietism upon Early American Mennonites." Unpublished paper, Lancaster County Mennonite History Society, n.d.

——————. "Influences Contributing to an Early River Brethren Confession of Faith." *Mennonite Quarterly Review* 38 (October 1964): 344-53.

Smith, Timothy L. "Congregation, State, and Denomination: The Forming of the American Religious Structure." *William and Mary Quarterly* 25 (April 1968): 155-76.

Stange, Douglas C. "Lutheran Involvement in the American Colonization Society." *Mid-America* 49 (April 1967): 140-51.

Stout, John Joseph. "Count Zinzendorf and the Pennsylvania Congregation of God in the Spirit: The First American Oecumenical Movement." *Church History* 9 (December 1940).

Sutter, Sem C. "Mennonites and the Pennsylvania German Revival." *Mennonite Quarterly Review* 50 (January 1976): 37-57.

Tappert, Theodore G. "John Caspar Stoever and the Ministerium of Pennsylvania." *Lutheran Church Quarterly* 21 (April 1948): 180-4.

Tharp, Daniel B. "Chattel with a Soul: The Autobiography of a Moravian Slave." *Pennsylvania Magazine of History and Biography* 112 (July 1988): 433-52.

Tully, Alan. "Patterns of Slaveholding in Colonial Pennsylvania: Chester and Lancaster Counties, 1729-1758." *Journal of Social History* 6 (Spring 1973): 284-305.

Wentz, Abdel. "Relations between the Lutheran and Reformed Churches in the Eighteenth and Nineteenth Centuries." *Lutheran Church Quarterly* 6 (1933): 300-27.

Wittlinger, Carlton O. "The Vision of the River Brethren." Unpublished paper, Lancaster Mennonite Historical Society, n. d.

Music and Hymnals

Bach, Johann Sebastian. *Wachet auf: ruft uns die Stimme.* The score of the New Bach Edition: Backgrounds, Analysis, Views, and Comments by Gerhard Herz. New York: W. W. Norton, 1972.

By a Committee of Mennonites. *A Selection of Psalms, Hymns, and Spiritual Songs, from the Most Approved Authors Suited to the Various Occasions of Public Worship and Private Devotion, of the Church of Christ.* Harrisonburg, Va.: J. H. Wartman and Bros., 1847.

The Christian's Duty, Exibited in a Series of Hymns, Collected from Various Authors, Designed for the Worship of God, and for the Edification of Christians, Recommended to the Serious of All Denominations, By the Fraternity of Baptists. Philadelphia: Peter Leibert, 1813.

Service Book and Hymnal of the Lutheran Church in America. Minneapolis, Minn.: Augsburg Publishing House, 1958.

Index

About the Author

STEPHEN L. LONGENECKER (B.S., Shippensburg University; M.A., West Virginia University; Ph.D., The Johns Hopkins University) is an Assistant Professor of History and a member of the Forum for Religious Studies at Bridgewater College in Bridgewater, Va. Dr. Longenecker has also taught at Towson State University and Franklin and Marshall College. He has previously published *Selma's Peacemaker: Ralph Smeltzer and Civil Rights Mediation* (Temple University Press, 1987) and *The Christopher Sauers* (The Brethren Press, 1981).